3 1000 00044364 1

D0938657

Garden of Dreams

Garden of Dreams

KINGSMERE AND MACKENZIE KING

Edwinna von Baeyer

Dundurn Press
Toronto and Oxford
1990

Editor: Mark Fenton
Design and Production: JAQ
Printing and Binding: Gagné Printing Ltd., Louiseville, Quebec, Canada

The writing of this manuscript and the publication of this book were made possible by support from several sources. The publisher wishes to acknowledge the generous assistance and ongoing support of **The Canada Council**, **The Book Publishing Industry Development Programme** of the **Department of Communications**, and **The Ontario Arts Council.**

J. Kirk Howard, Publisher

Dundurn Press Limited
2181 Queen Street East, Suite 301
Toronto, Canada
M4E 1E5

Dundurn Distribution
73 Lime Walk
Headington
Oxford 0X3 7AD
England

Canadian Cataloguing in Publication Data

Von Baeyer, Edwinna, 1947–
Garden of dreams

Includes index.
ISBN 1-55002-080-3

1. Kingsmere (Quebec) – History. 2. King, William Lyon Mackenzie, 1874–1950.
3. Gardens, Canadian – Quebec (Province) – Gatineau Park. I. Title.

SB 466.C33K56 1990 712'.6'09714221 C90–095679–8

To my family

Table of Contents

The Mackenzie King Estate today

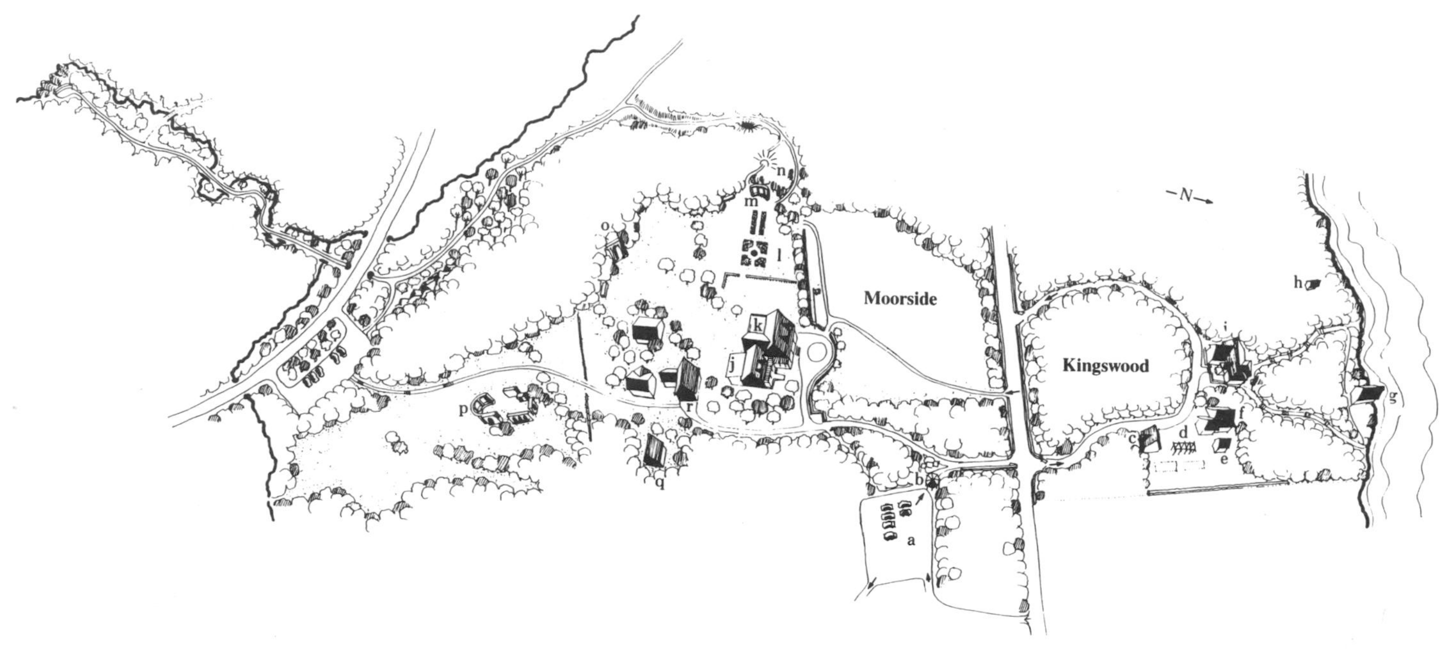

a — Parking

b — Visitors' kiosk

c — Garage

d — Pergola

e — Ice house

f — Guest house

g — Boat house

h — Pump house

i — Kingswood cottage

j — Tea room

k — Moorside cottage

l — Garden

m — Window on the Forest

n — Hidden Garden

o — Arc de Triomphe

p — Abbey Ruins

q — Forge

r — Garage/Theatre

PREFACE

GARDEN OF DREAMS IS THE STORY OF FORMER PRIME MINISTER WILLIAM Lyon Mackenzie King's other life, his fifty years on his country estate in the Gatineau Hills. It is an odyssey through the landscape King loved so well. Again and again, from 1901 to 1950, he wrote in his diaries that his country activities "filled him with delight" — as well as a full measure of joy, heartbreak, passion, and spiritual renewal. His Kingsmere story also has a larger dimension. Mackenzie King's progress from cottager to country squire, with a brief period as a gentleman farmer, mirrored the leisure-time preoccupations of many Canadians. Through King's example, we can examine the broader themes of the summer holiday, the country estate and the urge to garden. By watching King build his dream garden we can learn a bit about ourselves.

The political Mackenzie King is only allowed on the Kingsmere stage for brief appearances. This side of his life has been recounted in great detail by many other historians. It is the horticultural King who is highlighted here.

To piece together the story of his Kingsmere years, I combed the William Lyon Mackenzie King papers held at the National Archives of Canada — an incredibly rich collection. His private diaries turned out to be the most important source on his years in the Gatineau Hills. Reading them was, in itself, a fascinating journey through King's mind and emotions, which he painstakingly recorded from age nineteen to his death at seventy-four. The diary was his best friend, a constant, non-critical audience of the day's activities, and a welcome creative outlet for the controlled political man. King's private correspondence, collection of clippings, photographs, and memorabilia were also mined for supporting material. For landscape historians especially, the Kingsmere files contain an unusual amount of information on a private Canadian landscape. Unfortunately his financial papers are closed until 2001, limiting research into his methods of hiring and using gardeners. As well, King's spiritualism papers are also closed until then, blocking further exploration of possible connections with his Kingsmere life.

It is to be noted that the frequent quotations from the diaries (kept in the National Archives of Canada) in the text are not identified by footnotes, but only by date.

Many people helped me unravel this unique story. Janet Leduc, of the National Capital Commission (NCC), first suggested I look into the Kingsmere papers. Her continued support for the project during the three years of research and writing is greatly appreciated. Robert Smythe freely shared the insights into King and Kingsmere he gathered during his pioneering research on King's Kingsmere years. Susan MacGregor, who oversaw the King estate for the NCC, was constantly helpful by making available NCC reports, photographs, and people to interview. Alan Sibley, of the Visitor and Heritage Services Branch, has generously lent numerous photographs from the NCC collection for the book. I would also like to thank those who helped my research by pointing out promising leads, granting interviews, or sending along helpful articles: Susan Buggey, Sally Coutts, Pleasance Crawford, Mrs. John Fraser, Molly Hirsch, Robert Hunter, John Lay, Tom Nesmith, Cecelia Paine, Jim Taylor, Ina Vrugtman, Janet Wright, and the ever helpful staff at the National Archives of Canada and the Canadian Agriculture Library of Agriculture Canada.

My family's support, especially my children's bemused encouragement, is, as always, very much appreciated. I could not have persevered without them or their encouragement. A very special thanks again to Cornelius who often said he could not bear to hear another quote from the diaries, but was always there to hear more. His helpful comments on the text were, as always, welcomed, even when it meant rewriting.

The NCC deserves special thanks for its preservation and restoration of the King estate over the past forty years. Not only has the Commission kept alive a fascinating piece of our history but has also played a supportive role in Canada's expanding landscape preservation movement.

Although editors, friends and relations have read portions of the book, improving it with their suggestions and corrections, any errors or omissions are only mine.

Edwinna von Baeyer
Ottawa 1990

INTRODUCTION

Mackenzie King's Gardening

AND THE HORTICULTURAL TIMES

Lurking beneath William Lyon Mackenzie King's lacklustre exterior, was a complex, contradictory personality — sometimes colourful and often excitable. This inner man led an amazingly rich life, which was not revealed until the release of his extensive diaries. Admittedly, in the thousands of pages of intimate detail of King's daily life, there is much to reinforce his dull, serious image: a short, pudgy, plodding prime minister, an earnest Christian and a master of the compromise. He was our longest-serving prime minister and symbolized the status quo, security, and Victorian propriety. What would his contemporaries have thought if they had known that King, the supreme politician, the aloof prime minister, participated in seances and other "psychical research," where he spoke with Wilfrid Laurier, his mother, and even Lorenzo de Medici? An interest in spiritualism was not unusual in the early 1900s, but if it had been known that he also recorded and interpreted his dreams ("visions" he called them), as well as tea leaves and even the pictures his shaving lather made — what would have been his standing in a public opinion poll? Would King have served so long as prime minister had Canadians been aware of his ardent worship of his mother? For many years after her death, whenever he entered his library after a long absence, King kissed the marble lips of her statue. A sentimental regard for motherhood was common in the Victorian era, but how many other men constantly kept flowers and a light burning beneath their mother's portrait? His mother's influence continued long after she died. The diaries document his sustained friendships with a number of safe, married ladies, but King, with his lifelong devotion to his mother, never married.

The true, abiding passion of King's life was his estate in the Gatineau Hills. He lavished unwavering and uncritical devotion on it for all his years in Ottawa. King was more relaxed at Kingsmere, more inclined to give his "other life" fuller expres-

G. Lunney/National Archives of Canada/PA 116871

King always left a light burning beneath the portrait of his mother in the Laurier House library.

sion. During the half century of his life there, Kingsmere became many things to him: a refuge, a status symbol, an experimental station, and above all an enormous canvas for King to fill with a beautiful landscape of flowers, trees, picturesque roadways, and statuary. Kingsmere was a focal point for King's flights of romantic imagination and his profound emotional response to the landscape.

At Kingsmere, King continually marveled at the natural world. He was constantly thrilled by what he saw or did there, repeatedly exclaiming that each new view or object was the most beautiful he had ever seen. The contemporary reader of the diaries may find his effusions rather difficult to interpret, perhaps branding King a hypocrite. Yet his style of language, an emotional shorthand of overblown adjectives, extreme declarations, and ardent sentimentality, was common in the writings of 19th century evangelical Christians[1] — a literature the religious Mackenzie King was well acquainted with.

King revelled in sentimental and Romantic poetry, a taste which probably influenced his determination to build European-inspired ruins on the Canadian Shield. Guests were proudly shown these artificial ruins, were treated to poetry readings around the fire, or were given a glimpse of his passion for landscaping. However, what his guests, let alone the people of Canada, were not shown was the extra dimension of King's country life. The landscape reverberated with spiritual emanations, as gardens, forests and fields became physical projections of his fantasy life, his enchanted garden.

His was not a whimsical magical garden, but, reflecting King's personality, an earnest one. King's gardens were animated by the presence of God, the spirits of the dearly departed, and a multitude of auspicious signs and messengers from Heaven. His romanticism and active imagination combined to colour his perceptions of Kingsmere until he really could see an Athenian temple in his re-created ruins, an English gentleman's park in his turfed grounds, and a spiritual creation in his modest boathouse. Trees were more than inanimate scenery, birds were "messengers from heaven," and his ruins were the foundation for another Westminster Abbey.

Kingsmere was his sacred grove where he diligently tried to capture, then enhance, the *genius loci*, the spirit of the place.

Landscaping, his one great hobby, was a life-long creative outlet, an activity he said gave him "great joy." King transformed the primeval landscape of the Canadian Shield into a scene of British pastoral delights: rolling lawns, meadows filled with grazing sheep, woodland trails, flower gardens, and the deep mystery of the forest. Landscaping this paradise was part of his fight for goodness, truth and beauty, as he subdued nature and made the "wild places smooth." All this was created without committing a master plan to paper — King could simply refer to the model he obviously carried around in his head.

National Archives of Canada/PA 126203

Winston Churchill was only one of the many distinguished guests King invited to his estate.

Kingsmere was the best of all possible worlds in King's assessment. At Kingsmere he saw himself as he wanted to be: an ardent lover of nature, a sensitive, cultured soul, and a protector of a natural heritage. As the estate expanded, it became an expensively maintained stage set, where he changed roles whenever he wished — from humble cottager to gentleman farmer to country squire.

His realistic side tempered his romantic, imaginative feelings toward the estate. He could have emulated his peers and built an elaborate country house and created lavish gardens, but King's habitual frugality and his dislike of ostentatious display stifled any such desire. King frequently justified improvements or land purchases by reassuring himself that these were very good investments, either for his financial position or for his health. He continually noted in his diaries that his ability to carry on the onerous duties of high office was enhanced by the estate's privacy and by his rejuvenating contact with nature there.

Politically and socially King felt that Kingsmere reflected his status as prime minister and provided a fitting place to bring occasional guests: royalty, politicians, clerics, party workers, friends and family. Owning an estate was yet another sign, along with invitations to Rideau Hall and other houses of the prominent, that he had arrived. It also signified that the son of a lacklustre lawyer and grandson of a maligned reformer had rescued and glorified the family name. Yet, apart from necessary entertaining, King jealously guarded his garden paradise from unwanted intrusions. Even his family was given limited access, although he was a very lonely man, and professed to be very close to his family. He begrudged visits from his nieces and nephews and rarely invited his only surviving sister to visit him there.

National Archives of Canada/C 7352

The King children: William (age 7), Bella, Max and Jennie.

The estate was not for his family to inherit or enjoy. To soothe his nervousness over acquiring so much property, King reassured himself that building up the estate was an investment for the nation. Through conversations with friends, employees and the sympathetic diary, he gradually refined his idea of preserving a spot of beauty for all time into a legacy for the people of Canada, and willed it to the nation. Instead of creating a family property, he would establish a memorial to outlast any vestiges of the King family or vicissitudes of the family fortunes.

His fantasies were not always strong enough to repel the real world, for reality could intrude rather roughly into his idylls at the estate. The lustre of the enchanted garden was dimmed for a while when his sheep died, a neighbour contested his water rights, labourers cut down the wrong trees, slanted newspaper stories blighted his happiness in land purchases, and his servants caused domestic upsets. Despite the frustrations and disappointments, King continually marvelled over what he had created: "I could scarcely believe," he wrote in 1935, "such a place could be my own as I saw today with the mountain and the forests and the distant valley and the great sky overhead — and all the beauty of the house and grounds." And we marvel too how King managed to create such a personal, horticultural statement which encompassed not only his eccentricity, his romanticism, and his aesthetics, but also his special, eclectic reflection of the gardening spirit of early 20th century North America.

The Woodside Years — King's Horticultural Roots

King's interest and participation in gardening began during his childhood years at Woodside, his family's rented home in Berlin (now Kitchener, Ontario). In 1869 John King, Mackenzie King's father, established a law practice in Berlin. He married Isabel Mackenzie (the youngest of W.L. Mackenzie's thirteen children) in 1872. They began a family in 1873 with the birth of Isabel (nicknamed Bella). William Lyon Mackenzie was born the following year, 1874, christened with the burdensome name of his grandfather — the ardent reformer and leader of the rebellion in 1837. Two years later his sister Janet (Jennie) was born, followed by Dougal Macdougall (Max) in 1878.

The family lived in two other rental homes in the city before moving to the outskirts of Berlin in 1886 to rent the estate-like Woodside. Although the Kings lived in this house for only seven years (1886-1893), this fifteen acre (10 ha) wooded property became the focal point of family nostalgia. Over the years it was always associated with the best in their family life. Mackenzie King wrote in his seventies: "As Woodside is the only place of residence in which I have shared in those joys and sorrows which belong to family life, it is perhaps natural that, to me, Woodside should speak more of home than either of the other homes I have had."[2]

The family moved to Toronto in 1893, hoping to better their fortunes on John King's expectations of a career advancement which never materialized. During the King's twenty-three years in Toronto, the family moved four times. By then Mackenzie King was in university and never really at home after that.

The Kings' financial plight had worsened — debts were owed everywhere. The parents were ailing and unable to afford domestic help. Bella, who was a serious woman devoted to good works, wanted to become a nurse and trained at a Boston hospital while King was doing graduate studies at Harvard. Her career aspirations were destroyed by King's continual disparagment of her training, even though he loved to date nurses, and was briefly engaged to a Chicago nurse. Nursing was not considered an appropriate profession for a gentlewoman, or a King. Pressure from King and his parents, to devote herself to those at home rather than strangers, was steadily applied until she returned to Toronto. Ironically, Bella, to help with family finances, soon went to work in a bank. The worry and exhaustion of caring for her parents, working and looking after the house undermined her health. Bella died in 1915 at the age of forty-two. The next year John King died, soon followed by King's beloved mother in 1917. Max's debilitating illness and death was the final family tragedy. After working his way through medical school, Max had served as a military doctor in South Africa, then worked in the United States before coming to Ottawa to practice. After marrying and having twin boys, Max was forced to move to Denver to cure himself of tuberculosis. He regained his health only to be stricken with an incurable muscular disease which led to his death at age forty-four in 1922.[3]

During these stressful years it was not surprising that the thought of "dear old Woodside" instantly transported any King family member back to happier times. King never failed to look for the house from the train on his many campaign journeys. Family letters often referred to it: King's mother once wrote that although she was looking forward to Christmas, she wished "...we had the red berries and periwinkle of old Woodside to decorate our table."[4] While on holiday, Jennie wrote to her brother: "Mr. McMurrick has just come home from his paddle and brought the most beautiful armful of white water lilies. You know I never see them without the strangest feeling of homesickness coming over me. I am glad we have Woodside to remember as our childhood home."[5]

Woodside was a small, Picturesque-style brick and stone house set within a landscape of trees, a white picket fence, running water, lawn and flower beds. A narrow, winding road led up to the vine-draped house, whose large verandah was a focus for family activities. Lilacs, cherry trees, honeysuckle, bittersweet vines, maple, elms and linden trees softened the house facade. A

National Archives of Canada/C 8313

King and his sister, Jennie, on the Woodside Lover's Walk.

tulip tree and a pond filled with white water lilies were visible from the library.

Flower beds filled with various annuals, lily-of-the-valley, periwinkle, and violets graced the south lawn. Many of Isabel's garden parties, often enlivened by dancing on a removable platform, were held there. One such garden party was written up in the local newspaper: "The warm weather precluded much dancing...The grounds were beautifully illuminated and the winding walks lined with Chinese lanterns made a very inviting promenade..."[6] An apple orchard, a kitchen garden, as well as a small area planted with hay for the cow and horse were part of this pastoral landscape. The property even included a "lover's walk" through the woods and over the hills.[7]

Although maintaining the Woodside ornamental grounds (*de rigueur* for aspiring members of Society), neither parent seemed interested in any aspect of gardening. The teen-aged King, either by parental command or natural inclination, assumed the gardening chores. The Kings had a hired man to do the heavy work while Mackenzie King weeded and cultivated the gardens. He also harvested apples, cherries and other wild berries, sold the surplus, sharing the profits with his mother.[8] Foreshadowing his own gentleman farming attempts in the late 1920s, King also tended the family cow, chickens, horse, and, for a while, pigs. His Woodside years were an idyllic, pastoral interlude before the cares and challenges of adulthood preoccupied him.

By his seventies, Woodside had attained mythic proportions. When he was approached by prominent Liberals in 1946 who wanted to buy and restore Woodside as a memorial, King was quite delighted. But he demurred from any overt fund-raising during his time in office. This reticence did not curtail his long letters to the chairman of the Mackenzie King Woodside Trust, full of detailed suggestions for its restoration. However, as often happened during any of his private projects, King had his moments of doubt: "I can see that in my own mind, I idealize these things very much. It all looks easy to the imagination. When the time comes to acquiring the articles of furniture, travelling back and forth, I am afraid I shall become greatly disillusioned and perhaps disheartened" (1 October 1946). These misgivings evaporated the following year when King made yet another nostalgic visit to Woodside. Although distressed by the dilapidated state of house and grounds, King could immediately visualize its restored beauty. In 1947 he enthused in the diary over "...the real delight I felt at seeing...its possibilities as a park," for landscaping was of as great importance to King as the house restoration. To the end of his life, landscaping continued to challenge and delight him.

The Horticultural Temper of the Times

King's interest in gardening and landscaping was nurtured at Woodside and sustained by visits to estates in Britain, Europe, and North America. As well his landscaping attitudes were probably affected by the upsurge of interest in landscaping and gardening in North America by the late 1800s. In Berlin and later during his University of Toronto days, as well as his early years in Ottawa, he would have witnessed the beginnings of civic beautification — horticultural and architectural.

From the late 1800s up into the 1920s, Canadian society was characterized by a reforming zeal, and buoyed up by a spirit of optimism. This would be Canada's century! By 1900 Canada had emerged from the effects of a world-wide depression. New lands and markets opened in the west as a result of massive immigration and of technological advances in the wake of the rapid rise of industrialization. For some, the standard of living improved. But not every Canadian benefitted from the economic recovery. Rapid industrialization and urbanization coupled with waves of immigration inflicted misery on many, especially labourers who were low-paid, ill-housed, and ill-educated. Changes in the structures of their lives were unsettling for many Canadians, who, in this period of transition, attempted to redesign and adapt existing institutions to conform to the new reality. As well, between 1900 and 1910, the urban population increased by sixty-two per cent. Existing welfare institutions (charitable organizations, religious orders, and government agencies) were unable to cope with the resulting social ills: poverty, disease, intemperance, crime, prostitution, child abuse, and political unrest. The problems were not new but they had multiplied to such an extent that they could no longer be so easily ignored by society.[9]

Reform leaders and their followers were mainly drawn from an urban middle class intent on stabilizing and improving society according to their own values. Mackenzie King was one of hundreds who believed in the ideals of participating in social reform programs. During his university years, King was involved in various good works. King taught Sunday School at the Toronto Children's Hospital, tried to reform prostitutes, and lectured on social issues to working class men's institutes. While attending graduate school at the University of Chicago, he toyed with the idea of working with the famous American reformer, Jane Addams at Hull House. And later while attending Harvard, King, in a series of newspaper articles and reports, brought the plight of Toronto's garment industry "sweat shops" before the Ontario public. King definitely felt the mantle of his reformer grandfather settle on his shoulders.

Horticulturally, reformers were also at work. Unplanned, unaesthetic, unlandscaped urban areas were often included on the list of social problems needing solutions. Professional as well as amateur efforts were directed into horticultural reform programs to create the "city beautiful," idealized as a community graced by parks, trees, boulevards and stately buildings. The beautifiers were convinced that society as a whole loved beauty, wanted to be surrounded by it, and did not differ in aesthetic taste from the reformers' own ideals.

National Archives of Canada/PA 27905

Main Street was a favourite focus for the activities of horticultural reformers. They beautified the city hall, post office, factories, libraries, railway stations and other public sites.

Horticultural reformers used current psychological theory, that an ugly environment damaged a viewer's mental health, to bolster their sense of purpose and duty. If the streetscape was cleaned up and beautified, a "social duty" would be performed:

> If we are to provoke a revulsion against untidy streets, hideous alleys, tumble down houses, repulsive garbage heaps, offensive advertisements of black and yellow on dead walls and mountain sides, we must become teachers of beauty...Missionaries of beauty are wanted to enlist in this crusade against ugliness.[10]

By 1910, many Canadians, especially in central and maritime Canada, were heeding the improvers' message by successfully initiating a variety of public plantings. Street tree planting was one of the earliest civic beautification projects, closely allied with the popularity of boulevarding: creating a strip of lawn and trees and sometimes flower beds alongside or down the centre of a city street. The planting campaign was further stimulated by claims that street trees attracted visitors and encouraged settlement.

Home owners did not escape the reformer's rhetoric, nor their vision of a beautified urban landscape. They were urged to clean up unsightly back yards where dishwater and other refuse was thrown, then to create gardens for their mental and spiritual welfare. For a home was not a home, these reformers noted, without floral embellishments.

Mackenzie King certainly agreed. While he did not landscape Laurier House with the same energy or on the same scale as he did Kingsmere, King did beautify his city property. He planted evergreens, flowering shrubs, and elm trees, sodded the lawn, and filled window boxes and stone urns with flowers. Not only motivated by City Beautiful ideals, King also acknowledged he wanted to create "a real memorial" to Laurier.

Although King never joined one, horticultural societies at this time increased their membership and civic improvement associations were established across Canada. Garden competitions were sponsored by these organizations to stimulate civic beautification. For example, during King's early years in Ottawa, Lady Minto and later Lady Grey gave vice-regal sponsorship through the Ottawa Horticultural Society for garden competitions in Ottawa. As well, weed-infested, debris-laden vacant lots were rented out to enthusiastic gardeners who transformed the plots into flower and vegetable gardens. Up into the 1920s, Mackenzie King would have seen these gardens, as well as a few classroom gardens on school grounds, whenever he ventured into Ottawa's Glebe area.

The enthusiasm which prompted neighbourhood clean-ups and municipal flower beds was also directed into park building, one of the most popular City Beautiful activities. The landscaped public park entered North America in the 1830s through the "rural cemetery" movement. These cemeteries were designed as pastoral landscapes — rolling hills, tree-shaded roadways, and flower beds. When a burial ground was landscaped, it served as "a quiet place in which to escape the bustle and clangor of the city — for strolling, for solitude, and even for family picnics."[11] By the late 1800s the need for public parks, aside from cemeteries or other open spaces, was increasingly recognized. Park promotion and creation were enthusiastically supported by private citizens anxious to duplicate some of the amenities of the "old country." In the larger centres, parks were promoted as the "lungs" of the city, where city dwellers could refresh themselves spiritually and bodily. In 1883 the Ontario legislature passed the Public Parks Act, enabling municipalities to appropriate land and vote funds for park creation. The number of parks soon burgeoned throughout urban Ontario.[12] Ottawa in 1898 had only one park, but by the time King was in cabinet, mainly through the efforts of the Ottawa Improvement Commission, the city was ornamented by six more.

National Archives of Canada/C38987

School gardens were a part of the primary school curriculum in the early 1900s. They were to promote a love of nature and rural living, while providing a concrete basis for the 3 Rs.

Mackenzie King continually supported City Beautiful activities in the nation's capital during his years in government. Laurier wanted to make Ottawa the "Washington of the north," and King also heartily endorsed the idea. In 1936 King met Jacques Gréber, a French town planner, at the International Exhibition in Paris. The two men had very productive talks, and King was impressed by the scope of Gréber's ideas: "I found him an exceptionally brilliant and interesting man, splendidly informed" (15 October 1936). In 1937 King invited Gréber to undertake the fourth city plan Ottawa had had since 1903. Gréber's report, approved in 1951, recommended a "green belt" around the capital, the removal of slums, the creation of parks and parkways, the acquisition of land on the outskirts for government

King and Pat, Laurier House, 1939.

buildings, the purchase of property in Quebec for the Gatineau Park, and the removal or relocation of railways in the area"[13] — all of which were eventually implemented.

King was able to initiate such programs, because, throughout his prime ministership, he kept cabinet control of the portfolio directing the activities of the Federal District Commission (the successor of the Ottawa Improvement Commission, and now called the National Capital Commission). King ensured that money was appropriated, legislation enacted, and sympathetic commissioners and chairmen were appointed — all to further his desire to create a truly beautiful and inspiring capital. King kept this portfolio not only because he thoroughly enjoyed beautification projects, but because he also thought that the other members of his cabinet lacked the imagination to make Ottawa a beautiful capital.

King actively intervened in Ottawa beautification decisions. King chose the site of the National War Memorial, oversaw the selection of the sculptor, and strongly suggested that the sculptor get away "from 'conventional' lines, giving the impression of carved granite rather than [that] cut by machine" (20 March 1926). He ruled on the final site of the Supreme Court building, insisting on a "...picturesque 'chateauesque' roof on top of...the starkly cubic 'modern classic' design."[14] In 1936 he changed the roadway leading through the Experimental Farm: "The route laid out & agreed to by the Farm is no good at all, no scenic beauty — there is one *through* the Farm by a row of trees planted years ago, which is just the thing, and if brought via the arboretum would command one of the finest views in Ottawa. It will be opposed strongly by the Farm, but I shall press for it in the Cabinet & believe it will be possible to secure it. The Ottawa Experimental Farm & arboretum are "show" places & should be brought into the driveway picture..." (11 May 1936). By the next year, the scenic route was in service and King congratulated himself: "I felt *I* had made a real contribution to the beauty of the capital..." (30 September 1937). King also chose the colour of bricks for a new building at the Experimental Farm. And he joined a neighbourhood crusade to save Laurier Avenue trees from destruction. The city was going to widen the street which meant destroying the grassy boulevards and its 117 trees — mainly elms — some of which were nearly a century old. King obviously enjoyed this work for he stated, like Laurier, he would like to be the Chairman of the F.D.C. when he retired. He reluctantly abandoned the idea when his health began to fail after he left office.

Just as other social movements lost their sustaining energy and reforming zeal in the 1920s, so did the urban beautification movement. However, certain ideals stayed in the public mind. The moralistic rhetoric had ceased, but parks, tree-lined streets, well-tended front lawns and public plantings never really lost their champions. Neither was the home garden abandoned. In fact, having trowel in hand became the "thing to do," and many "right-thinking," middle and upper class people supported and engaged in gardening at this time. The upsurge in home gardening was supported by the burgeoning Canadian nursery industry and the expansion of our horticultural media. The proliferation of nurseries and development of improved delivery methods, provided greater varieties of plants and hardier plant material for the nation's gardeners. Although our gardening media had to compete against the more numerous British and American horticultural publications (articles, books and pamphlets), Canadian design possibilities, descriptions of new varieties, and some local cultivation tips were actively published in pre-World War II Canada.[15]

National Archives of Canada/PA 13022

Colonel By Driveway was an early beautification project of the Ottawa Improvement Commission.

Neither did Mackenzie King lose his active interest in gardening. From the time he began spending summers on his Kingsmere property until his death, he continually improved the landscape. The application of his landscaping ideals on the Canadian Shield were strongly influenced by the prevailing horticultural ethos — social necessity, duty and the creation of beauty. However, King's eccentricities led him down garden paths uniquely his, even though fashioned from the common elements of his horticultural time.

King standing in front of Beaver Rock.

CHAPTER ONE

The Road to Kingswood

On Thanksgiving Day 1900, William Lyon Mackenzie King and his best friend, Bert Harper, bicycled the twenty-four kilometers north from Ottawa into the Gatineau Hills. Their destination and purpose on this crisp, clear autumn day was to climb the auspiciously named King Mountain overlooking the equally well-named Kingsmere Lake — definite attractions for King although neither spot was named after him. After hiking to the top of the mountain, the two men shared a picnic lunch and marvelled at the fall colours. It was just the right setting for one of their favourite discussions on man, nature and God. In all, a propitious beginning to many days spent in the area King would later call his real home.

The twenty-six year old King had arrived in Ottawa late that summer, fresh from a European tour after finishing graduate studies at Harvard and the London School of Economics. He had accepted the editorship of the *Labour Gazette* to be published by the newly created Department of Labour. He had agonized all across Italy whether or not to accept the offer. Not only would it mean cutting short his holiday, but also delaying his plans to write his Ph.D. thesis at Harvard, and thus stalling his intention to pursue an academic career. However, he chose the Department of Labour, and Harper, a close friend from his University of Toronto undergraduate days, resigned as a reporter on the *Montreal Herald* to become King's assistant. King found Harper's company congenial, for they shared the same high moral purpose, the same belief in God and nature, and the same recognition of King's future greatness.

Earnest and energetic, King and Harper entered Ottawa society with verve. They joined a rowing club, they were invited to dinner parties, balls, and skating parties, and they were often among the eligible, promising young men invited to vice-regal affairs at Rideau Hall. They also began attending St. Andrew's

National Archives of Canada/C 14180

King, Mrs. King (seated on the ground), possibly Mrs. Herridge and Bert Harper enjoying their Kingsmere holiday.

> We will have tents, and likely sleep in them all the time. Mother can have my room, and during the day while we are in at the office there will be nothing for her to do but read, or go out and sit by the water, or off into the woods, or walk to meet us, on our way in at night....It is right in the heart of nature, no hotels or the like.[1]

The plan matured and was realized. King, his mother, Harper and the Herridge family became a close, happy group. Often Mrs. Herridge and Mrs. King walked the few kilometers into a nearby village to meet King's afternoon train, and escort him back to Kingsmere. "Mother waiting like a picture at the top of the hill for me," King typically emoted in his diary (13 August 1901). In between bouts at the office, King expended his energy in outdoor activities such as hiking, canoeing and swimming. On warm summer evenings King was fond of looking at the stars with Mrs. Herridge: "After dinner tonight we lay out on the moor in the moonlight drawing into our souls the inspiration of the Heavens swept with stars" (21 August 1901). The summer quickly passed, King enjoying inspirational evenings of reading and star-gazing, days of strenuous physical activity, and nights of serious talk and speculation. When Dr. Herridge returned in early September from his solitary holiday, he was immediately drawn into plans to build a cottage on Kingsmere Lake. King greatly enjoyed planning projects of this kind: "I drew a plan of the house, and we agreed — the entire night discussing it, framing dimensions, etc. etc." (6 September 1901). Ironically, King would buy this cottage from Reverend Herridge nearly thirty years later.

Presbyterian Church, one of Ottawa's richest and most prestigious churches. There King met and evidently impressed the minister, the Reverend W.T. Herridge, and his wife, Marjorie. This developing friendship was to have a profound effect, not only on King's personal life, but also on his life in the Gatineau Hills.

Hearing the Herridges' enthusiastic reports on a summer spent at Kingsmere, King and Harper, the next summer, took rooms for the season at Mrs. McMinn's boarding house, along with Mrs. Herridge and her children. They commuted daily by rail and hired coach to the office and back. As a treat (he had been living away from home for nearly four years) King invited his beloved mother to "camp out" for a few weeks:

Love of Nature

National Archives of Canada/C 46560

King and his mother at Kingswood.

What really lured King into the Gatineau Hills? Fellowship certainly, but there was a deeper attraction — the potent lure of nature. King fervently appreciated nature, his enjoyment of natural scenery could be intense and emotional. Listen to the young Mackenzie King enthuse as he travelled over two continents from 1894 to 1900. In the Muskokas: "I could sit silently for hours and look at the wonders of nature" (7 August 1894). In the U.S.: "I was greatly pleased with the scenery from Albany to Boston...How I love Nature" (4 January 1898). In England: "I love nature above all handiwork of man, nothing compares with beautiful scenery..." (25 October 1899). And in Germany: "I have learned that to me nature is the best friend I have..." (25 March 1900). Initially ambivalent about working in Ottawa, King listed as one of the positive elements of his decision his enjoyment of the area's dramatic natural scenery.

King's passionate outpourings were similar in tone and language to the reactions of many Victorian Canadians to the natural world, reactions which were often expressed in words and images highly influenced by British and American writings. Mackenzie King had inherited the cultural baggage of early British settlers.

The British Romantic movement in the late 1700s and early 1800s glorified the natural world as an expression of untouched beauty, simplicity, goodness, and as an object eliciting a "spontaneous overflow of powerful feeling." Men and women, the Romantics proclaimed, had lost the ancient connections to this world, and needed to refresh and invigorate their minds, bodies and souls by returning to it. Europeans "sought nature anew," communed with the elemental force of the wilderness by admiring its scenery. Travelling into the countryside became easier because of more roads and signposts, stronger horses, and better maps. These amenities enabled greater numbers of Europeans to experience nature, to escape the increasingly unpleasant living conditions of large European cities.[2]

Intellectually, the appeal of wild landscapes was stimulated by a sophisticated knowledge of the traditions of European painting, especially the romantic, imaginative landscapes of Salvador Rosa, Claude or Poussin, who painted in the 1600s.[3] By the 1800s, sensitivity to the sublime emotions engendered by the sight of a waterfall, a picturesque wild ravine, or a robin building a nest indicated that one was cultured and classically educated.

National Archives of Canada/C 8051

Picnic at Chaplain Island in the Muskokas. The potent lure of nature drew Mackenzie King and thousands of other Canadians into the countryside.

Also packed in the English settler's portmanteau were the theories of Natural Theology. Mackenzie King certainly tried these ideas out for size. This movement, significant in Britain since the seventeenth century, portrayed nature not only as a stimulus for inspiring profound emotions and aesthetic admiration, but also as an illustration of God's grand design, where nothing was wasted and things of beauty could also be utilitarian. For example, mountains were extolled as beautiful *and* useful "...whether in creating rivers, providing natural frontiers or offering a congenial home for goats."[4] Appreciation of nature had become not only an aesthetic experience, but also a religious act. Wilderness was healing, beautiful, and spiritually powerful. By the end of the 18th century, the combination of Natural Theology and Romanticism had changed European attitudes toward the natural world. No longer did the rural scene symbolize backwardness and the wilderness, evil and disorder.

In Canada the reality of the bush was at first difficult to reconcile with Romantic ideals. Coming from a gentler landscape, British immigrants were ambivalent in their responses to Canadian nature. Awe-inspiring scenery mingled with blackflies and interminable forests frequently reduced Romantic emotional outbursts to a minimum. Nature was frequently viewed as irrationally threatening, uncontrollable and actively hostile to human endeavours.[5] However, as the terrors of the bush receded before the advance of cities and towns, nature, for some, reappeared dressed in Romantic clothing. Living on a crowded street without trees or flowers to soften the architectural hardness, some urban dwellers found the idea of the forest glen and sparkling lake immensely appealing.

Victorian Canada was familiar with the idea of the revelation of God-in-nature through sermons, children's stories, and publications.[6] Canadians were taught that nature was benevolent because God was benevolent. Nature as the handiwork of God was therefore an object worthy of study and meditation. "I never felt," King wrote from a Muskoka cottage in 1896, "so deeply impressed with the all pervading presence of an infinite God who inhabits Eternity as in this delightful spot. Nature in all its purity & beauty proclaims on every side the magnificence of his handywork & my soul enjovs a communion with His world about not to be expressed in words."

To experience nature was to see God, and not to be terrified by an incomprehensible force. Not for these Victorian enthusiasts was the pioneer's fear of raw Canadian nature, the encroaching forest, the log cabin vulnerable to the bitter cold of winter, or the crop-destroying drought or insect swarm.

The popularization of nature as a manifestation of God led directly to the formation and popularity of natural science clubs in central Canada and the Maritimes. The study of nature became a "...disciplined, scientific quest...a fashionable diversion,"[7] as well as a study of the ways of God. Natural history activities, such as botanizing or shell collecting, were characterized as edifying, morally upraising activities, suitably filling the leisure hours of educated, cultured people. Details of floras (plant collections) compiled during weekend rambles were often published in the late 1880s. Scenery was admired and captured in watercolours, and later in photographs taken with a family's first box camera.

Mackenzie King was not a true collector, for he loved "nature without a name" and his naturalizing was decidedly haphazard. One August morning King and a friend set out from a cottage on Gore Bay, Manitoulin Island to gather fossils: "We got a good deal of petrified moss, wood, &c., a couple of shells &c took two big hammers, & a small one also 2 valises with us" (16 August 1894). However these specimens seemed to suffer the usual fate of summer souvenirs — forgotten to gather dust in some dim corner of the house.

Country Versus City

The attractions of nature — spiritual and worldly — lured King and many others like him into the wilderness. However many Canadians were driven into the bush to escape the negative aspects of city living. From the late 1800s into the early 1900s migrants from rural areas and immigrants from abroad crowded into our cities and towns. Overcrowded and under-planned, the Canadian city was criticized for its physical and spiritual unhealthiness, for the accessibility of its dissipations, and the opportunities for moral backsliding. City life was also considered harmful to one's mental health, which was supposedly undermined by exposure to the ugliness of a typical urban streetscape — a profusion of utility poles, billboards, garbage heaps, chaotic mixtures of architectural styles, lack of vegetation, and a general drabness. Mental upset, nervous disorders and bad health were further aggravated by the hurly-burly and competitiveness of urban life.

Not surprisingly, the artificiality and unhealthiness of urban life was contrasted with the clean, simple, natural life in the country, a pastoral conceit present in Western literature since the Greeks and Romans, and echoed by the Canadian poets, Archibald Lampman, Duncan Campbell Scott, Bliss Carmen and Wilfrid Campbell:

> Are you bowed and bended double
> With a weight of care and trouble,
> Are you spectral with a skin like a sheet?
>
> Take your body and your soul to the woods,
> To the tonic and control of its moods...[8]

Well within this literary tradition, J.S. Woodsworth, the Canadian social activist, wrote in the common rhetoric of the period:

> The higher the buildings, the less sunshine; the bigger the crowds, the less fresh air....We become weary in the unceasing rush, and feel utterly lonely in the crowded

streets. There comes a wistful longing for the happy life of "God's out-of-doors" with the perfume of the flowers and the singing of the birds.[9]

However, the city/country contrast was emphasized for a deeper reason, beyond a guardianship of our morals or an indulgence of our "wistful longings." The flood of rural migrants into eastern Canadian cities provoked fears that the collapse of rural society was just around the corner. Abandoned farm houses became mute symbols of a growing rural malaise. Farmers left the land, discouraged by social isolation, unprofitable returns from farming, and a decreased farm labour market due to mechanization. Or they abandoned their farms simply lured by "city lights," and the promise of an easier life in town. Social commentators warned Canadians that their agricultural industry was deteriorating, which would severely weaken the nation.

To keep people happily on the farm, writings appeared idealizing the virtues of country living, and playing down traditionally negative stereotypes. The country bumpkin living in a stagnant backwater was replaced by a "son of the soil" living in the best of all possible worlds. Fresh, untainted air, beautiful surroundings, healthful exercise, innocent pastimes, and a sense of community were contrasted with the polluted air, ugly cityscape, anonymity, vices and the fast pace of city life. Even King, a very urban fellow himself, could comfortably echo these sentiments in 1900:

> I find myself more out of harmony with cities the more I see of them, they seem to me an abnormal growth, marking the triumph of mammon, and as such destined to suck the life blood from the vitals of their people. Men have succeeded in caging themselves like beasts, & will suffer for it as beasts do when caged (19 April 1900).

Mackenzie King throughout his life subscribed to the idealization of the countryside, and continually thrilled to scenes of rural activity. At age twenty, on holiday in the Muskokas, he marvelled: "...I sat in the waiting room of the Queens Hotel. The old settlers were sitting around a big stove and in little groups making a very pleasant little picture of 'life in a lonesome village'" (20 August 1894). In his seventies, King could still wonder: "It was a beautiful sight to see the hay wagon with the farmer's children helping in the loading of the hay, one of the boys holding a dog with a rope. It would be difficult to describe the loveliness of this rural scene...." (11 July 1945).

No matter how appealing the picture or how strong the nostalgic pull of the countryside, many urbanites did not intend to give up their metropolitan amenities. As well, many had to live in the city for their livelihoods. For these people, turn-of-the-century social commentators had a simple message: live in the countryside if only for short periods. Even a brief exposure would soothe life's cares and restore one's mental, moral and physical health as vacationers enjoyed "...this bracing, unbreathed, and untainted atmosphere."[10] As well, the nation would be strengthened if all urban young men would take rural holidays:

> ...after a few weeks' residence amongst these islands, living on the finest fish fresh water can produce, it is no wonder that our young men return to the city with their perceptive power increased, and just ache to take part in the controversy entailed on some vital question...[11]

In this context, Mackenzie King wrote to a friend from the Muskokas in 1892: "Getting brown as an Indian, also building up a good constitution for next year."[12] Recognizing the curative powers of nature, a group of philanthropists in 1874 built the Convalescent Home at Murray Bay (now La Malbaie), a popular resort on the lower St. Lawrence praised for its healthy climate. Invalids and the sick who could not afford a healthful summer in the country were sent there on the recommendation of Montreal charities. Room and board was paid by donation and, as a public duty, the summer residents helped to administer the home.[13]

As the cult of nature worship increased, and more people discovered the appeal of the great outdoors, a literature sprang up, intertwining itself with the other movements. Popularizations of nature lore, animal stories and romanticized accounts of Indian life added to the allure of the wilderness. To vicariously experience the idealized life of the forests or of the noble savage became part of the mystique:

> There is something of the savage in all of us, and after civilization has done its best, there is left that nomadic instinct which impels us periodically to seek new camping grounds.[14]

British Antecedents of Summer Resorts

Healthy though a country holiday might be, it was also judged by Mackenzie King and many other Canadians to be quite fashionable. Just as Canadian interpretations of nature had been directly influenced by British activity, thought and writing, so too was the urge to summer at a resort hotel or boarding house, or, later, a cottage of one's own. Long before the country holiday had become fashionable, the British aristocracy habitually spent part of the year on their country estates, an exodus which shaped the activities of London society. As well, wealthier members of the middle class from the late Middle Ages onward had summer homes in the country.[15] This movement out of London was motivated not only by the annual Parliamentary recess, but also by

National Archives of Canada/C 6313

Pauline Johnson, the "Mohawk Princess," evoked through her poetry the romantic allure of the wilderness — the beat of the tom-tom, the hush of the forest.

National Archives of Canada/C 58762

Resorts, such as Murray Bay, thrived as transportation links multiplied: excursion steamers traversed the Great Lakes and the St. Lawrence, railway lines were extended, and more roads were laid into the wilderness.

the threat to health and life. When rudimentary sanitary systems combined with summer heat, cholera and typhus became frequent hazards of summer life in large cities.

While country life was praised by many, and defined as a quintessentially English life style, some did dissent. An ambivalent attitude towards the countryside was always present — a nice place to visit, but not to live. High society, whose members' wealth and titles stemmed from their country estates, enjoyed seasonal, organized activities of country life. However, this did not preclude aristocratic, nor urban middle class, snobbery towards rural England — they did not fancy being permanently surrounded by what they thought of as yokels or being bored by bucolic activities. The Reverend Sydney Smith, one of England's foremost preachers and writers of the late 18th century, once wrote a friend from his Yorkshire country parish: "I have no relish for the country; it is a kind of healthy grave."

On the other hand, by the early 18th century, wealthy patrons might spend part of the social season in country resorts or spas — "country" defined as "not London." At the time, these resorts or spas were the only places outside London or the country estates of the wealthy[16] where leisure entertainment could be enjoyed. Spas were built around mineral springs, holy wells or streams with reputed therapeutic value. The sick were sent to specific sites, depending on their ailments to "take the waters."

By mid-18th century, "taking the waters" was not only a medical necessity, but had become a social one as well, as attendance during the season became an integral part of the upper class social round. Spa life changed when the middle classes began visiting the glittering, prestigious resorts. Exclusiveness decreased — attendance at a spa was transformed from a social necessity of the leisure class into a break in the working life of a family. By the 19th century, many less affluent people were taking holidays, usually within the British Isles.

The domestic holiday was further stimulated by increased leisure time, better transportation, and more money for luxuries, as well as by the writings of the Romantics. Seaside resorts began to flourish by the early 1800s and successfully challenged the supremacy of the spa. Increasingly, the new seaside resorts had less to do with health and much more to do with pleasure.

Central Canadian Summer Resorts

By the time of Mackenzie King's birth in the 1870s, resorting had progressed from its humble beginnings. At first "away from it all" meant an excursion into the bush, sleeping in tents and travelling by canoe. Roughing it for pleasure was an elitist activity up into the late 1800s. The beautiful scenery of lakes and forest, and its abundant wildlife and fish drew many affluent sportsmen to lake and river for a holiday. For example, in the 1850s a number of British army and navy officers built "fishing and hunting boxes" on Rice Lake in Upper Canada to take advantage of the abundant game and to stage hunting parties in the style of the "old country." By 1858 a regatta was held on the lake.[17] Although recreational tent camping was originally linked to men's hunting camps, by the 1880s families were camping together — either as part of a religious camp meeting, or as an affordable way of spending the summer on a lakeshore. In time some tenting sites were replaced by cottages or resorts.[18]

National Archives of Canada/C 58765

St. Lawrence Hall, a popular Cacouna, Quebec, resort hotel, offered many diversions. Here the ladies indluge in a bit of bowling after breakfast.

The most powerful catalyst in the promotion and growth of the central Canadian resort industry was the steamship — offering comfort, ease and accessibility of transport. Early resort development in Ontario and Quebec (along the St. Lawrence, in the Kawarthas, along the small ports of Lakes Erie and Ontario, around the Rideau Lakes, and in the Muskokas) boomed when regular steamboat routes were established. The Thousand Islands area had steamships plying its waters by the 1840s:

> ...assembled by some sedgy brook,
> A pic-nic party, resting in the shade,
> Spring pleasedly to their feet to catch a look
> At the strong steamer, through the watery glade,
> Ploughing, like a huge serpent from its ambuscade.[19]

In the St. Lawrence, steamships provided regular service between Montreal, Quebec and the Saguenay by 1853, especially after the construction of a new, enlarged wharf at Pointe-au-Pic near Murray Bay in the Charlevoix region. At first frequented by a few sportsmen, the Charlevoix area tourist trade was stimulated by the regularization of steamship schedules and the expansion of accommodations.

Laden steamships became a common sight: "To look at the piles of baggage and furniture, the hosts of children and servants, the household goods, the dogs, cats and birds, one might think the Canadians were emigrating *en masse*."[20] For those unwilling to spend the summer, three-day excursions from Quebec City to Murray Bay with a day's exploration of the Saguenay were offered for twelve dollars in 1853.[21] By the 1880s steamships, or *bateaux blancs* (so-called because of their gleaming white paint), were outfitted so elegantly and luxuriously, they were called floating palaces. For example, the three hundred passengers on the *Montréal* could dine in a magnificent salon ornamented with bronze bas-reliefs depicting the four seasons.[22]

Steamboat excursions by the 1870s had become standard holiday fare for many central Canadians — Mackenzie King among them. As a treat in June 1894, the high-spirited King and a friend enjoyed the delights, including flirting with young ladies, of an overnight excursion aboard the *Chippewa* from Toronto to Niagara. They had such fun, they extended the trip another day and journeyed on to Buffalo, arranging the boat trip to maximize the number of free on-board meals. There they met a couple of girls, walked and talked in the rain, and in general had "a splendid time." King also had opportunities to go on day excursions to popular picnic grounds — always a favourite with large groups such as Sunday schools, Farmers' Institutes, and schools.

Murray Bay (now La Malbaie) was one of the most popular St. Lawrence resorts. Arthur Buies, a Quebec social activist and man of letters, praised Murray Bay in 1878 as "...la plus pittoresque et la plus poétique des places d'eau, l'Eden du Canada, le rêve du poète."[23] William H. Taft, twenty-seventh president of the United States, who summered at Murray Bay for nearly forty years, unreservedly praised the resort: "The invigorating air of Murray Bay exhilarates like champagne without the effects of the morning after."[24]

Annie Fréchette, a journalist who wrote for the American journal, *Harper's*, had another opinion. In 1884 she described the resort life, where mainly women and their children were found on week days, as subdued and exhibiting "none of the mad gayety of the fashionable watering-places."

> No matter if people go there bent upon being systematically frivolous, Nature takes them in hand and teaches them a perhaps unrealized lesson at every turn.... Certainly these do essay, night after night, to bring into the primitive ball-rooms of the hotels something like the giddy dance; but either because most of the participants are already weary of limb from climbing hills or rowing about the bay, or because piano-forte music, a dearth of young gentlemen, and a not overabundance of coal-oil lamps do not combine readily to form an exhilarating atmosphere, the dance soon languishes.[25]

The early Quebec resorts were often compared with fashionable Newport, Rhode Island society life. St. Lawrence society was usually judged the more wholesome and low-keyed, but lacked the glamour of Newport with its "...scandals, its petty quarrels, its frivolous affectations, its conceits and its attempt at semi-respectability!"[26] Yet, Murray Bay, a quiet, conservative resort, inspired vociferous loyalty from families who returned year after year. French and English Canadian high society were well represented: Louis Fréchette (the "poet laureate of French Canada"), Sir Adolphe Routhier (judge and author of "O, Canada"), Sir Rodolphe Forget (industrialist), the historian George M. Wrong. American notables such as the widowed Mary Todd Lincoln, and some American Cabots also summered there.

The construction of the Manoir Richelieu in 1899 by the Montreal architects Maxwell and Shattuck, gave the resort an air of luxury and exclusivity. Among the usual amenities of good food and stupendous views, the hotel, novel for its time, also provided a barber shop, beauty shop, swimming pool, golf course, resident doctor, and an orchestra which played every afternoon as well as four evening concerts per week.[27] The hotel, burned to the ground in 1928, was rebuilt in stone, resembling a French château.[28] By the 1930s, Murray Bay had outgrown its conservative reputation and had been dubbed the "Newport of the North."[29]

A.M. Ross/National Archives of Canada/PA 120309

Tenting was popular with families by the late 1880s. A tent was often the precursor to a family cottage.

Tadoussac, at the mouth of the Saguenay River, acquired a glamorous image when the Earl of Dufferin built a summer home there during his tenure as Governor General. Tadoussac, frequented since the mid-1850s by a quieter crowd, had become, due to the Governor General, "...the chosen resort of some of the most fashionable French families of Quebec...and a very entertaining, lively society has formed itself."[30] Tourists were attracted to the area by the salmon fishing, the chance of sighting porpoises, seals and whales, the Saguenay's beauty, and the luxurious Tadoussac hotel built in 1865.

After the Civil War ended in 1865, ever-increasing numbers of Americans frequented St. Lawrence resorts. The Americans were said to be especially attracted by the Quebec resorts, where they could hear "...snatches of conversation, carried on in French and English, which they have caught as picturesque un-American-looking people strolled past them."[31] The *habitants* were an additional attraction. As one British visitor remarked, the locals seemed to be "one of the happiest, most contented peasantries probably in the world, and not by any means the least picturesque."[32]

The Maritimes also attracted summer vacationers. New Brunswick resorts were once whimsically described as excellent places with the "...most liberal licence laws; first class cuisine and a bar in the hotel. No tourists, no golf, too cold to swim — just the place to enjoy oneself."[33] St. Andrews, New Brunswick on Passamoquoddy Bay, founded in 1783, was a Loyalist town renowned for its shipbuilding. Thrown into decline when it lost its economic rivalry with Saint John, the beautiful small seaport was saved by the substantial American and Canadian summer resort colony. William Van Horne, Sir Charles Tupper, Sir James Dunn and Thomas Shaughnessy built summer homes there. Later the Algonquin Hotel became the centre of St. Andrews' thriving resort industry.[34]

Nova Scotia was also touted as "ideal vacation land" due to its invigorating atmosphere, lack of insects, and healthy climate — "Nature's sanatorium."[35] Digby, for example, was promoted as a resort town, advertising such attractions as deep sea fishing, moose hunting, sightseeing (the Micmac "camps" were highly recommended), in addition to the usual resort activities. Lour Lodge, as late as 1913, charged $14 a week for a room in high season. Its eleven cottages were the main rental accommodation in the town. In addition to tennis courts, croquet lawns and a sheltered, comfortable verandah, Lour Lodge also advertised "a cosy and attractive sitting room and a fine large parlour well adapted to card parties or afternoon teas."[36]

Some Thousand Islands resorts were originally sites of religious camp meetings. Attended by less affluent holidayers, they came from Toronto, Hamilton, and other Ontario towns to such campgrounds as Grimsby Park, Niagara-on-the-Lake and Thousand Islands Park on Wellesley Island.[37] By the 1870s, reflecting the rising popularity of summer resort living, many of these camp-meeting sites had become secularized and drawn into the fashionable social round.[38] On one former campsite, called Thousand Islands Park, cottage lots were sold by the Reverend J.F. Dayan to fellow Methodists. These lots were said to be an "outgrowth of a sincere desire to glorify God, and yet, in doing so, to make summer homes where families could receive the benefits of change of scene and of air and perhaps in the manner of living."[39] The Park was praised as a place where a man could leave his wife and family for the season without fear they would be exposed to any harmful influences.[40] Steamers were not allowed to dock there on Sundays.

The Muskokas

The young, high-spirited Mackenzie King holidayed in the resort area preferred by many Torontonians — the Muskokas. Sited on the southern edge of the Canadian Shield, the area appealed to Mackenzie King and other Ontarians because of the abundance of lakes and rivers, its picturesque scenery of islands, forest, and water, its range of accommodations, and, with the coming of the steamship and railroad, its accessibility.

For many Canadians, the Shield, a primeval bedrock covering half of Canada, epitomized the raw, wild, primitive wilderness and symbolized the colourful, adventurous life of the voyageur. The Shield discouraged settlers attempting to farm the thin soil which barely covered the Precambian rock, but yielded more to others. Hudson's Bay Company trappers saw the Shield as a mother-lode of furs, and its rivers and lakes as a main water route into distant trapping areas. Lumbermen and prospectors exploited the Shield's rich reserves of timber (conifers, maples, beeches, hemlocks) and minerals. It was a naturalist's paradise, with swamps and bogs, mountains and meadows contributing their unique flora and fauna — fish, wildflowers, insects (unfortunately endless swarms of mosquitoes and black flies among them), and wildlife.[41]

The rise of the Muskokas as a prime resort can be traced to the enterprise of one man, A.P. Cockburn, who believed in the area's potential. In the late 1860s he built the first steamships on the three Muskoka lakes after local Indian bands ceded the land to Canada and the government opened it to colonization.[42] When railway lines, superseding the lumpy corduroy roads, were extended into the Muskokas, travel from eastern Ontario became much less arduous. Cockburn effectively promoted the scenic attractions of the area and its transportation facilities in pamphlets and newspapers. In 1866 his first steamer, the *Winonah*, was on the lakes, and within four years the first resort hotel, Rosseau Hotel on Lake Rosseau, was in operation.[43] By 1871 a cut at Port Sandfield joined all three lakes — Muskoka, Joseph and Rosseau — thus making the area even more accessible.

Steamers became increasingly important in the Muskoka holiday scene when railway schedules were meshed with those of the ships. The Grand Trunk's *Muskoka Express* from Toronto discharged its passengers onto Gravenhurst's Muskoka Wharf Station, which jutted nearly seventy meters out into the lake.[44] It was the major embarkation point for a summer holiday. To the right of the gingerbread-trimmed, clapboard station house, the commercial steamboats, the *Muskoka*, the *Nipissing*, the *Medora*, the *Kenozha*, as well as private hotel launches, waited to take on passengers. Steamship journeys provided the venue for annual reunions of habitual Muskoka holidayers, as well as opportunities to make new and valuable contacts. King enjoyed meeting "jolly sorts of girls," buying them little boxes of candy, dancing and promenading on deck. He was never adverse to meeting important people, and certainly enjoyed the trip he shared with the Bishop of Algoma and his daughter. Shipboard amusements were genteel. Social activities centred around polite conversation, dancing, admiring the scenery, hymns around the piano after breakfast, and eating.

F.W. Micklethwaite/National Archives of Canada/PA 132116

Windermere Hotel on Lake Rosseau was one of the most luxurious of the grand Muskoka hotels.

Hotel development was slow before Cockburn began promoting the area. Many hotels began as private homes where rooms were occasionally rented to visiting fishermen and sportsmen. Gradually extensions were built when the owners realized there was money to be made housing and feeding tourists. In time, these homes became summer boarding houses, some later evolving into sizable hotels.[45] When steamer-docking wharfs were built in front of the larger hotels, commercial success was nearly guaranteed.

The newly built hotels were usually quite large, ornate wooden buildings, two to three stories high, characterized by: "...towers, turrets and gables, lavishly trimmed with lattice and gingerbread fretwork," and full-length balconies and verandahs.[46] Verandahs were important social centres, where tea, gossip and covert assessments of new arrivals were the main amusements.

F.W. Micklethwaite/National Archives of Canada/PA 129995

Fisher Island, Lake Joseph, ca. 1910. Some families built elaborate cottages, influenced by the example of grand Newport, Rhode Island cottages.

At night, in the verandah's dark corners "...confidences and an occasional pressure of the hand (possibly a kiss)..."[47] were exchanged. Some hotels provided a separate dining room for children and their nannies, as well as for the guests' personal maids.[48] No matter what style they were built in, or what amenities they offered, the hotels were united by the ever-present threat of fire. Over the years, quite a number were destroyed by sparks and untended fires.

Hotel grounds could be landscaped elaborately, such as Maplehurst Hotel on Lake Rosseau, with lawn, flower beds, trellised arbours, and gazebos overlooking the lake.[49] To supply their dining rooms, some hotels cultivated vegetable gardens and orchards. In addition to good food, hotels provided boat rentals, dance halls, scenic cruises, archery ranges, tennis courts, croquet lawns, bowling greens, shuffleboard courts, and later, golf courses.[50] For $2.50 per day, visitors to the Georgian Bay House, Penetanguishene, could enjoy hot and cold sulfur baths, an excellent livery, drives and picnic parties.[51] Regattas often highlighted the summer season. The friendly competition between hotels and cottagers, over trophies and ribbons for canoe and boat races and other aquatic events, drew huge crowds each year.

Resorts also offered social status. Although to the modern reader their rates seem reasonable, resort holidays were often beyond the resources of the average worker. Exclusivity was determined by transportation costs and the leisure to enjoy these escapes into the wild. By the 1890s the news of Society's summer entertainments was eminently reportable:

> Columns of print were given over to cataloguing the names of visitors at the hotels. Whole sections in the weekend editions described the romantic activities at the resorts, the regattas on Rice Lake, Burlington Bay, Lake Rosseau, and the Bay of Quinte; the picnics on Strawberry Island, a speck in the northern part of Lake Simcoe; the taffy pulls at Rosebank, on the Rouge River just east of Toronto; the dances and the visits and the fishing.[52]

King and Muskoka

The young King found the carefree, eventful Muskoka life to his liking. In fact, he entered into his Muskoka holidays with great gusto — often the guest of his Kappa Alpha fraternity brothers, or friendly Alpha Deltas. In 1894 he travelled "back to nature" with a smoking jacket, cricket blazer, dancing pumps, hymnal and Bible (Diary endpapers, 1894). Other members of the King family were "farmed out" to friends' cottages — his parents and younger brother went to a Mr. Dickie's cottage at Port Sandfield, his two sisters to an unnamed cottage elsewhere in the Muskokas. This seemed to be a family pattern, not unusual for other middle class Ontarians. At other times, the Kings, not wealthy enough to own their own cottage, stayed with friends or rented rooms in a resort hotel. However, by the time King was holidaying in the Muskokas, building a cottage of one's own had become quite fashionable.

National Archives of Canada/PA 124450

King loved to canoe — here he paddles with his friend, Joan Patteson, in the mid-1920s.

The Riordan cottage on Lake Rosseau where King frequently visited was an example of a summer cottage where the owner had (in King's words) "spared neither time or money in making this a lovely spot:"

> All the woods have been cleared out, no dead wood is lying about. Splendid walks run around & through different parts of the Island. Seats are scattered around in favourite spots. In front of the house is a large clearing which allows one to see a long way down the lake. A great many beautiful flowers have been planted in different places and are now in splendid bloom. Near the wharf are 3 boat & bathing houses, sail boats canoes row boats etc. To the left of the house is a beautiful grove filled with hammocks, a most inviting place. The large verandah which surrounds the house itself affords 27 laps to the mile....A tennis court is made in a beautiful locality among the trees....A windmill at one end forces up the water from the lake.... (22 August 1895).

Mackenzie King enjoyed all the typical cottaging activities. Canoeing was a favoured sport, although most cottagers of means also had yachts and later motorboats. The Macdonalds at Kagawong Lake, Manitoulin Island, where King spent two weeks in August 1894, had a yacht, the *Vega*, large enough to carry nearly twenty passengers. But the canoe was the romantic favourite. A canoe was a passport into the wilderness, into remote, inaccessible spots: "...canoes are for pleasure...canoes are natural....In a canoe you can steal up to her [Nature's] bower and peep into her very bosom."[53] Whether it was the exercise or the peeping, canoeing was promoted as a restorative activity, promising a simple, elemental life on the water. Canoeing allegedly provided not only health, but also solid character-building — "All gentlemen are not canoeists, but all canoeists are gentlemen."[54]

Mackenzie King particularly enjoyed the fellowship of canoe excursions, songs around the picnic campfire, and glimpses of inspiring nature:

> The new moon came up to lend extra beauty to all surroundings and the paddle home by moonlight both down the river and over the smooth lake among the many islands can only be thought of by the imagination. Every star in the Heavens was reflected in the waters. We sang, whistled and kept time with our paddles, Oh what a Heaven this earth can be! (5 September 1894)

He especially enjoyed taking young ladies "for a paddle," to commune with nature and discuss the meaning of life. King also canoed to build up his constitution. One energetic day a friend and he paddled twenty miles on Lake Rosseau.

As well King hiked and swam. Swimming also offered chances for mild flirtations, when King and his friends taught young women to swim. King also enjoyed tennis on private courts, a common feature on the affluent cottage landscape. King delighted in winning, but looked on others who did not take their losses well as behaving "...not in any manner becoming a gentleman..." (27 August 1895). He also burned up excess energy by rowing for supplies, or participating in boxing bouts.

Other diversions were less strenuous. King once spent three hours reading from Ruskin and Gibbon to young ladies at the Riordans' cottage:

> I have had moreover as a delightful audience, two bright intellectual and beautiful young ladies who swing in hammocks or sit at my side as I read aloud. I will hear their silvery voices in a moment or two telling me that they are ready for more..."Will, are you ready?" and of course I answered "always."[55]

Visits to other cottagers, Sunday church attendance, and tea with friends at nearby hotels punctuated long summer days. Intense discussions on the verities of life were also part of the entertainment for King:

> Tonight I had a most delightful walk & talk with Amy. We started walking round the verandah & kept it up from 7 till 9.40 must have gone nearly 10 miles. Spoke mostly of God, Eternity, Immortality, Life, &c. Both were confidential & earnest (13 September 1896).

Evenings were enlivened by hymn sings, fortune telling, card games ("...had a splendid game of 'snap pack' ...we all had our hands badly damaged" 8 August 1894), and always food. Formal entertainments such as fancy dress balls were organized. In August 1894, King attended a masquerade as a young lady, "Clementine," wearing a borrowed dress from one of the "silvery voiced" young ladies at the cottage and having his hair frizzed by the other. The following year, as the "Heavenly Twins" King and Jack Falconbridge "....dressed in long baby robes with little hoods & ribbons, we were blackened with corks, he was 'Angelica' I was 'Diabolo'" (9 August 1895). "Walk rounds" were also staged. In one a Mr. Burson led the cottage group in a grand parade around the cottage grounds playing a bugle and wearing a tea cosy on his head (11 August 1894).

Flirtations also helped to pass the time. In the late 1800s cottage house parties offered a conducive, yet safe, venue for the "mingling of the sexes." In August 1895 while staying at the Douglas' cottage, "Highlands" on Lake Rosseau, King enjoyed a brief flirtation with Kitty, the seventeen-year-old daughter of the house. It began with a moonlight canoe ride and serious conversation:

> We got talking along different lines, historical, economic, religious. The stars were beautiful above [over?] head and we exchanged our thoughts freely. Kitty has a beautiful mind indeed, a wonderful mind for a girl of 17. She is very original and a charming girl to talk to (12 August 1895).

It progressed over two weeks, King read poetry and Gibbon in the boathouse for hours on end to her. Finally he admitted to himself that he had fallen "insensibly in love" with Kitty. Then he panicked, and confessed all to her, saying it was not right:

> ...I had conquered myself enough to know that all I felt towards her now & henceforth was nothing but pure friendship and a sincere interest in her welfare & happiness thro' life....When we began talking the moon passed through the clouds, appearing hiding and reappearing at times and as we confessed all it shone brightly out behind a dark cloud which shrouded half the sky. So was my confession....May its remembrance bring no sorrow to the heart but like the brightness of that heavenly sphere, may it shine forth as a little bright page in the history of a life just beginning to unfold not in one life only but in two (27 August 1895).

A few days later he could not understand why she was so unpleasant: "I do not like such an exhibition of feigned unconcernedness in such a young girl" (30 August 1895). This experience did not seem to leave any internal scars as King continued to gleefully record his canoeing, hiking and reading with young women on subsequent Muskoka holidays.

King and Newport

The innocent fun and high spirits of his Canadian cottaging experience sharply contrasted with his stay in Newport, Rhode Island in August 1899. Mackenzie King had been hired to tutor his Harvard classmates, Peter and Robert Gerry, in French and German.[56] Newport, a fishing and trading port on the windy, rocky coast of Rhode Island, was transformed into a summer resort in the early 1800s. Wealthy Southerners sailed up from the tide-water regions, and rented or built summer homes to escape the South's summer heat, humidity and malaria.[57] By the 1880s wealthy New Yorkers followed, building palatial summer homes, called "cottages," along Bellevue Avenue. With their arrival, Newport became the archetypical fashionable resort — where who you were mattered more than what you were. Mrs. William Astor, the proclaimed leader of Society, ruled Newport resort life, characterized by opulence, propriety, and a set round of activities. In her autobiography, Edith Wharton reminisced about her Newport days — days filled with the ardours of "calling," of the daily carriage drives accompanied by liveried footmen and dressed "as elegantly as for a race-meeting at Auteuil or Ascot."[58] Although she later admitted that this social set was not very intellectually stimulating, as a young girl she fully enjoyed her summers at Pencraig:

> Every room in our house was always full in summer, and I remember jolly bathing parties from the floating boat-landing at the foot of the lawn, mackerel-fishing, races in rival 'cat-boats,' and an occasional excursion up the bay, or out to sea...on one of the pretty white steam-yachts which were beginning to be the favourite toys of the rich.[59]

"Rich" was certainly the operative word. The "cottages" were ornate, theatrical backdrops for the ostentatious activities enacted each season. That August, Mackenzie King entered a world he had never seen before and mixed for the first time with people who were not his social equals. It was not a heady experience, but rather one of self-revelation and at times revulsion.

From the first day when he sailed to Newport on the Gerry's yacht, the *Electra* (all mahogany and cherry wood with brass fittings), King was alternately impressed and appalled by the trappings of great wealth. He greatly admired the stately grounds surrounding the Bellevue mansions. Sea Verge, the Gerry's cottage-cum-mansion, sported beautiful lawns leading down to the ocean, hydrangeas lending blue and pink accents to graceful flower borders, a conservatory filled with roses, grape vines and exotic plants. But he probably would not have admired the ostentatious Rogers estate, which was elaborately landscaped to imitate one of Mr. Roger's magnificent Persian carpets. Luckily King did not visit the gardens at Bois Doré where the owner hung his trees with 14K gold apples.[60] Yet, he admired the interiors of the "cottages," especially the Vanderbilt's Marble House. It was all gilt and marble and costly furnishings. The ballroom, modeled after the Petit Trianon at Versailles, was embellished with crystal chandeliers, carved gold leaf wall panels, and a magnificent marble fireplace.[61] In the end, all this glitter did not sway the young King:

> I judge not the man by his possessions but by himself, to be made to feel that I am beneath another, raises all the blood in my veins....I will never bow to wealth...I would write were I able over the skies of this place "Vanity vanity, all is vanity" (15 August 1899).

This "true Christian in the den of iniquity" was appalled by the lack of church attendance on a Sunday morning in contrast with full attendance at the Casino the same evening. His opinion of Newport society was further lowered when he attended a charity theatre performance:

> As I looked down from the gallery on the women below, the sight was intoxicating. Women with all the adornment wealth could bestow, in low necked dresses bare arms, many displayed their breasts almost entirely...As I looked at a group of them in pale blue with white gauze etc., it was like looking into a sea in which mermaids were bathing. Society runs close to the border of abandonment. Yet these people believe themselves to be above all others in the world! (5 September 1899).

Although abstaining from drinking and gambling, King led a typical Newport resort life: swimming, sunbathing, walking, bicycle polo, driving, horseback riding and attending parties. He maintained his friendship with Peter Gerry until the end of his life, although the lessons of Newport were never forgotten — King's lifelong distrust of great wealth was implanted amidst the glamour of the New England resort. When he began to create his Gatineau estate, King emulated the style of the staid Muskokas rather than the opulence of Newport.

Ottawa Resorts

By the time King arrived in Ottawa in 1900, he had holidayed from Muskoka to Newport, from the country houses of England to the palaces of Italy and France. The Ottawa resort and cottage areas offered a much narrower choice.

The resort holiday was part of Ottawa society's summer plans by the turn of the century. The wealthy left the city for extended periods: "...the chief charm of September lies in the fact that it brings people back to town."[62] To escape Ottawa's stultifying heat and humidity, Ottawans travelled by rail and steamer to resorts along the St. Lawrence. Others (less affluent or less able to leave their jobs) sought shorter holidays closer to town or within the city limits, easily reached by carriage, or the cheaper transportation of the street railway. Rockcliffe Park, created in the late 1800s, was advertized as a place unfortunately overlooked by "the younger generation," where "...nature appears to have outshone herself in her efforts to provide food for the tired brain and rest for the weary body."[63] Sited on the banks of the Ottawa River in the northeast section of the city, the park's beauty was enhanced by its large stand of native trees, scenic drives, a rock escarpment, and wild flowers in abundance.

National Archives of Canada/C 10842

Britannia-on-the-Bay, a favoured Ottawa resort, was easily reached by streetcar.

Located on the other side of the city, Hog's Back fishing grounds were the oldest public camping grounds in the area. It supposedly received its name from a prominent rock formation which looked like the back of a hog: a formation "...no one whose imagination is at all defective can detect..."[64] The Rideau River widened into a small lake at this spot, at one end of the lake a natural rock dam supplemented by sluice gates turned the river into a series of cascades.

Another favourite resort was Britannia (west of Ottawa), a small village on Lake Deschenes on the Ottawa River. By 1880 Britannia, a small community of labourers and carpenters, was enlarged by ten cottage families. Ten years later, sixty cottagers (senior civil servants, lawyers, merchants, and other professionals) summered in the area.[65] Dr. E. Stone Wiggins, B.A., M.A., LL.D., M.D., a Finance Department official, built a summer home called Arbor House, which later became his primary residence. He was noted for his amazing weather forecasts: "I shall never forget how, in 1883, we did all watch for that storm he predicted for March 5th. None of us believed that such a thing was possible for any living man to say...when it came exactly to the day as he had said, our surprise was unbounded..."[66] When he predicted in 1894 that an earthquake would hit Ottawa in the fall of 1904 and it did, his prestige was assured. Other less exciting, but socially prominent cottagers who built at Britannia were the under-Minister of Agriculture Sidney Fisher; the ex-mayor of Ottawa, Frederick Cook; the son of a Chief Justice; and

National Archives of Canada/C 22762

Queen's Park, an Aylmer, Quebec resort, offered a variety of amusements.

Robert Burland, manager of the British Bank Note Company.[67]

Resort life was nothing without hotels. By the 1890s the Balmoral and the Chateau Von Charles offered rooms to summer visitors at Britannia. The Chateau Von Charles was operated by Frederica de Vallier Von Charles, a French immigrant, who came to Ottawa in 1888. The Chateau was known for its cuisine as well as the charming personality of its owner. The Balmoral, sited on the same intersection as the Chateau, boasted "every modern convenience, superior cuisine, and reasonable rates."[68]

In 1900 the first street railway route to Britannia was inaugurated, opening it to people other than summer resorters. Before then Britannia could be reached only by train or by horse-and-carriage. The Ottawa Electric Railway Company (O.E.R.) during the 1890s replaced horse-drawn trams with electric ones and extended the lines of operation. The first tracks, laid along Ottawa's main streets, terminated at the Central Canada Exhibition grounds. This was a typical development pattern for North American streetcar lines. In order to popularize streetcar use and increase profits, many companies built amusement parks, connecting them by track to the downtown core. This enabled companies to fill cars with workers during the weekdays, and excursionists on the weekends.[69] The O.E.R. was no exception. It had already extended lines to popular Sunday picnic and strolling sites such as Rockcliffe Park and the Central Experimental Farm. Around the same time the company bought land on the bay at Britannia to develop an amusement and recreation area. To promote their investment the O.E.R. laid tracks out to the resort.

The *Ottawa Free Press* boldly proclaimed that the resort "...would compare favourably with Coney Island, Newport or any of the great American watering places..."[70] Certainly the common elements of popular seaside resorts were present: numerous bath houses, a refreshment pavilion, fishing sites and picnic grounds. An auditorium, featuring vaudeville performances, plays, band concerts and later movies, was built near a long pier and riverside boardwalk. Band concerts were held once a week by a military band such as the Govenor General's Footguards Band. Like a noisy Pied Piper, a band would lead music lovers out to the resort, playing in a special open-air streetcar, decorated with a banner announcing "Band concert at Britannia tonight."

Visitors to Britannia could also take day trips on paddle wheelers and later steam yachts. For fifty cents one could go on a day excursion up the Ottawa River, picnic at Fitzroy Harbour and enjoy the scenery. The most popular was the C.B. Green's moonlight excursion where one could dance into the night to the music of a live orchestra.[71] Wealthier boating enthusiasts had their own yachts and belonged to the Britannia Boathouse Club.

The O.E.R. was anxious to develop Britannia-on-the-Bay to offset the growing popularity of a resort across the river in Aylmer, Quebec. The Hull-Aylmer Electric Railway ran a line, inaugurated in 1896, up to their resort, Queen's Park. The scenery viewed on the half hour trip from downtown Ottawa to the resort was said to be well worth the ten cent fare. Queen's Park offered the usual recreations: swimming, fishing, strolling, and amusements at the entertainment pavilions, as well as boat excursions up the Ottawa River. One building housed "The Maze" where even "the most ingenious person can get lost."[72] Another favourite amusement was "shooting" the water chute. Passengers, seated in "a huge boat shaped like an old fashioned rocker," were winched to the top of a wooden structure "up to heights which make you dizzy" then sent whooshing down: "The first time you are on you invariably grasp the seat on which you are sitting, hold down your head, shut your eyes and say nothing. Later you grow accustomed to it...."[73] Queen's Park was patronized during the parliamentary session by M.P.s, senators and cabinet ministers — who along with their ladies — enjoyed a few hours of "needed rest, away from the heat of the city."[74]

The Hotel Victoria, sited on top of a hill which sloped down to the beach, offered accommodation for those who did not want to rent or buy cottages in the area. Boating, swimming, tennis, golf, and promenading down wooded walks were standard activities there. Cottages were built near the hotel in forest clearings owned by the Hull-Aylmer Electric Railway. Not to be outdone by Britannia, one commentator said those who did not patronize Queen's Park were missing "pleasures nearer to home which equal Bar Harbor..."[75] Others who rejected the pleasures of home-grown Newports or Bar Harbors sought the quiet, undeveloped Gatineau hills.

Chelsea

In 1900 when King first went up into the Gatineaus, the villages of Chelsea and Kingsmere were noted for their quiet, restful atmosphere in contrast to the "more crowded resorts." Lumbering and farming, the area's main industries, were slowly supplemented by tourism. Mainly settled by Irish immigrants, Chelsea was the religious centre of the surrounding farming community, including Kingsmere. Before the Ottawa and Gatineau Valley Railway was built, visitors to Chelsea had to endure a long stage ride to and from Ottawa. Chelsea was a favourite spot for picnickers, who favoured the grove of pine trees near the railway station[76] and the rushing waters of the Cascades on the Gatineau River. The railway, to encourage more custom, distributed illus-

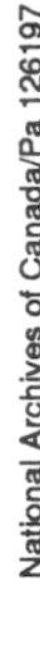

A view of the village of Kingsmere from the stage coach.

trated booklets describing the Gatineau district, its game laws for hunters, and accommodations for nature lovers.[77] Chelsea supported a number of hotels, among these in the 1860s was the O'Neill Temperance Inn.[78]

By the late 1800s Chelsea had attracted a number of prominent cottagers: John Sharpe, the sculptor; high-ranking civil servants such as George Johnson, the Dominion Statistician; ministers, and newspaper editors.[79] One of the summer residents, Mike Bristow, built a clay court behind his house and organized a tennis club. He also hosted dances lit by Japanese lanterns and accompanied by a hired military band.[80] Another of Chelsea's early summer residents was Mary McKay Scott who wrote inspirational articles for Ottawa newspapers under the penname "Yarrow" — the name of her cottage. Her summers spent at Chelsea were the subject of many articles: "All thoughts of too near file cases, dusty offices, banging typewriters, bells, screeching whistles, and granolithic pavements, faded away, and the peace and comfort of the hills was ours."[81] Here she was surrounded by the serenity her religious temperament required: "...there is nothing so reposeful as the everlasting hills, with the shadows on them so refreshing to the spirit."[82] She wrote of her pansies, forget-me-nots, and sweet-peas, roses, hedges of peonies, and how she was surrounded by "...the things she loved — blue china, old books, flowers, pictures, and her beloved piano...."[83]

Kingsmere

Tourists and cottagers did not appear at Kingsmere until the late 1800s. Dating from 1792, the area was part of York County, Quebec. For the next fourteen years, the present Kingsmere area was known only as Range 7 and 8. The area, opened for colonization in 1800, was settled at first by Americans. The first settler, William Jeff (after whom the lake was first named) in 1824 took lot 20 of Range 7 which bordered on the lake. The area developed slowly as a farming settlement over the next twenty years.[84] The descendants of some of these early farming families (the Mulvihills, Murphys, Fleurys and Deans) played important roles in the development of the cottage community (and Mackenzie King's estate) by providing labour, provisions, equipment and expertise in building boathouses and cottages and erecting fences.

The 1870s saw some tourist activity in the area. Although not substantiated, some claimed that Edward VII when he was the Prince of Wales (and not so portly) was taken up King Mountain as part of his 1860 Canadian tour. However, another royal, Princess Louise (one of Queen Victoria's daughters), during the time of her husband's Governor Generalship (1878-83) definitely visited the lake, climbing King Mountain on a path that was cut especially for her. She was said to be delighted with the "unusual beauty and panorama" of the place.[85]

National Archives of Canada/PA 126162

View of Kingsmere Lake taken from the Kingswood shore.

Although undeveloped, the attractions of lake and mountain only eight kilometers from the Chelsea railway station were prophetically praised in 1873: "...we would be quite content if we could in the cool of the evening leave the dusty, pent-up city, and seek repose in some cottage overlooking the Gatineau....The hotels and cottages in the neighbouring mountains are among the illusions of the future..."[86] When one of the farm families began operating a stage between the Chelsea station and Kingsmere, the area became more accessible as a popular weekend picnicking and hiking site. The Ottawa Field Naturalists' Club enjoyed combining their naturalizing with picnicking near Kingsmere. In May 1879 the club went by horse-drawn van out to Kingsmere to sketch the scenery and collect specimens on King Mountain. A good day was had by all but one luckless collector who fell over a log, crushing a bottleful of beetles. These excursions became so popular that by 1902, 300 members participated in expeditions to Chelsea and the surrounding countryside.[87]

The first cottagers were drawn to Kingsmere by its accessible wilderness and scenic grandeur, the stirring scenery of the southern Shield. In 1875 the first cottage was built by John Chamberlain for the Deputy-Minister of the Department of Interior, Colonel J.D. Dennis. Soon J.S. Bourinot, the Clerk of the House of Commons and man of letters, joined him.[88] Bourinot bought the Jeffs' original log farm house with its large orchard, and grape vines. In a hired furniture van, Bourinot moved not only his family, pets and piano but also parts of his library to Kingsmere for the summer months when the House of Commons adjourned.[89] There he wrote his essays, historical studies and biographical sketches.[90]

In 1880 Dennis, Bourinot and a new arrival, H.V. Noel (a

National Capital Commission

Kingsmere Lake.

bank manager) decided to have the name of the lake changed when the little village needed a post office, thus an official name. Inspired by the English lakes Grassmere and Windermere, they named it Kingsmere Lake — the lake of the king,[91] probably influenced by the proximity of King Mountain.

By the early 1890s the little lake resort appeared more settled as cottages and year-round homes began filling up the lakeshore. Neighbouring farmers serviced the small summer community with transportation, water, ice and labour. The village was now subject to the seasonal rhythms of cottage life: from closing up in the fall to opening the cottage with its attendant removal from the city:

> We packed our belongings on a covered furniture van, piano, sewing machine, typewriter, furniture and pretty china, and left our rooms on the top flat of an apartment house and hied us to the country...let us recommend a drive in the country on a high seat furniture van.[92]

The lake continued to be a major attraction. Mrs. Herridge, Mackenzie King's good friend, said the lake had medicinal properties: "...it has made her a new woman....She likes it better than the ocean, and thinks it as beautiful as Switzerland."[93] King said he immediately fell in love with Kingsmere — its hills, water, and forest cover. However, his romantic reaction was probably also influenced by his realistic appraisal of the area. The class of summer people living at the lake was decidedly "the right sort," owning a cottage had not only a health appeal but also a social one, important for a man who repeatedly sought out the right connections, made the proper contacts. But beyond the scenery and the social cachet, the deciding factor could have been the presence of Mrs. Herridge who was to be a very real part of King's early Kingsmere life.

CHAPTER TWO

Kingswood

OUT INTO THE LANDSCAPE

KING'S YEARS AT KINGSWOOD, AS HE CAME TO CALL HIS LAKESIDE cottages, were set against a backdrop of turmoil in his personal life and a time of growth and decision-making in his professional and political life. The Kingswood era also witnessed the beginning of the fantasy he wove of his life in the Gatineau Hills — a fantasy related to the way King was to shape his landscape. Kingswood set the stage for King to act out the patterns of thought and behaviour which were later magnified and embellished as his estate grew and his involvement in landscaping deepened.

Mrs. Herridge

Mackenzie King returned to Mrs. McMinn's Kingsmere boarding house for the summer of 1902. The winter had been traumatic for King. His closest friend and fellow Kingsmere enthusiast, Bert Harper, had drowned during Governor General Minto's skating party in December 1901. With a cry of "What else can I do?" he jumped into the dark, icy waters of the Ottawa River to save Bessie Blair who had skated onto thin ice and fallen through. The strong current swept them both away. Understandably King was bereft. He turned, in particular, to Mrs. Herridge ("...full of fun, and a bright, kind-hearted woman"[1]) for friendship and consolation. King was soon an intimate of the Herridge family circle in the St. Andrew's manse. He sang hymns with the family, read essays aloud, played with the children, sat with Mrs. Herridge in church, talked and talked with her, and shared new poems. The dour Reverend Herridge ignored these goings-on for some time, but finally lost his ministerial calm one night when King and Mrs. Herridge returned to the manse at midnight:

> When we came to the front door it was locked, Mrs. H. rang twice and then the Dr. came himself unlocked the

> door & stepped back. When I sd. good night to him, he did not reply, but in the most direct manner possible slammed the inside door shut on both of us. It was in so many words 'You may both go your way, I scorn you both' (26 February 1902).

King managed to patch things up, for King, Mrs. Herridge and her children made a jolly group at Mrs. McMinn's that summer — the Reverend had gone off again on a solitary summer holiday. What had been building up during the winter seems to have flourished in the invigorating Kingsmere air. Diary entries were very sketchy during this intriguing period, when King began calling Mrs. Herridge, "Child." However by September a mild cottage flirtation may have developed into something more serious:

> The story of my life for the present is the story of its relation to the Child. Our summer has been lived together, lived to ourselves, and now the fall and winter has come and we are to live apart, and the duties of life rather than its pleasures are to receive their emphasis. What is to be the outcome of this love, the love which binds her to me and me to her, that is the problem now. She loves me more deeply than ever before if that is possible, and can do less well without me. I have reason to love her as I never had reason to before. I tremble at moments when I think of what our lives are to each other. The solution will not come in seeking to turn away, or in ceasing to be, it must be worked out in the full presence of each other by a fuller presence of God...working for the uplifting and purifying of self, and the betterment of others is the only rational, as it appears to be the only tolerable view to take....The Child looked beautiful today, so fair — oh Child! (21 September 1902)

King's involvement with a married woman twelve years older than himself was not to bring either of them joy. The passionate declarations, the evening visits to King's rooms, the exchange of meaningful gifts and flowers lessened over the years, eventually to be replaced in King's feelings by declarations of strong friendship. This romantic interlude was the first of many strong memories to form the associative undercurrents so important in King's perception of his Kingsmere life.

The First Cottage

In 1901 King considered buying a Kingsmere lot from a local farmer for $200: "this is a valuable summer locality & few places near Ottawa compare with it."[2] But inexplicably he did not carry it through. There were no diary entries for the next important summer — 1903 — when on September 24th he bought 2.9 acres (a hectare) for $400 from Isabelle Bourinot a year after her husband, Sir John Bourinot, died. The lot was bounded on the south by the lake and on the north by the division line between ranges 7 and 8 of the Township of Hull, County of Hull. Traversed by rudimentary paths, it was densely wooded, rocky in places, swampy in others, in short, a typical cottage lot. No records survive to date cottage construction or identify the contractor, although King did mention in his 1936 diary that his first cottage (a simple four-room framed shell, clad in clapboard siding) was completed in 1903. The size and layout were ideally suited to his bachelor life. At the end of the summer, his parents and younger sister, Jennie, spent five weeks with him in his small cottage. King slept in his tent when his parents visited, otherwise guests were accommodated there. The tent, 14 x 10 feet (4 by 3 m), was pitched near the cottage's south-east corner on a

W.J. Topley/National Archives of Canada/PA 141392

National Archives of Canada/C 3176

National Archives of Canada/PA 12444

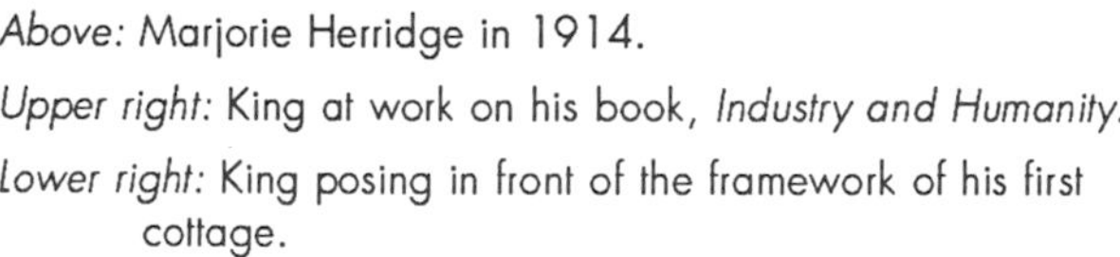

Above: Marjorie Herridge in 1914.

Upper right: King at work on his book, *Industry and Humanity.*

Lower right: King posing in front of the framework of his first cottage.

National Archives of Canada/C 46545

King enjoying his favourite Kingswood exercise — underbrushing.

wooden platform underneath large White pines.[3] Jennie slept in "the big room" and the other bedroom was used as a dining room. It is not clear where the elder Kings slept. The twenty-eight year old Jennie praised the cottage ("as quaint as it can be...certainly awfully pretty...") and her brother's decorating ("He has shown remarkably good taste in his curtains etc...All his doors, windows etc. are painted white and it makes the place so fresh").[4]

Hidden from the main road, "embowered in trees," over-looking Kingsmere Lake, the secluded setting reflected King's life-long admiration of British landscape styles, especially the placing of English country homes and cottages.[5] However, the design and the modest extent of his cottage beginnings were dictated by finances, rather than style. In 1903-04 when King built his first cottage, he had only been working for three years, and was also helping to pay off his father's debts. Yet, even in times of affluence, the style and scope of King's efforts were shaped by his rather conventional tastes: he preferred the old-fashioned and the familiar.[6] King's informal, rustic, wood-frame cottage was definitely modelled on the humble Muskoka cottages of his youth.[7]

However, signs of his imaginative eccentricities were already appearing — highly personal symbolisms and associations he enjoyed finding or creating at Kingsmere — which would culminate in the building of his Abbey ruin. The first hint of King's "extra dimensional" thinking was his design and installation, in his rather nondescript cottage, of a model of the large fireplace at Shakespeare's Stratford-on-Avon home. He inaugurated the cottage and fireplace by having Mrs. Herridge read from Matthew Arnold's works, after which King dedicated the fireplace to the memory of Bert Harper. When the fire was lit, it was said that the fireplace refused to draw, driving the guests out of the cottage.[8]

King's early years at Kingswood centred around Mrs. Herridge who had a cottage "up the hill" from King. He spent most evenings at Edgmoor reading aloud, singing hymns and talking with her and the children. As well, they often prayed together. During this first summer of cottage ownership, King initiated what would evolve into an annual ritual — prayers at the beginning and end of a Kingsmere season. Mrs. Herridge accompanied him to a secluded spot, their favourite prayer site, to commune with God-in-Nature, to implore "...his Guidance...that we might carry into our City tasks the teachings of the solitude & the seasons here — the transitoriness of life, as witnessed by nature around us, the...presence of God as witnessed by the mountains and the [skies]" (22 September 1904).

National ARchives of Canada/PA 124445

The sleeping tent.

Mrs. Herridge also influenced the early shaping of the Kingswood landscape. She was very fond of flowers and gardening — garden lists from the late 1800s, possibly in Mrs. Herridge's handwriting, were found in King's papers. The number of flower seeds sowed, bulbs forced, and roses planted, evidently at the manse in Ottawa, were noted. However, it is not known to what extent she gardened at her Kingsmere cottage. King's earliest recorded cottage landscaping was noted in September 1904, when Mrs. Herridge and he dug out Virginia creeper in the woods where it was climbing over a wild plum tree. She planted some of the vine around Edgmoor, but King preferred to plant his vines "...around the w.c. hoping it might cover the premises in the near future" (25 September 1904). Digging up wildflowers, vines and shrubs from the bush was common practice in pre-World War I Canada.

Landscaping records are skimpy from 1905 to 1915, when King was busy professionally. Within months of his arrival in Ottawa as the editor of the *Labour Gazette*, King advanced to deputy minister of labour. In 1906 he was awarded, through the instigation of his patron Governor General Grey, the Commander of the Order of St. Michael and St. George[9] — an action resented by many other civil servants. His rising political ambitions were stoked by Mrs. Herridge — it was like tossing a burning branch into a forest fire: "She feels that public life with all its risks to be better for me than the civil service. She has often told me I should be my own master & would only realize my best self when I was" (27 July 1907). His pressure on Laurier to find him a Parliamentary seat finally yielded results. In 1908 he entered political life when he was elected to Parliament from Ontario's North Waterloo riding.

Soon after, King was en route to England, India, Japan and China as a member of the British delegation to an anti-opium congress in Shanghai.[10] On his return Laurier appointed King minister of labour. As a minister, King no longer travelled to Kingsmere by train or bicycle, rather he rented a horse and carriage in Ottawa, and delegated his private secretary to drive it. F.A. McGregor noted: "Conversation, although it tended to be one-sided, never lagged...the emphasis was always on politics and social reform, but religion, art, and music crowded in."[11] After the Laurier government and King were defeated in 1911, King searched for three years for a public service position worthy of his talents, but was unsuccessful in finding another riding. Unemployment after eleven years in government was not pleasant for the energetic King. In spite of his inaction, he rejected various newspaper jobs, and the leadership of the Ontario Liberal Party. Finally he assumed the task of organizing a Liberal Party Information Office in Ottawa. Then he worked for a time in the United States with John D. Rockefeller, Jr. and the Rockefeller Foundation as a labour conciliator. In 1915 he returned to Ottawa to write a book on labour relations, deciding unequivocally to remain in Canada to work out his destiny. Kingswood and its development — architectural and horticultural — played a major role in his future Ottawa life.

Like his first architectural project, his early landscaping efforts at Kingsmere were low-key and unambitious, most often restricted to clean-up operations. Occasionally the wild grass, weeds, and wildflowers near the cottage were scythed, seeds or shrubs were sporadically planted, and more paths added. The site was so overgrown that King's usual outdoor exercise (ceasing only with age and the burden of work) was underbrushing and culling trees that were damaged, dead or spoiled the view. After 1915 the tempo of his Kingswood improvements increased significantly. His decision to cast his fate in Canadian affairs, combined with the financial gains of his Rockefeller employment, for the first time allowed King to focus money and energy on Kingswood.

Cottage Renovations

Horticultural changes to the landscape in 1916 were modest. Three trees were removed to accommodate an addition to the cottage. But other than underbrushing and cutting the grass, King did not substantially change his surroundings. His cottage by 1916 just seemed too small: "...I want to feel I can have a guest in my own home. These domestic joys I have never permitted myself. All such things in large measure have been sacrificed to saving. Now I feel I have earned this right..." (22 June 1916). To remedy the lack of space, an addition was built by an Ottawa contractor, a member of the Kingsmere Murphy family who were to help King in other construction projects.

Giving the "go-ahead" to John Murphy, who had built many cottages in the area,[12] worried King. Spending significant amounts of money on himself always made him nervous. This was partly due to his upbringing. His childhood was coloured by his mother's stories of her years of poverty when her father (William Lyon Mackenzie) was in exile in the United States. And his early adulthood was affected by his father's lack of financial success, and King's subsequent shouldering of his father's debts. The planning of costly projects always tested King's habitual frugality, although he usually mustered the right rationalizations to proceed: "It is well too to cultivate inexpensive habits of living. But I think, too, that a man's inner life is affected by his daily & immediate surroundings & associations to a degree to which he hardly believes possible, & *good things* have a real influence. When a purchase is an ultimate necessity, there is no economy in a *cheap* bargain." (24 January 1902). He rationalized that the cottage addition, costing $400, would "...fill my heart with joy, my mind with noble thoughts, my body with health....I want the memory ever of happiness beneath this roof with mother and father, to do my work, and to have them here during August" (22 June 1916).

Once the financial hurdle was surmounted, King greatly enjoyed planning improvements. He fussed over the details until everything was just right, bringing to his Kingswood projects the same passion for painstaking care, the same intense attention to detail, that he practiced in his political and professional life. Taken to extremes, this personality trait often infuriated his Parliament Hill employees as well as his estate labourers.

National Archives of Canada/PA 124447

Mr. and Mrs. John King enjoying the Kingsmere air.

The cottage plan was meticulously thought out. King stipulated in a closely typed four-page letter the size of bedroom cupboards, bedroom windows, method of staining the shingles, etc. The original cottage had been designed as a rather squat L-shape: the living room and breakfast room overlooking the lake, and a small kitchen and bedroom behind. Onto this King added a western extension: two bedrooms (each with doors opening out onto an enlarged lakeside verandah), a back verandah, and a servant's bedroom — which was separated from the adjoining bedroom by extra boarding and an air space "to prevent sound."[13] The placing of the servant's bedroom (transformed from a shed, originally standing to the west of the cottage) was well thought out, and discreetly placed at the rear of the cottage, just a short verandah away from the kitchen.

Although the addition ostensibly provided room for guests, King was never completely at ease when sharing his living space with others. With a hint of what would later develop into an occasional reclusiveness, King wrote in his diary that he would give much to be "...uninterrupted, alone...I could think, reflect, & not be obliged to talk" (25 September 1904). In 1904 when his parents and Jennie stayed at Kingswood for five weeks, King expressed his happiness in a rather stilted form:

> I never saw father & mother looking better, and the pleasure & happiness I feel, in knowing that their little visit with me has contributed to this is for real. How thankful one should be that one has an opportunity so to help those who are most dear to one. I hope the benefit of their holiday will long be with them... (12 September 1904).

As soon as the 1916 addition was finished, King invited his parents for a short holiday. Their enjoyment of the typical

National Archives of Canada/C 46539

King designed a boathouse in keeping with his ideas of a proper summer residence.

Kingsmere pastimes of hiking, underbrushing and swimming were curtailed by health and age. His mother could not hike far, nor could she enter the lake without her daughter's assistance. It was his father's last summer there. Ailing and nearly blind, John King posed for innumerable photographs in front of the cottage, next to the tent, and walking through the trees. He died later in the year in Toronto. This was the beginning of King's *memento mori* attitude to Kingswood. The following year when his mother spent the last summer of her life at Kingswood, the obsession grew and Kingswood slowly evolved into "sacred ground."

King often described his family as his refuge, but with the death of his sister and father, his brother's tuberculosis, and his mother's wasting illness, that bastion was tottering. With the family rapidly diminishing, it is not surprising King began constructing another refuge — that of his country home:

> Such happiness as I felt in being beneath my own roof, amid the trees, away from the world of humans and with nature and solitude for a time. I have literally fled here, to get back to the quiet of deep thought and peaceful living — fled with the city's unrest and burning in my veins to seek God and live again with my own soul (22 June 1916).

When King took his terminally-ill mother out to Kingswood for the summer of 1917, he thought the magic of Kingswood and the healing powers of nature would do what the doctors could not — restore her health. He painted one of the bedrooms hospital white and installed a nurse to look after his mother while he worked on *Industry and Humanity*, solidified his political position, and prepared for the upcoming election. He rejoiced at every sign of recovery and felt despondent when these brief rallies subsided once again.

Boathouse and Wharf

In amongst these domestic and political concerns, King found the time and energy to plan the next phase of landscape changes, again taking an architectural form. In late July 1917 he decided a boathouse, a common structure on cottage landscapes, was needed to house the canoe and to provide a proper place for ladies to change and to have a "lake bath" in privacy. After drawing a rough plan for John Murphy, King said he could hardly sleep for thinking of it: "I love work of construction of the kind, and the joy that comes in planning anything, seeing it realized in accordance with the picture of one's imagination is as pure a delight as any I know" (7 August 1917). King's ability to fantasize, to create vivid mental pictures, was exercised frequently during any improvement to the estate. These images, when coupled with the right rationalizations, usually allayed his turmoil when the estimates came in.

Edwinna von Baeyer

Boathouse as seen across Kingsmere Lake.

King justified the boathouse, by noting it "completed" a summer residence and thus would be a good investment all round whether he sold, rented out or continued to live there himself. Perhaps, he reasoned, the materials would be more expensive next year. However, his mother's association with building the boathouse overrode all other justifications. King's relationship with his mother, during and even beyond her lifetime, was a complex and ambiguous one. Along with adulation, he felt guilt over his neglecting her, instances often magnified in his mind, and ultimately over his absence at her death. Over the years he wove a fantasy of their relationship as he transformed his mother into the epitome of "truth, goodness, purity and beauty."[14] The boathouse was included in the transforming fantasy. As a memorial of her summer at Kingsmere, King told his mother he was going to name the boathouse after her:

> ...for like her, it was a 'spiritual creation'....this little child of my thought & spirit which delights my heart and which she has watched grow into being...So it shall be the *Isabel Grace Mackenzie*, a thing beautiful in itself & in all that it expresses (18 August 1917).

Building the boathouse signalled the beginning of King's enjoyment in creating memorials, and associative structures on his Kingsmere landscape.

Every step of construction thrilled King: "Especially enchanting was the sight of the first rafters of the roof with a pitch at an angle of 45 degrees giving fine proportions to the whole structure" (9 August 1917). As usual, he agonized over the details: "During the afternoon they stained the shingles. I was afraid at first that the stain would be too light, & was going to wait for the dark green I had ordered, but consented to it going on to save time. I am glad I so decided as it is just the colour of the trees, and looks quite beautiful" (14 August 1917).

Swept on by this wave of excitement, King had a 4 x 13 foot

(1.2 by 4 m) wharf built, with protecting gangway sides, and small posts for mooring boats. It hugged the shore rather than extending out into the lake. King marvelled:

> Curiously enough father over & over again spoke to me about constructing a wharf & boathouse, but especially a wharf....we would call the boathouse after her, & the wharf after father. Now it is just the anniversary of the day he left Kingsmere & said 'farewell'... (21 August 1917).

The Murphys were instructed to finish the wharf with a detachable flagpole and the white-painted crisscross railing design of the boathouse, keeping it, as King wrote, compatible with the boathouse and cottage. King liked flagpoles on the landscape. When a white-painted flagpole near the cottage, erected early in King's residence, deteriorated, King had Paddy Murphy rebuild it and strengthen it by piling rocks around the base. Watching the raising of the Union Jack each summer, especially during the war years, never failed to move King: "...I thought of all the flag has meant & cost across the seas" (28 June 1918).

After completing the construction, King then made new paths uniting cottage, boathouse and wharf. The Murphys were commissioned to further link the house to the wharf by building wooden stairs descending the hill: "The stairs are necessary if use is to be made of the boat & bathhouse by ladies, or elderly people & may save a twisted ankle or a broken neck in getting up & down hills." (10 August 1917). The stairs were also designed in keeping with the other architectural elements.

When both structures were completed in late August, King persuaded his mother, who was daily worsening, to christen them. He wrapped her up in a blanket and with the help of the nurse, carried her down the steep hill to the water's edge:

> She christened the wharf 'John' by dipping her hand into the water & sprinkling it, uttered a little cry as it were, part laugh, part cry, when she had done it. Later she christened the boathouse 'Isabel Grace Mackenzie' (26 August 1917).

Landscaping did not keep pace with the architectural improvements. On his small, steep lot, King seemed content with planting the occasional shrub around the cottage. In a sense, he was paralleling the pattern of the original settlers, as he first cleared, and then ornamented. There is some evidence that he planted vines, rose bushes (perhaps the hardy rugosa) and other unnamed shrubs at the front and alongside the cottage, as well as a few shrubs on the lawn leading down to the lake.[15] In 1917 he planted hollyhocks around the ice house and the "closet," possibly following contemporary gardening advice urging gardeners to conceal outbuildings on home and cottage property either with vines or other plant material. However, no further mention of the Virginia creeper he had lovingly planted the year before with Mrs. Herridge was ever made.

Each fall King hired the Murphys to cover plants and shrubs with manure for winter protection. In 1916 he hired Willie Murphy to sow grass seed around the cottage: "...if you think it would do any good and would improve the appearance of the lawn for this year...."[16] Evidently some of the grass took because by June he was mowing it.

Unfortunately these plantings were often unspecified. This was not only due to the sparse records he kept in the early years, but also to King's indifference to specific plant names. For example he noted in 1916 that he planted a vine from a house in Toronto where his family had lived, as well as "a blue flower" a neighbour had given him. Often he recorded that he had sowed "some seeds" or had the gardener put in a "few plants." The effect on the landscape or in King's mind was the true value of an individual plant — not its name.

Kingswood Life

1921 was a turning point not only in King's political life, but in his Kingswood life as well. King became prime minister in the December 1921 election. He had by then published two books, received valued experience and exposure as a Rockefeller consultant and his financial status had also risen. Summers were no longer idyllic communions with nature and Mrs. Herridge. After those first few intense summers, they had grown apart, and King had seemingly grown tired of what he termed her occasional overbearing emotional outbursts. "I must forget," Mrs. Herridge wrote him in 1912, "and you must forget, 'not because one will, but because one must.'" Then in a horticultural aside, she wrote: "Hearts are not like gardens — one cannot throw out one plant and put another in its place."[17] However, it seems that King could easily replace plants or people in his affections, but not his passion for his Kingsmere property.

Over these twenty years, his Kingswood life was shaped by small ceremonies and evolving habits. The first ride out to Kingswood, when trees had just begun leafing out, the first sighting of lily-of-the-valley (his mother's favourite flower), and the first flag-raising gradually assumed an immense importance to King. Prayers continued to accompany the opening and closing of the cottage : "Grant oh God," King recorded in his diary, "that I may attain in some degree to the higher ideals & aspirations which have come to me in the quiet of this place, in its happy and restful hours..." (25 September 1904).

His sense of well-being was partly dependant on an increasing number of servants in his employ. Servants had become visibly numerous on the Kingswood landscape, for King enjoyed having his tea and meals prepared and his fire tended by others. Yet King frequently tired of organizing people to serve his comforts, especially when the servants began getting into each other's hair. In a vehement outburst, King exploded in his diary: "What a dam-d nuisance servants are. It is no job for a man alone running a house & a country at the same time & laid up with grippe to boot" (28 February 1923). Other aspects of the upkeep of Kingswood were less troublesome. The Murphys often supplied the ice to keep perishables cool and the wood for cooking and heating; other farm families supplied milk, butter, and eggs. King was, however, annoyed by occasional unauthorized charges to his bill by his guests or servants. King sharply reminded Willie Murphy in 1916 that he was not liable for his guest's milk orders or stage rides — his private secretary F.A. McGregor now had to pay the twenty-five cent stage fare himself. King parsimoniously noted at the end of his letter to Willie: "...I am sure you will agree that it is better in money matters that we should err on the side of not leaving room for any possible mistake."[18]

However much King fussed with his employees and cottage upkeep, his life at Kingswood amply made up for any frustration. King continued to delight in his summer idyll. As the years progressed and he became more deeply involved in political life, Kingswood became a summer extension of his Parliament Hill offices. Secretaries and other support staff made the hour-long journey by train and stage to King's cottage, some office staff sleeping in the tent. Whether or not they enjoyed working there made no difference, King certainly did. A long meditative walk through his woods, perhaps stopping to admire a new flower, and on down the access road and out into the moor, followed by a restoring swim in the lake often helped King unravel a perplexing question. Or he simply enjoyed walking through the colourful autumn landscapes to "...drink their beauty into my soul" (24 September 1924). He might also sing hymns or practice an upcoming speech. Or he might read his favourite poets — Arnold, Tennyson and Wordsworth — during his woodland walks. Poetry was a solace, an entertainment, and an inspiration in King's life at Kingsmere. He shared favourite poems during evening readings with Mrs. Herridge and later other guests. A stormy, windy night at the Herridge cottage inspired King in 1901 to write a poem ("The Wind and the Soul"): "The Wind knoweth not where it listeth/Yet it findest a home in the trees./ A flower may bloom, alone in the gloom/Yet its fragrance is borne on the breeze..."[19]

The Kingsmere area attracted *bona fide* Canadian poets as well. By the late 1800s a few major poets were employed in the federal civil service in Ottawa. Archibald Lampman and Charles Sangster worked in the Post Office, and Wilfrid Campbell (who left the Episcopalian ministry in 1891) in various departments including the Privy Council and Archives. Duncan Campbell Scott rose to a high position in the Department of Indian Affairs.[20] These poets and other literary figures were a close-knit circle in bureaucratic Ottawa. The proximity of the Gatineau Hills was said to enhance their Ottawa life. Lampman even suggested that the crisp northern air of Ottawa was conducive to poetry and art. "A certain atmosphere flows about its walls," he said, "borne upon the breath of the prevailing north-west wind, an intellectual elixir, an oxygenic essence thrown off by immeasurable tracts of pine-clad mountain and crystal lake."[21] Rupert Brooke, the English poet who died in World War I, was also impressed by the Gatineau landscape. In 1913 on a visit to Meech Lake he wrote: "We went by little French villages and fields at first, and then through rocky, tangled woods of birch and poplar, rich with milkweed and blue cornflowers, and the aromatic thimble-berry blossom, and that romantic, light purple-red flower which is called the fireweed..."[22]

Archibald Lampman knew the Kingsmere area well — his famous poem "Heat" resulted from a walk he took near Ironside, a neighbouring village: "From plains that reel to southward dim,/ The road runs by me white and bare;/Up the steep hill it seems to swim/Beyond, and melt into the glare.[23] Lampman's sister, Annie Jenkins, had a cottage near King's for a number of years. Duncan Campbell Scott, Lampman's best friend, often accompanied him on forays into the Gatineaus. Scott also wrote poetry inspired by visits to Kingsmere: "Last Night a Storm Fell on the World" and "Spring Midnight, Deepwood" were written at Arthur Bourinot's cottage, next door to Kingswood. Bourinot was the son of Sir J.S. and Lady Bourinot from whom King had bought his first land. Arthur, a poet and a lawyer, frequently presented his books of poetry to King: "It makes me very happy," King acknowledged one gift, "to see you adding so much of beauty, alike in thought and expression, to an environment which holds for each of us so much in the way of close association."[24]

During his early Kingsmere years, the genial Mackenzie King integrated himself into the small summer community. He exchanged pleasantries and advice with fellow passengers on the stage ride from Dunn's Hotel to the Chelsea station. King was also an active benefactor. With his connections to the Post Office (his mentor, William Mulock was the postmaster general under whom the department of labour was initially established), King petitioned the deputy postmaster-general to "loan, sell or give" the Kingsmere farmer who acted as postmaster, a letter box to be placed at the side of his farm door: "The facilities he possesses for collecting mail are most inadequate, and I have felt it would be a protection to myself and other summer residents of the locality...."[25] Within a week Kingsmere residents could proudly drop letters into a two dollar refurbished letter box.

King also delighted in visiting various Kingsmere residents. Sipping tea and sharing genteel conversation with the Crannel sisters in their impressive picturesque-style wooden cottage, enjoyably passed a Sunday afternoon. Inviting neighbouring young ladies for canoe rides or to tea on the verandah was also one of King's entertainments. In 1918, at age forty-four, a year before becoming leader of the Liberal Party, King entertained the daughter of Annie Jenkins to canoe rides, dinners, picnics, etc., but did not allow her (as Kitty did so many years ago) to misunderstand his intentions. His rather charming arch exchanges with Dorothy and her friend culminated in a Christmas present of a small photo album entitled: "A Summer's Idyll — Kingsmere 1918." The girls were called "sweet singers" and King "their philosopher friend." Under the last photograph, King wrote: "The sweet singers pause a moment on their journey for a last farewell. 'Rex' [their dog] remains faithful to the end. The philosopher friend unable to endure a second parting has left him there and sought Nature anew for consolation. The summer is ended."[26]

National Archives of Canada/C53484

Duncan Campbell Scott and Rupert Brooke walking at Meech Lake.

Although King found these rather homey visits with his neighbours enjoyable, when he became prime minister this free and easy camaraderie lessened. More prestigious visitors began walking the property and admiring the little cottages. For example, Stanley Baldwin and his wife visited Kingswood in August 1927. The two men became quite informal, removing their coats and vests as King delightedly showed his British counterpart his holdings. In memory of the visit King presented Baldwin with a cane, its gold band engraved "Kingsmere 4.8.1927." Baldwin was amazed that King slept alone in the cottage without a security guard or locked doors (4 August 1927).

Another visitor to the area could not believe the prime minister lived in "that quaint little place." When her guide referred to "Mr. King, the prime minister," this American lady grew quite indignant. Whispering loudly to her companion, she said, "I thought he was an awful liar and now I know it!...He told me that place back there was the summer home of the King and the prime minister. Such nonsense! I know the King never crosses the ocean. They won't let him."[27]

Kingswood Expansion

His election as prime minister, an office King had long thought he was destined for, had a definite impact on his Kingswood holdings. His perception of his status as prime minister and of the consequent need for more privacy stimulated a number of changes to the Kingswood landscape. The first significant alteration was in the size of his property.

In 1922 and 1923 King purchased lakeside property which doubled the size of his holdings, and "squared off" the boundary lines giving King sole control over nearly seven acres (3 ha) bounded on the north and south by the lake and the public access road. As early as 1916, King tried to buy more property from Lady Bourinot, from whom he had purchased his original land in 1903, stating he would be willing to purchase an additional lakeside lot or two from her — "...rather than risk having an uncongenial neighbour at any time in the future, or seeing any of the trees cut down...."[28]

In 1924 the thought of undesirable neighbours bothered other residents as well. The summer community of forty-five households gathered together to form the Kingsmere Property Holders Association for "...the good of all...the betterment of Kingsmere...the beautifying of the community."[29] A board of directors was elected (King was made honourary president) and an annual fee of five dollars charged. This fee, combined with a grant from the Chelsea Council, would be used for community betterment. Roads were to be properly maintained, fences and boathouses repaired and painted. One resident was advised by the Association to use her cottage rental money to fix her fences because her cattle had been wandering down the Kingsmere roads and "doing considerable damage."[30] To further beautify the surroundings, brush alongside the access road was to be cut twice a year and safely burned. The lake was to be protected from contamination, cleaned of floating debris and stocked with fish. In 1925 King, through his office, contacted the Quebec provincial fish hatchery in Magog for five cans of brown trout fry. In later years, other residents saw to the restocking. A game warden was to be hired not only to prohibit poaching, but also to limit the daily fish catch by each resident.

The Association's active policy of excluding "undesirables" was the dark side of its activities. The charter stated that "all property for sale or rent be submitted to the Association with a view of keeping out undesirables."[31] Some unwelcome visitors had been discovered swimming in the lake after having undressed in their automobiles or in the roadside bushes.[32] Undesirables were not only those "not our kind," but more often Jews. Anti-Semitism was quite prevalent in early 20th century Canada, reaching almost virulent levels in the 1930s and early 1940s. The Kingsmere Association's "Christians Only" policy was common at this time in a number of private clubs, resorts and hotels.

In 1925, George P. Harris, president of the Kingsmere Association, wrote King that three Jews had rented cottages at Kingsmere, and one "intimated" that he would either buy the house he was in or buy a lot and build: "This would be very harmful to the Community and it would also give them a Lake frontage near Stewarts."[33] To prevent this transaction Harris wanted King to join him in buying the suspect property to "seal our end up."[34] King never wrote answers to letters of this type, but he was by no means free from prejudice. In 1927 after securing more property he noted: "... if I had not purchased the properties, they might have been secured by Jews or other undesirables..." (14 August 1927). On the other hand, in 1936 King could admit to himself in response to ferment in Germany: "My own view is there are good as well as bad Jews and it is wrong to indict, a nation or a race" (9 August 1936). His government's non-action, however, during World War II toward the plight of European Jews was a shameful episode in modern Canadian history.[35]

Topley Studio/National Archives of Canada/PA 144966

Thomas 'Carbide' Wilson's summer home on Meech Lake.

King's brand of anti-Semitism was perhaps more insidious than overt prejudice. He kept his opinions to himself, opinions which ranged the full spectrum from Christian compassion to outright hostility. While he was capable of benevolence towards Jews in private, he was also capable of doing nothing to help this community.

His ambivalence towards Jews was longstanding. It is evident in his reactions to his government's defeat in 1925. King had predicted a majority Liberal government and was stunned by the results — he even lost his own seat. As he searched for explanations, King wrote down various speculative causes in his diary: the Progressives for dividing the vote, the jealousies of the French and Irish Catholics within his party, the appeal of Tory protectionism, and the non-support of influential Jews who believed they were being excluded from his government. King did not confirm or deny this charge, but he certainly took remedial action. King successfully courted Archibald J. Freiman and his wife, owners of a large Ottawa department store and influential in the Canadian Jewish community. They had actively campaigned against him in the federal election. By 1930 King was visiting them at their summer cottage on 525 acres (212 ha) overlooking Meech Lake not far from Kingsmere.[36]

The contrast between King's humble Kingswood property and the Freiman's was considerable. Even King admitted to himself that their house was "much more beautiful" than his. Their estate was originally established by Thomas "Carbide" Wilson, an inventor, engineer, and wealthy industrialist who discovered the means to produce calcium carbide.[37] Although a

The guest cottage.

few cottages had been built at Meech Lake, the area was not developed until after 1903 because the summer commuting distance from Ottawa seemed so great. At that time many Ottawans were still building summer homes in Rockcliffe and Britannia Bay. Allegedly, Wilson's summer home, built in 1907, was designed by Edgar L. Horwood, a prominent Ottawa architect. The two-and-one-half storey, eleven bedroom house was built of wood and pink granite quarried on the site. Much of the stone originated from a rock ledge at the high point of the rise overlooking the lake, which was cut back to allow room to build the house. A long, winding, tree-shaded entrance drive led the way up to the house. The drive was ornamented by an imposing gate of pink granite and wrought iron, low stone walls, ornamental light poles, and various outbuildings: a chapel, stable and carriage house, woodshed and garage with caretaker's quarters. As at Kingswood, all outbuildings were designed to complement the house style. Extensive landscaping was undertaken, including tree clearing and planting, as well as creation of formal gardens, an ornamental fish pond, and a grassed terrace overlooking the lake. The overall feeling was rustic and pastoral — cleared, grassy spaces bordered by trees and shrubs, near the lake. King was quite impressed with Meech Lake: "...the great beauty of the mountains fold beyond fold, with wooded islands & heavily wooded hills rising on both sides from the water's edge, like Northern Italy & Switzerland quite as fine" (1 September 1932).

In spite of his enjoyable visits to Meech Lake, Freiman's efforts to gain Jewish community support for the Liberals, and King's admission that Freiman was a good man, he never awarded Freiman his desired senatorship. How much was political revenge, and how much was anti-Semitism?

Jews were not the only "undesirables" singled out by the Kingsmere Property Holders' Association. The indefatigable George Harris in 1927 wrote heatedly to King that Dr. Charles Saunders (a plant hybridist who developed Marquis wheat) was thinking of selling his property to the Joan of Arc Institute, a Roman Catholic organization which provided a residence for young girls and women.[38] The Institute intended to erect "several small buildings...for the purpose of housing Ladies of the Institution who need a rest. This I think would be detrimental to

Kingsmere."[39] Harris and another property holder tried to raise funds to buy the property themselves. He then implored King to intercede with Saunders to stop the sale. However, King wisely did not interfere, perhaps because the founder of the Institute, Sister Marie de St. Thomas d'Aquinas, was King's friend. Saunders, who had promised to take the Association's wishes into consideration, went ahead and sold it to the Institute: "I am very disappointed in the attitude of Dr. Saunders," Harris disconsolately wrote to King.[40]

National Archives of Canada/C 2128

King and his sister at Kingswood.

Meanwhile King had also been trying, not always successfully, to buy more land to ensure privacy and distance from uncongenial neighbours. Lady Bourinot had replied to King's request to buy additional land from her, by saying she would be willing to sell an adjoining lot for $600, although King had already purchased "...the largest & best of these four lots for so little...."[41] King did not like the price and dropped the matter until summer 1922 when he resumed negotiations with her son, Arthur. They dickered over the price and size of a lot on the west side of King's property. During the negotiations, King attempted to convince Bourinot of his indifference to the transaction by stating he might sell all his property and buy land in a more secluded section of the upper Gatineaus. This threat evaporated into the Kingswood air, replaced by King's attempt to regulate the type of building on the land in question and to be granted an option for fifteen years on the adjoining land which Bourinot might want to sell in the future.

Bourinot rejected these proposals, calling King's bluff. King then quietly acquiesced and purchased 2.9 acres (a little over a hectare) for $1,100 — the same size lot he bought in 1903. Word must have spread around the Kingsmere community, for soon a neighbouring cottager, A.J. Cameron, offered to sell his entire holdings for $1,800. But King demurred, perhaps because he was negotiating with another neighbour, Cyril Cunningham for an acre (half ha) on the east side of his property. The sale of this lot plus cottage for $2,500 was concluded rapidly and smoothly by October. To square off his lakeside holdings, King reopened discussions with the Camerons for a corner half acre (quarter ha). The purchase (for $150) was completed by King's secretary on September 26, 1922, while King was out of town.

The purchase of the Cunningham cottage initiated a pleasing new round of planning for King. King justified the "little extra cottage" as a good investment for a proper "sleeping cottage." Paddy Murphy was hired to do the extensive renovations. The interior was completely panelled in B.C. fir, King's favourite wood. Two bedrooms, separated by a bathroom, were created. A kitchen and servant's bedroom were attached to the back, extensive verandahs built on the side and front of the cottage, and a smaller porch added at the kitchen entrance: "It is hard to hold the proportions down but harder not to permit them to enlarge," King ruefully noted (17 October 1922). All external detailing matched the main cottage: clapboarding, gangway porch railings, paint scheme of white and yellow and green.

King at the time had the additional stress of renovating and furnishing Laurier House, just inherited from Lady Laurier in Ottawa:

> I sometimes feel that with my new house in the city and my larger estate here I am taking on too much, getting away from the simpler & humbler methods of living. I do it not from any love of possession but solely for the greater authority which these things seem to give in filling the position I hold. I want my life to be lived only in the service of God and as a follower of Jesus Christ....These things are but means to the end of greater efficiency in the handling of men as instruments to carry out this purpose (9 October 1922).

Did he fear he was sinking into a rural version of Newport resort life?

Landscaping Kingswood

Within the framework of board and stone and road, the challenges to formal gardening at Kingswood were numerous: the lack of adequate sunlight due to the dense forest cover, the thin, rocky soil of the Shield, the swampy areas, the sharp slope of the ground from the cottage down to the lakeshore, and the short growing season. King was always sensitive to his surroundings and by this time had seen a great variety of gardens, ranging from Ontario to New England, to the country homes of his British friends. He had also gathered landscaping ideas on trips to Europe and the Orient.

The doubling of his Kingswood holdings was a strong incentive for unifying the treatment of the landscape. Although the forty-eight year old King feared the corrupting influence of increasing wealth and possessions, he continually felt renewed as he "redeemed the wilderness," cultivated and rearranged the Kingswood landscape. He also continued to enjoy underbrushing and cutting down trees. His pleasure in wielding an axe was transformed by the press in 1924 into an "instinct of the coureurs de bois, and our trailblazing, tree-felling forebears."[42] This manly image was further strengthened when the reporter compared his activities with those of the leader of the opposition: "Arthur Meighen goes to Quebec like a professor of languistics [sic] to study the language. Mackenzie King goes like a Samuel Chapdelaine [sic] to clear the soil and 'make land.' The leader of the opposition blisters his tongue. The premier blisters his knuckles."[43]

Even before King acquired the 1922 property, he had debated whether to shape the landscape in a more formal, designed manner. The subsequent development of the Kingswood landscape set the pattern for the next twenty-eight years of landscaping on his expanding estate. The landscaping would proceed in unplanned stages (in future years as well) without a master design, and with the paid labour of the Murphy family and the unpaid aid or advice of various government officials.

At Kingswood, King thought he might concentrate on ornamentals: shrubs, flowers and trees, probably realizing the futility of growing vegetables and fruits on this site. King requested advice in 1922 from the Dominion Horticulturist, W.T. Macoun, on how to beautify his grounds. W.T. Macoun was certainly the right man to contact. By 1922 he was one of the most renowned horticulturists in Canada. The son of John Macoun, Dominion Botanist of the Geological Survey of Canada, Macoun began his government career in 1888 as a day labourer at the Central Experimental Farm (C.E.F.) in Ottawa. He rose through the ranks, and by 1898 he was appointed Horticulturist to the C.E.F. and curator of the Arboretum. In 1910 he was promoted to Dominion Horticulturist overseeing the horticultural activities of the entire Experimental Farm System comprising, at that time, twenty-four stations across Canada.

Macoun was characterized as a tireless worker for the betterment of horticulture. He wrote and lectured extensively on fruit and ornamentals, giving special attention to fruit breeding, especially apples. His originations, the 'Melba,' 'Joyce' and 'Lobo' apples, won recognition and awards. Macoun held a variety of influential positions ranging from president of the American Society for Horticultural Science to commissioner of the Ottawa Improvement Commission. A good Presbyterian, Macoun probably impressed King not only by his horticultural knowledge, but also by his quiet, dignified and gentlemanly manner. He, like King, enjoyed quoting poetry at appropriate moments.[44]

However Macoun did not go out to Kingswood the first time King requested help. He sent out two members of his staff, T.F. Ritchie who was the "Assistant in Vegetable Growing" and Isabella Preston (new to the Division of Horticulture, but to become the "Specialist in Ornamental Horticulture" and later one of our foremost plant hybridists). They duly drove to Kingswood one fine August day to consider the possibilities. They suggested a very naturalistic style of planting to take advantage of the picturesque qualities of the site. The design was colourful, rustically elegant, and seasonally interesting. Not knowing if the prime minister used the proper botanical names of plants (as did Miss Preston), she very tactfully used the common and Latin names of each plant in the list submitted with the Kingswood planting plan. Miss Preston chose shrubs and trees either for the colour of their foliage (Golden Elder/*Sambus nigro aurea)*, berries (Snowberry/ *Symphoricarpos racemosus*), flowers (Lilacs, Crab apple/*Pyrus baccata*), or autumn foliage (Ginnalian Maple/*Acer tataricum ginnale*).

Along the main road into the cottage (before the serpentine road was built), Miss Preston planned a judicious mixture of flowering shrubs, perennials and roses planted in large sweeping masses. Around the cottage she suggested placing a combination of vines, perennials and shrubs. For the very shady, road-facing cottage entrance, *Hydrangea arborescens* and *H. paniculata* were advised. On the lakeside verandah Miss Preston was quite exuberant with a variety of climbers: Dutchman's Pipe, Clematis Jackmani, and Climbing Bittersweet. Lily of the Valley was to be planted in the crook of the 'L' of the cottage. To provide privacy between King's cottage and the one he subsequently bought, a massive lilac hedge was to be planted. Shrubs were suggested for the top of the hill near the flagpole and birdbath, as well as for the slope. Miss Preston also attempted to highlight the winding path system down to the lake with plantings of *Rosa rugosa*, buckthorn, hawthorn, and dogwood. At the shore to the right of the boathouse, bordering on the land he bought that fall, a very striking spring and fall grouping of honeysuckle and spiraea, asters, helianthus, heliopsis, rudbeckia, and golden rod were planned. Along the shore line itself between the wharf and the boathouse, four varieties of moisture-loving iris were advised. Miss Preston rightly observed that "a Weeping Willow, Salix niobe, would be very effective near the water."[45] Another attractive touch was her typically British suggestion that "very beautiful effects could be had in spring by naturalizing bulbs under deciduous trees."[46]

She was confident the plan would "add to the beauty of the place," but was a bit worried about the soil condition. Miss Preston cautioned King to mix the surface leaf soil with the subsoil where shrubs were to be planted and to add loam or manure to the flower borders around the cottage to make the soil more suitable for flowers. Then King could plant such annuals as snapdragons, calendula, marigolds, and pansies.

The plan sat on King's desk for a month before he replied. He apologized profusely to Macoun and Preston pleading pressure of work ("I have been more than busy with pressing matters of urgent public importance..."[47]), and the property expansion which "...necessitated additional fencing, road making, etc."[48] However, he had not abandoned the idea of landscaping, and soon hoped to have a man prepare the soil for eventual root and seed planting. Then in a rather carefully worded aside King noted:

> It has been mentioned to me that in the Autumn and Spring months, you sometimes thin out some of the shrubs and plants at the Farm and that nothing more than an application would be necessary to secure a few roots which would otherwise be thrown away. I do not wish to take advantage of my relation to the Government to suggest any contribution from Experimental Farm sources, but if an opportunity of the kind does present itself, I should be grateful if you would let me know, that I might take some advantage of it. Please understand that this is not even indirectly a request; I am only asking for information so as to be able to benefit by a chance which may offer, in the event of my being credibly informed.[49]

Well, even if King did not call it a request, Macoun certainly treated it as such — from the prime minister as well as a fellow member of the St. Andrew's Presbyterian Church. King was never loathe to secure goods and services at bargain prices. He had tried to buy used garden hoses from the Department of Public Works, only to receive a rather curt reply, noting that when the department finished with their hoses, they generally were so worn out to be worthless. However, King was much luckier with Macoun.[50]

Ten days after receiving King's letter, Macoun, accompanied by the minister of agriculture, W.R. Motherwell, his wife and daughter, drove to Kingsmere to consult King. Motherwell, an enthusiastic gardener himself, telephoned King to say he was "very much interested in shrubs and would like to look over the property," before sending along a shipment of plants. He also noted that the shrubs would "take up a lot of room and would make a mess in the motor car."[51]

> We had a good hour's talk together, & then took a hurried walk over the property during which time Macoun made notes of certain plants and shrubs & flowers which are to be sent out from the experimental farms on a truck on Wednesday for planting. They are from the surplus and thinning out (9 October 1922).

After this visit, Macoun sent out the chief gardener from the C.E.F., Mr. Taggart, along with three helpers to plant a number of "hardy perennials and several shrubs and vines, & 'willows...'" (11 October 1922). It is not clear where this material was planted. One supposes that some attention was paid to Miss Preston's plan, although no one ever alluded to it again. In 1924 Macoun sent King a list of shrubs to be planted at specific locations, some of which (at the two entrances) were either replantings or additional plantings suggested in the Preston plan.

National Archives of Canada/PA 124707

A small flagstone entranceway was created for the original cottage in 1924.

Macoun's staff also planted shrubs near the new garage: large-flowering elder, wayfaring tree, hydrangea, and the ubiquitous Virginia creeper. King had a twinge of conscience when the new plant material either died or barely thrived: "It is possible, however, that some special knowledge of horticulture may be necessary...I may not be giving the plants the kind of care or nourishment which they require."[52] Macoun tactfully pointed out that: "Owing to the many native trees at your place and the shade and network of roots in the soil, shrubs which are planted do not make the showing that they would if planted in the open..."[53] But King still fretted, finally confiding that he wanted to "make a real demonstration" of the plants he was given. Whether he really thought he could establish a trial garden, it certainly was in character for King to visualize his few acres as a Gatineau substation of the Experimental Farm System.

King also began container planting once a second series of renovations was finished on the original cottage. To enhance the outside entrance, King had the ever-faithful Murphys construct low stone walls, enclosing the entrance court (paved with flagstones), and topping the walls with the same style of stone posts as at his front gates. The tops had small square holes to anchor stone flower pots, which were often filled with geraniums and dracaena "spikes." Small flower boxes on the entranceway windows added to the floral charm of the cottage.

The following year King and his gardener and general servant, Perriman, discussed plans to make "the worst spot of all into a beautiful garden." The first phase was to erect a stone wall between his eastern neighbour and himself: "...the present arrangement being altogether too open. No privacy, and often unpleasant visitors." A stone wall, he felt, would allow the construction of a "...garden of some size and effect, and will add immensely to the appearance of this part" (18 April 1925). Soon King was rejoicing over the beginnings of "something quite ef-

Evidently the journalist Frederick Griffin agreed. In a plimentary article written in 1928, Griffin enthusiastically raised the beauty of this small area:

> Behind this house [guest cottage] is a rectangle of level lawn, edged by beautiful beds of larkspur and other perennials. It is a delightful plaisance, given a quality of cool and cloistered peace, not only by the great trees that surround it shutting out the world but by a wall which Mr. King has built along one side. It might be the wall of an old monastery garden. For in it is a postern gate of some dark wood beside which hangs a black lantern. The whole effect is monkish and very soothing, a pleasure to the eye and balm to the spirit. Only an artist could have achieved it.[54]

King's admiration of "old world" charm and atmosphere was to resurface in later years when he conceived and built the "ruins" at Moorside.

Bordering this "monkish" spot was a large rustic pergola, built in 1925, painted white and constructed of six huge stripped cedar logs, and a dozen boards for the top lattice. The use of pergolas was influenced by a revival of interest in Italian Renaissance gardens. Originally designed to provide relief from the Mediterranean sun, pergolas by the early 1900s were popular British garden structures. In Britain, pergolas were utilized as aesthetic structures designed to show off flowering climbers, especially roses, rather than as shady retreats. The pergola had become so popular that Gertrude Jekyll, a renowned and influential British gardener, announced that "there is scarcely an example of modern garden design in which it does not find a place."[55] Pergolas were not common elements in the Canadian garden until the mid-1920s. In the *Canadian Florist*, a professional gardener described his Ottawa employer's pergola, built in 1912, as "probably the only one of its kind in the Dominion."[56]

The setting for King's first pergola was a bit strange. King placed it under the trees between the guest cottage and the garage, leading from nowhere to nowhere. King obviously had not heeded garden designers who urged care in siting:

> The pergola is of great value for marking the boundary line between two distinct portions of the garden, usually the lawns and highly cultivated parts, and the wilder section leading maybe to the orchard or fields beyond.... A short pergola would prepare us for a change of scene...[57]

"A sunny aspect...is best," cautioned another garden commentator, "for a cool, sunless place is practically useless for climbers, and anything but a healthy resting place."[58] Shade was something Kingswood had in abundance. As well, the gardener was warned that surrounding trees eventually deprive climbers of needed nourishment as tree roots encroach upon the pergola ground.

Caution was also urged in suiting the style of the pergola to the style of house and garden. Pergolas were built of various materials ranging from marble to tree branches. However, builders were warned not to construct the pergola with flimsy materials: "Nothing looks weaker or less satisfactory than a cross-beam that swags downwards...."[59] The unpretentious Kingswood setting was ideal for King's choice of a rustic cedar construction.

King followed the standard height and spacing dimensions: "Simplicity and a certain degree of solidity are the main points to be considered...."[60] In these pre-metric times, the magic number was eight — columns eight feet (2.4 m) high and eight feet apart in both width and length, provided the most pleasing dimensions. The minimum distance of eight feet across prevented a "mere tunnel of greenery, obstructing the light and making it difficult for more than one person to pass through at a time."[61] Wood and concrete columns were to be sunk four feet (1.2 m) into the ground.

King placed flagstone paving beneath it, probably to tie into the flagstone entranceways of both cottages, or perhaps because this use of flagstone was recommended in a book he had in his library: Charles Thonger's *A Book of Garden Furniture* published in 1903.

There was no strict unanimity on plant material, although the preference certainly was for flowering vines, especially climbing roses. Depending on the climate, a wide range of climbers was recommended: clematis, Dutchman's Pipe, honeysuckle, Virginia creeper, wisteria, *Bignonia radicans*, climbing nasturtium, Canary creeper, bittersweet, and cobea. Grape vines for the overhead rafters were especially favoured not only for foliage cover, but also for the decorative appeal of grape clusters. The optimum effect was a heavy foliage cover for the top and lighter "vine drapery" trained with galvanized wire supports onto the side pillars.

National Capital Commission

The garage and pergola.

King questioned W.T. Macoun regarding the choice of vines for his pergola. In spring 1926 Macoun replied, promising twenty-five climbing bittersweet vines from the C.E.F., rather than the Virginia creeper King wanted which was not in stock. Macoun also recommended four climbing roses, evidently for the pergola: 'Dorothy Perkins,' 'Dr. VanFleet,' 'Hiawatha,' and 'Paul's Scarlet.' The roses as well as *Clemantis jackmanni*, Macoun noted, could only be obtained from the Ottawa florist, Kenneth McDonald and Sons.[62] Which vines were actually planted, is not known; however, given the conditions at Kingswood, it is doubtful that climbing roses thrived. By June of the next year King happily noted in his diary that the pergola was beginning to be covered with vines — typically he did not specify which vines. Contemporary photos also show a small perennial border next to the Kingswood pergola — a recommended planting to "...set off the sunny front side" of the structure.[63]

Fencing

After the 1922 property was acquired, King immediately directed Paddy Murphy to define the boundaries of his property with wood fences and stone walls, and later, as the estate grew, with wire fencing. Enclosing the property, giving it an "air" of seclusion appealed to King's romanticism. Fencing also appealed to his philosophical side. While piling up rotten fence posts, King once mused on the "lesson" they provided. These posts, he wrote, "...have been in for twenty-three years...what will be the shape of the new ones 23 years hence & where will we all be! It is a commentary on our vanity that a fence post survives a man" (9 September 1924).

Fencing prevented livestock and other unwanted visitors entering the property. Fencing was utilitarian, but it also had an aesthetic value. By the 1920s fencing materials ranged from stone, wood, hedging, and wrought iron, to wire and brick. Owners were cautioned to consider not only the use of the fence, but also how it would blend with the surroundings, the style of the house and the location of the property: "It is wise...to avoid bizarre effects or too startling and unexpected use of materials. Simplicity never goes out of style...."[64]

This credo was close to King's frugal heart. He wisely and economically had his labourers use the natural materials at hand. Available stone was heaped into low piles along the public road — typical of stone fence construction at the edges of a farmer's field.[65] King greatly admired the effect of the stone fence: "Was delighted when I reached my gate to notice that the fence to the left had been put up for a good part of the way. The improvement was even more marked than one would have imagined.... What greater joy than working on a place of one's own like this" (31 August 1924). The original wall, which was stacked very high, incorporated various trees, giving the boundary a naturalistic look, as if it had been in place for years. During his Kingswood years the boundary walls were often rebuilt to accommodate changing property lines. At one time the stone wall was restacked into a wider, shorter structure than originally made, and some of the trees destroyed.[66] As the property expanded, King used white rail fencing and wire strung between cedar posts along the extensive boundaries. The posts and rails were whitewashed periodically. At the Kingswood entrance King had fieldstones set into cement and topped by a double-coursed cap (a common design in the Kingsmere area, as well as on other Ontario country estates) and wooden gates attached. The effect of this rustic, neat, tree-shaded, welcoming entrance was entirely in keeping with the tenor of the Kingswood property.

The "Serpentine" Road

The design of the entrance path also reflected the rustic character of the site. As soon as King expanded his holdings, he altered the narrow, grassy lane which led through a wire gate from the access road to the door of the first cottage. He designed an ambitious road with the ever-helpful Paddy Murphy: "We have marked out a splendid route, coming into the grounds by a gate which points in an opposite direction and then winding in serpentine fashion through a bit of swamp which will be redeemed into a fine road with stone walls either side" (3 October 1922). The word "serpentine" signalled King's knowledge of the ideals of the English Landscape Style, popular in the 18th century — ideals which would also influence his subsequent landscaping.

William Kent, a prominent 18th century British landscape gardener, reacted against the formalism of previous landscaping "schools" by treating estate landscapes in a more naturalistic manner. Kent began by freeing water from its confines of canals, fountains and basins, and allowing streams to wander or "serpentize" where they would.[67] "Nature abhors a straight line" became the designer's credo. The idea of a winding line of graceful curves was translated into other landscape elements, especially roadways. By the 20th century serpentine design was a commonplace treatment of an approach road, or a path though the garden.

Construction of the new part of the "serpentine" Kingswood roadway was a particular delight for King: "When I woke at 8 I heard the wagons at work on the road and jumped out of bed rejoicing that the new roadway was being pushed on" (16 October 1922). He was also thrilled when the route revealed "...three large elms which are most graceful and beautiful trees. There is great grace & dignity & 'refinement' about an elm. The one near the gate in its graceful purity & aristocratic bearing makes me think of dear Mother" (3 October 1922). The final result was a U-shaped road terminating in two sets of gates at the western and eastern sides of the property. The original path, also constructed in well thought-out curves, was widened to accommodate King's new motor car. King at first was dismayed when he saw the final effect : "I felt I had widened the road a little too much & that it had lost some of its character of an English lane" (5 November 1922).

National Archives of Canada/PA 126144

King greatly admired the effect of a stone fence wall incorporating a favourite tree.

Garden Ornaments

The increasingly designed look of the Kingswood landscape by 1926 was also enhanced by the number of decorative elements on the grounds. One of King's favourite ornaments, also one of his earliest, was the sundial. In July 1915 he erected a sundial he had wanted in place since 1911 when he found it in a second hand shop in Boston. He was thrilled to see the date 1777 engraved upon it, for it established an illusion of historic importance which King loved: "The fires of the forge in which it was made had been hot in their resentment toward Britain. With changed location [Kingswood], its pedestal had become the near companion of a staff flying the British flag."[68] For a number of years this "sentinel of time" sat humbly on a tree stump, until King found a handyman to make a proper wooden base and top, which were then painted white, a faint echo of the traditional marble. The first night he took it out to the cottage, King was so eager to see it in place, he cut the long grass with his scythe, and erected it before having supper (14 July 1915). A few years later

King had a permanent square concrete base for the dial set into the ground about a third of the distance between the cottage and the lake shoreline.[69] Whenever King looked at it he was "filled with delight," for he said he preferred "sun time" over any other.

King's capacity for casting a romantic and exaggerated glow of importance over his possessions was also directed onto the sundial. In 1917-18 during the writing of *Industry and Humanity* (demonstrating his belief in the possible synthesis of the labour movement, Christianity, and the capitalist system) he described, in rather tortured prose, the sundial as a symbol of

> ...a perfect order and a complete harmony in all that pertains to Time and Space throughout the physical universe....if all material things of the heavens and of the earth are thus related in a perfect harmony which the human intelligence is able to grasp; is it conceivable, is it rational to believe that underlying the social relations of men and of nations, an order is not discoverable somewhere, obedience to which will bring as perfect a harmony? ...We have turned the dials of human conduct to commercial uses when they were intended as guides to the divinity which lies everywhere about us.[70]

But it was even more. It was an emblem of Faith. "Since I know the sun is which I cannot see. So God though hidden by the cloud of our material existence," he wrote in his diary, "is nevertheless everywhere about us & some day shall be revealed. As I stood in position before the dial's face, the *shadow* began to emerge. So it is with our attitude towards God" (16 September 1918).

Early twentieth-century garden commentators wrote enthusiastically about sundials: "There is something so suggestive in the thin band of shadow cast by the finger of the old dial, that even the most frivolous feel sobered, almost awed, when we see one of these quaint objects in the garden."[71] Garden writers counselled proper placement of a dial in the garden to highlight its sentimental interest and ornamental effect: "Sundials...depend more for their decorative success on their right placing than on their intrinsic merit as garden sculpture."[72] The sundial was frequently used as a focal point: the centre of a rose garden, or a feature at the intersection of two paths. Minimal planting around it was recommended (a few roses, ferns, or a small vine clinging to the base) to highlight this rather moralistic garden feature. King planted only grass around his. By the 1920s many Canadian gardens incorporated sun dials. They ranged in style from humble wooden based dials topped by a simple brass gnomen to marble, stone and statuary-based models. Lady Eaton in her "Ardwold" garden in Toronto had an elaborate dial ornamented with dancing cherubim carved in bas relief around the stone base. The sun dial at the Royal Canadian Yacht Club in Toronto served as a war memorial.[73]

Surprisingly, for he loved these little tasks, King did not compose a proper motto (an integral component of the sun dial) for his Kingswood dial. Collections of mottos, as well as instructions on the proper composition and subject matter of these brief, gentle morals, were often published. A perennial favourite was "I mark only the bright hours." But mottos could also be didactic: "I count the time, dost thou?" or "Time's too short to dream away; All men ought to watch and pray."[74]

Although an antique European stone or marble sun dial was the preferred ornament, abundant advice had been published on how to construct a home-built dial.[75] A rustic model made from a tree trunk and a hand-engraved dial of brass, iron or slate was the most inexpensive and easiest to make. The challenge was in properly aligning the dial to display an accurate time: "...one will be led into exciting excursions into the mysteries of time and the realm of higher mathematics and even astronomy."[76]

Described by a contemporary garden writer, in terms King would have approved, as a "source of inspiration and delight," the bird bath was another common feature of the early twentieth century garden. King acquired a bird bath a few years after erecting his sun dial. Admired not only for its decorative appeal, the bird bath was also promoted as a necessary component in the movement to protect beneficial birds. This movement, influenced partly by the Victorian love of nature, stimulated the formulation of a conservation ethic, urging farmers and hunters not to destroy birds. As well, there was a strong reaction against slaughtering birds for their feathers to be used as hat trimmings. Information on the amount of harmful insects consumed by birds was widely circulated, as well as the ways to attract song birds into the garden.

National Archives of Canada/PA 126189

King and his first sundial.

King certainly delighted in birds as part of his "God's little creatures" attitude toward nature. He received, in June 1917, a bird bath as a gift from Mr. and Mrs. Welborn, an American industrialist King had met during his years as a labour conciliator for the Rockefeller Foundation.[77] King was thrilled with the gift: "It is a beautiful garden ornament and adds wonderfully to the charm of the little cottage & its surroundings," he wrote in his diary..."It will ever be memorable as marking this day, the arrival of dear mother in Kingsmere for the summer of 1917" (27 June 1917). The bird bath unfortunately arrived without directions for assembly, so King wrote the Howard Studios of New York. This company, specializing in marble, stone and cement garden decorations, duly sent along detailed instructions for constructing the foundation, and cementing bowl and pedestal together. When the construction was finished, King had the Murphys place the bird bath near the northeast corner of his cottage, so that he could comfortably watch birds frolic in its waters.

King wrote, thanking the Welborns:

> ...I seldom look into the water of the basin in which by day the pine tree branches, the sky and the clouds are perfectly mirrored and at night, the stars and the moon, that I do not think of those lines so true to the profoundest spiritual meanings of life and with the

birdbath offering itself to the reflected universe inevitably suggest:

> Only as the heart is pure
> Shall larger visions still be mine
> For mirror'd in its depths are seen
> The things Divine
>
> Were I able to do so I would carve those words around the rim of the basin, that everyone who looks into its waters and sees the wonders of earth and sky reflected there might gain some suggestion of the possibilities of his own soul in unbroken communion with God....To have the larger vision is to be indifferent to lesser ones, and it is the larger vision you have helped to give both in inspiration and companionship and the wonderfully beautiful symbol — which fills my heart with delight as I write... (15 July 1917).

By this time King believed birds, as agents from Heaven, would contact him, to let him know all was well and he was being guided and protected. King was thrilled to provide a place where these agents would stay close to him. As he wrote the word "symbol" in the letter to the Welborn's thanking for the bird bath, King noted in his diary:

> ...a little bird that has a nest above one of the windows came and stood on the rim [of the bird bath] and in a minute or so plunged into the centre of it and flew off rejoicing. It was one of the most beautiful and playful things I have ever witnessed and it made my heart leap with joy. I was very much struck with the wonderful coincidence....It is one of the most remarkable coincidences I have known in life (15 July 1917).

It was not to be the last, nor the most remarkable. As early as 1918 he mused: "I sometimes wonder if those we love do not control the spirits of birds & the fragrance & beauty of flowers & caused them to cheer [?] & speak to us. Why should it not be so" (5 April 1918). King's increasingly fantastical interpretations of his interactions with nature were in their infancy during his Kingswood years, and would later mature to play a major role in his enchanted garden during his residence at Moorside.

Garden Furniture

By 1928 the Kingswood landscape was a well-organized combination of decorative and utilitarian structures and ornaments, including garden furniture. Outdoor furniture elicited a myriad of "dos and don'ts" from garden designers. Although necessary, the consensus was "...the less of it the better...good of its kind, simple and artistic in construction."[78] Furniture of marble, concrete and wood were highly recommended: "...formal pieces resemble well-bred people. They fit suitably into any place in their surroundings."[79] However, no matter which design or material was used, the furniture should not detract from the landscaping. King's furniture was not bought and placed for artistic enhancement of his landscape, but rather for comfort, mobility (following the sun or shade), durability, and, King's ever-present concern, price. On the Kingswood grounds, the visitor would never find those impressive, but expensive, carved stone seats, typically placed in a mossy grotto upon a pavement of flagstone. Nor would a Kingswood guest ever sit on the distinctive camel-backed oak seats (designed by Edwin Lutyens, a noted English architect and garden planner) which weathered to a silvery hue, blending beautifully into the gardens of Britain's horticultural elite.

King had three types of furniture at Kingswood. Early photographs show rustic-work chairs made of branches and twigs.

Rustic-work was an outgrowth of the Picturesque movement in Europe in the 18th century when garden design mirrored nature, and ornaments made of natural materials were fanciful components in these gardens. To furnish the grottoes, follies and hermitages popular in this style, chairs, tables and other needed furniture were fashioned from twigs and branches of trees. Rustic work furnishings in late 19th century North American gardens allegedly symbolized the nostalgia for a rural life close to nature.[80]

One of the early Ontario suppliers of this furniture was the Rustique Work Manufacturing Company in Belle Ewart, Simcoe County, Ontario. The company supplied an amazing variety of objects: "summer houses, bowers, bridges, boat landings, park railing, settees, tete-a-tete chairs, vases, sparrow houses, hanging baskets, window boxes, brackets, dog kennels..."[81] The proprietor, with the imposing name of Prince Edward Drake, noted in his catalogue that his products were of higher quality than the U.S. imports. The home owner could also buy rustic-work from garden supply companies, nurseries, and general handymen.

King's rustic-work chairs, made by one of these unknown manufacturers, evidently did not last very long. In response to a local nurseryman's query if King needed any rustic seats for Kingswood, King replied: "...I found that the squirrels and the weather played such havoc with them that, after a year or two, I was glad to burn them."[82]

The next installment of furniture was more elegant. In 1927 King ordered six chairs and two settees from a Kitchener carpenter, A.W. Burke. The grouping was simple, straight backed, white painted, wooden furniture, common in the mid-20th century garden, sometimes called the Adirondack, or even Muskoka, style. The chairs and settees proved to be so compatible with King's taste and ideas of appropriate decoration, that in 1929 he ordered four more chairs and two additional settees from the same contractor.

The third type of garden furniture used at Kingswood was park benches. In the late 1920s, King once again attempted to buy "surplus" material from the Department of Public Works. King had his private secretary, W.H. Measures, phone the maintenance department to inquire if they had used park benches for sale. This request worked its way up to the deputy minister, who said there were no used benches available, and refused to sell King any new ones. He explained that the D.P.W. benches were marked with the Department's insignia. The deputy minister feared "...the public would never believe that Mr. King paid for the benches, and it would be said that Mr. King was taking public property up to Kingsmere."[83] Measures then contacted the superintendent of the Ottawa Improvement Commission, Alexander "Sandy" Stewart, who played a major role in King's future landscaping efforts. Mr. Stewart proved to be much more amenable. Within a week, ten O.I.C. benches ("hardwood slates with malleable iron supports") were delivered to Kingsmere at a cost of four dollars each.[84]

Waterfront Improvements

The last major landscaping projects King undertook at Kingswood were various waterfront improvements. Paddy Murphy began by constructing a low fieldstone and concrete retaining wall along the water's edge, with concrete and stone steps at both ends. This wall effectively straightened the shoreline, and the steps created a grander entrance from the lake. King said he was "well-nigh in raptures" over it. He was even more delighted when Nature gave a "sign" of her approval. As he made his first inspection of the work, a school of speckled trout swam close to the stones (18 October 1925). However, his neighbour, Arthur S. Bourinot, thought otherwise: "His shore line has been artificially reinforced with a stone wall and terraces which while excellently done rather mar the otherwise wild and natural beauty of the surroundings."[85] King's smooth, regular shoreline certainly contrasted with his neighbours.'[86]

The more formal treatment of this area was further emphasized when King had two lakeside terraces built, providing flat areas for sitting and sunning. They were yet another transitional device in the progression from the wildness of the forested entrance to the formality of the stone wall and steps at the lakeside.

The land was cleared of scrub and stumps, leveled, and prepared for sodding. Laying sod was a new enterprise for King. Usually Paddy Murphy sprinkled grass seed around the cottages, but King had caught the improving fever, and wanted to use more sophisticated methods and materials. For the lawn area between the stone wall and the pergola, King attempted to obtain some creeping bent fescue grass he saw on the Jasper National Park golf course. Maynard Rogers, superintendent of Jasper Park whom King had met on a recent Western tour, recommended it for the Kingswood conditions — thin soil, short growing season, etc. In 1924, Rogers passed on the request to the Stanley Thompson Company in Toronto who did nothing about it that fall. King once again contacted Rogers in spring 1925 to remind him of his promise of seed and sod. A flurry of telegrams from the Thompson Company followed, noting that the order was taken and sod from the company's laboratories would be sent. An equal number of sharp telegrams issued from King, asking when exactly the roots would arrive, etc. After a month of these communications, the creeping bent arrived in Ottawa without instructions. King, worried about incorrect planting, wrote: "Having understood from you that there would be two varieties of roots, one for nursery purposes and the other for lawn use, I was at a loss to know just for which purpose the sod was intended...."[87] The Thompson Company wired back just to "lay sod in ground temporarily as you would any ordinary sod. Soak thoroughly," and promised to send a company representative up to Kingswood to supervise the laying of this small plot. King noted in a letter to Rogers that he was rather put out by the delays and inadequate follow-up and finally had Paddy Murphy sod the area with a local grass variety.[88] With an almost audible sigh, he then remarked that he planted a dozen bags of the creeping bent roots "as a sort of nursery and from which in the course of a year or two I hope to be able to derive results."[89] However, the nursery seems to have died out.

Learning from this experience, King did not bother with special grasses when sodding the lakefront terraces. Paddy Murphy instead sodded it with a local variety of grass. When he inspected the final outcome in November of that year, King was simply delighted:

> As we came around the corner of my cottage and saw the green sod down by the water's edge near the stone wall I could have shouted for delight. Nothing in weeks past has brought such a feeling of pure joy to my heart and mind. The effect is wonderfully beautiful, to look from the verandah of the cottage and see the water's edge itself (22 November 1925).

The sod evidently was laid correctly, for the health of the lawns today attest to their proper preparation and siting.[90]

Miscellaneous Improvements — Water Supply

In addition to the landscaping, various buildings were added between 1922 and 1925. An ice house and shed were built in 1922, and the following year a garage near the guest cottage was built. The permanence of servants at Kingswood was further signified by building servants' quarters onto the second story of the garage. All the buildings conformed to the style, materials and paint schemes of the first cottage.

Affluence also allowed the upgrading of his water supply system, an alteration which had an effect upon the landscape. The first recorded mechanical device King used to get water from the lake was a hand pump connected with difficulty in 1917 to lengths of pipe laid out into the lake. The first pump did not work until a defective handle was replaced and the pump was moved twenty feet closer to the lake. This move was unfortunate, as King had obviously tried to avoid hauling water for any great distance up the steep hill. Annoyed when the defective pump and the unused piping were left lying around the cottage, King wrote the suppliers, F.G. Johnson & Co., that he was not liable for the equipment or the final bill. The Murphys, who constructed the pump, not King, were to pay the company when completed. F.G. Johnson and Co. replied, undaunted by King's strong words, that "...if do not receive paymt this month we have no other cause but to force payment....And if Mr Murphy do not hand over the cash you may have to pay."[91]

In keeping with the major improvements in his lifestyle, landscaping, and property holdings, King decided to replace the outdoor plumbing. But to provide constant running water for bathtub and kitchen sink, a water tower was required. This necessitated major engineering activity involving numerous plumbing firms, the Department of Public Works, King's office staff, and the ever-helpful Murphys.

Water towers, familiar structures on large estates and on some suburban lots, were often built to complement the neighbouring architecture. One garden writer noted: "It need not necessarily be expensive, but at least it should be picturesque...."[92] To achieve this decorative ideal, water towers were to be transformed from damp, hollow buildings. The first and second floors could be used as an "artistic or literary workshop," or the first floor could be entirely decorative, especially if it were designed as a pergola extension or an open-air retreat.[93] Water would be stored on the third floor. One rather pretentious summer home, Carleton Villa in the Thousand Islands, boasted a water tower nearly 111 foot (34 m) tall and 16 foot (1.5 m) square, storing 200 barrels of water. The second floor of the tower was used as a workroom and the top floor was fitted out as an observatory. At night the observatory was lit with gas lights as a signal to boaters. The owner connected the tower to the main house by two bridges and named the elegantly decorated connecting rooms "the bridge rooms."[94]

But King did none of these things. In keeping with his predilection for free government services, King had the chief architect of the Department of Public Works, R.C. Wright, draw up specifications and drawings of a steel-legged water tower. These were to be used by companies bidding on the project as well as for the construction itself. The tower was 32 feet (10 m) high, and the 5 foot (1.5 m) diameter tank held 1400 gallons (5300 litres) of water. These specifications were recorded by late summer 1923, but King did not proceed seriously until early July 1924.

Feverish activity commenced on July 31st, when the concrete foundations were laid. King, alternately enjoying and fussing over the details, was rather appalled when the supervisor of the tank tower team appeared: "A sickly mortal just out of

Edwinna von Baeyer

The pump house.

hospital arrived to do the superintending with one man, had I not had the Murphy staff to do the erecting & get everything in readiness it would not have been up till day of Judgment" (31 July 1924). But things moved apace. The pumping engine was installed, pipe laid to connect cottages and lake, and indoor plumbing fixtures installed. The tank was hoisted into place on August 2nd: "I felt rather nervous watching the hoisting operation for fear of a break or fall which might have seriously injured one of the men, but all went well. Paddy Murphy is a genius."

King also had the lake water tested and was not pleased to read the delicately worded report from the Assistant Chief Dominion Analyst of the Department of Health: a slight contamination of the water was possibly due to organisms "from the discharges from human beings."[95] However, in spite of the report, King waited seven years, until 1931, to have a well bored at Kingswood. He loaned the Kingswood cottage to his private secretary, H.R. Henry, and his family in August that year. While there, Henry's young son contracted a serious case of typhoid fever. King worried that the Kingsmere lake water may have been at fault, and began drilling.[96] It took ten days to drill through 70 feet (21 m) of Canadian Shield. King found well-drilling, in spite of the noise, "...a new & interesting experience" (24 September 1931). When the well was finished King was thrilled: "The well at the little cottage has come into being....To have a spring of living water from a well so near the little cottage where dear mother spent her last summer is to me an indescribable joy" (25 September 1931).

The Sacred Precinct

His mother's spirit seemingly hovered over Kingswood. King cherished certain spots as sacred or as especially conducive to serious thinking. One session in the cottage with "the tenderest and holiest of associations" produced one of King's infrequent self-assessments:

> I have decided it is well for me to mix all I can with people whilst reserving some time for study, to keep in touch, share the life of the community & of the nation. To live after the world but not in or of the world, to be a normal natural man full of the joy of life, not a prude or narrow, but not given to excess in anything. To be strong

in upholding the principles of right & honour, & good conduct, honesty, integrity of character — but enjoying life, not given to over-discipline in it, as I have perhaps to too great an extent this year. My role is that of a leader in public affairs, and to play that part contact with the public is essential, to set an example where I go may be & is right enough, but to go is increasingly a duty I can see. The little absence of three days in Toronto & the West has been all to the good, filled me with new zeal & refreshment & helped me to get away from unnecessary introspection & its fatal results.[97]

King probably was not much different from the average cottage owner in his delights and annoyances over the daily workings of an "inessential home," but the power of his imagination elevated his summer life onto an inviolable plane. At Kingswood he was surrounded by loving memory, by associations cleansed of any unpleasantness. Kingswood was where he had set his roots and where he said, years later, that his heart remained. By 1928, with help from various government departments and the Murphys, Kingswood had reached the height of its development — physically and spiritually. After that King began to transform it (mentally) into a museum, a historical site to be preserved without change. King would not alter any detail of house and grounds, perhaps afraid that the fragile connection with his mother's spirit might be broken, a connection King found particularly consoling:

> I went to the room dear mother was in last summer, and knelt by the side of the bed...and prayed that God would bless this summer to me, would guide and keep me. I prayed that dear mother would be near me, that I might work hard and conclude my book [*Industry and Humanity*] in a worthy manner...This little house is a sanctuary, these quiet hills & woods a refuge... (24 June 1918).

The connection was so potent in King's mind that even twenty years after his mother's death, he could be seriously upset by the most trivial unauthorized changes. In 1937 he rented out the little cottage. When he visited Kingswood at the end of that summer, he was shocked:

> Mrs. Coleman had on her own painted over the chairs...including the one in which mother was seated when her picture was painted. This hurt me very much, but I said nothing (11 July 1937)....I was terribly surprised and pained to see that Mrs. Coleman had painted the green table & window leaf — without asking any permission. It changed the whole character of the room, — robbed me in an instant of many of the associations shared with Mother & Father, Joan & Godfroy, Mrs. Herridge & others — a shocking thing to have done, the painting of the old chair was bad enough, but this was criminal....I shall just have to have the paint removed....I shall not let any of the cottages again to persons I do not know more about....I would not have taken the rent of both cottages for these alterations & what they do of injury to my heart & feelings (21 August 1937).

The presence of his mother's guiding love was a powerful component in his conviction that Kingsmere could strengthen his mental and physical health. By the late 1920s, the notion of seeking refuge at Kingswood from the cares of political office or the buffetings of everyday life, gained great significance for King. For example, after the turmoil of his 1926 constitutional battle with Governor General Byng, and King's subsequent resignation, he found solace at Kingswood:

> I walked over the grounds after looking at the trees and reciting to myself Lanier's lines "Into the woods the Master went" — I wish dear old Harper had been at my side thro' all this...Came and sat at the side of the little

> lake as the last reflections of the daylight sky were upon it — It was wonderfully beautiful, such a rest, such a rest — to be alone on this little spot...oh so glad to rest alone in my little cottage, alone in the midst of the trees, under the open sky (3 July 1926).

Although his later dabblings in the spirit world, his property expansion, and his significant landscaping projects were often influenced by his feelings of holding a sacred trust at Kingswood, ego overcame sentimentality. The solace, the spirituality of Kingswood was subordinated to King's interest in expansion, aggrandizement and social status. He would from now on cast himself into the role of a country gentleman, no longer a mere cottager.

Photo Credits for following pages:
Page 81: National Capital Commission.
Page 82: National Capital Commission.
Page 83: (clockwise) Edwinna von Baeyer; National Capital Commission; Edwinna von Baeyer.
Page 84: National Capital Commission.
Page 85: (clockwise) Edwinna von Baeyer; Edwinna von Baeyer; National Capital Commission.
Page 86: National Capital Commission.
Page 87: National Capital Commission.
Page 88: National Capital Commssion.

Moorside, King's cottage residence through much of the thirties, as seen from a side field.

Above: Moorside from the lower lawn.

Upper left: King's bedroom in the restored Kingswood cottage, King's first cottage.

Lower left: King's bedroom in the restored Moorside cottage.

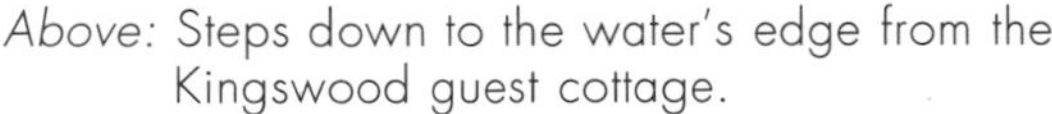

Above: Steps down to the water's edge from the Kingswood guest cottage.

Upper right: The main pathway of the Moorside garden leads down to a ruin King called "The Window on the Forest."

Lower right: The Moorside garden.

The farmhouse, now the residence of the speaker of the House of Commons.

Above: The waterfall.
Upper right: The waterfall trail.
Lower right: Kingswood cottage.

The first ruin he purchased, King placed high on a Moorside hill.

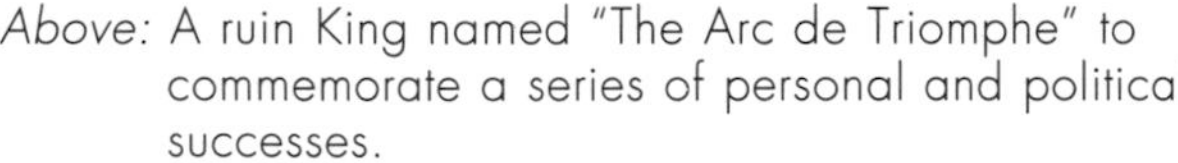

Above: A ruin King named "The Arc de Triomphe" to commemorate a series of personal and political successes.

Upper right: "The Doorway," part of "The Abbey Ruins," a collection of architectural fragments King built to suggest the ruins of an actual building.

Lower right: "The Fireplace Wall" formed the rear boundary of "The Abbey Ruins."

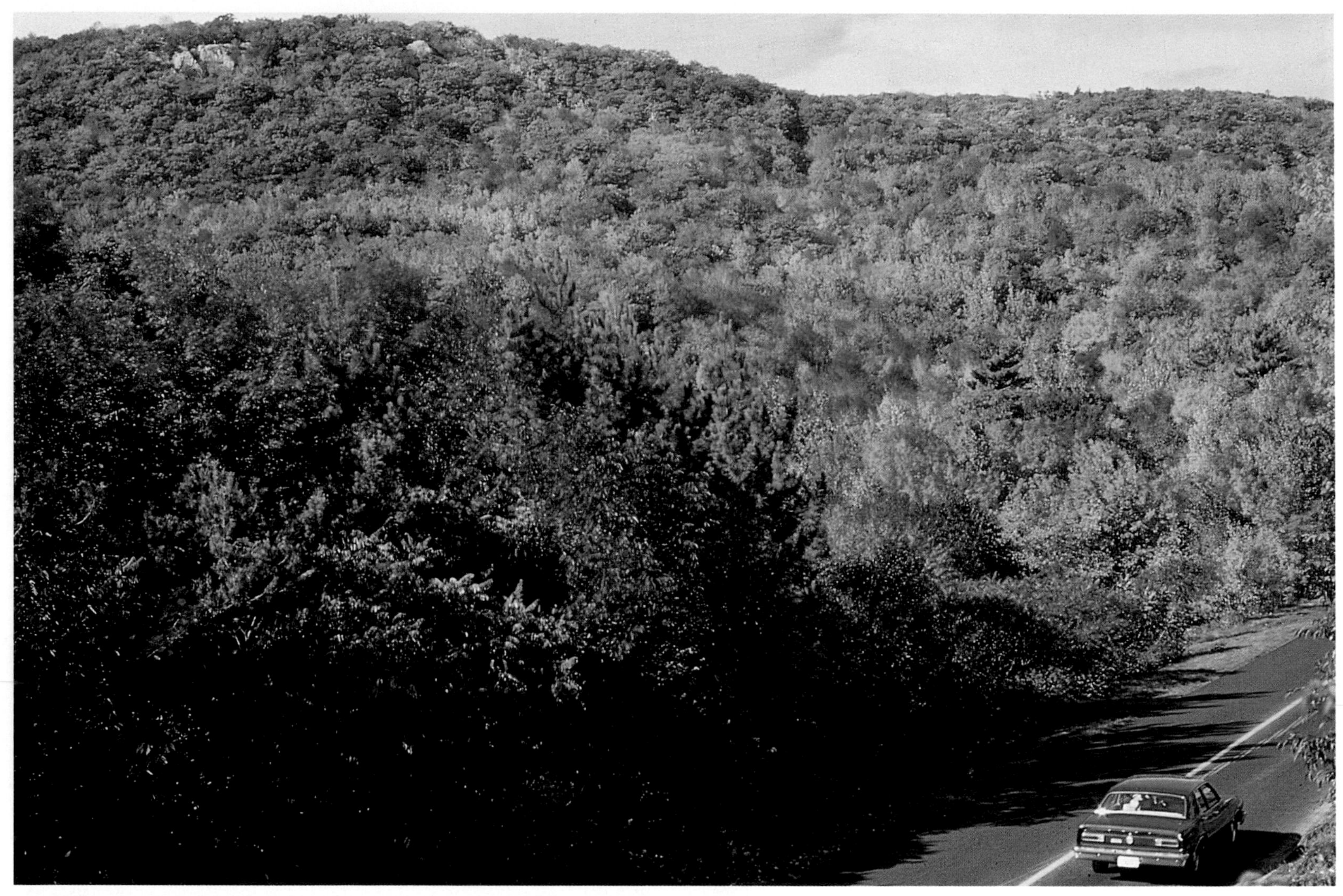

King Mountain.

CHAPTER THREE

Moorside

FROM COTTAGER TO COUNTRY GENTLEMAN

By 1928 Mackenzie King wanted to be labelled as more than just a cottager, he wanted that prestigious British label of landed proprietor. He was a man of means and position, and he had served as prime minister for nearly seven years. But to transform himself from cottager to country squire required leaving Kingswood. It was not a major move in terms of distance, but psychologically it was momentous. King left behind all the potent associations of his early Kingsmere life in favour of creating a new Kingsmere persona. His steady acquisition of property provided the means to realize his ambitions.

Property Acquisition

King acquired his property in the same way he pursued many major estate projects — piecemeal. Over a nine year period nearly 500 acres (202 ha) were accumulated in transactions involving one half acre to one hundred acre parcels. His first purchase, separate from his immediate Kingswood holdings, was a nine acre (4 ha) plot directly across the public road from his cottage property. This land was bought in April 1923 for $1,500 from Charles Fleury, a local farmer. A few months later, King purchased one half acre for $150 to square off the Kingswood property. This purchase established a precedent for his subsequent transactions — that of "completing" an area he had embarked upon, expanding and smoothing out the boundary lines.

In early fall 1923 when King visited the terminally-ill Marjorie Herridge for the last time, she said she would not be going to Kingsmere again. She offered to sell him her Edgmoor property, adjacent to the Fleury land, including cottage contents for $5,000. King seemingly dismissed the idea, noting to himself

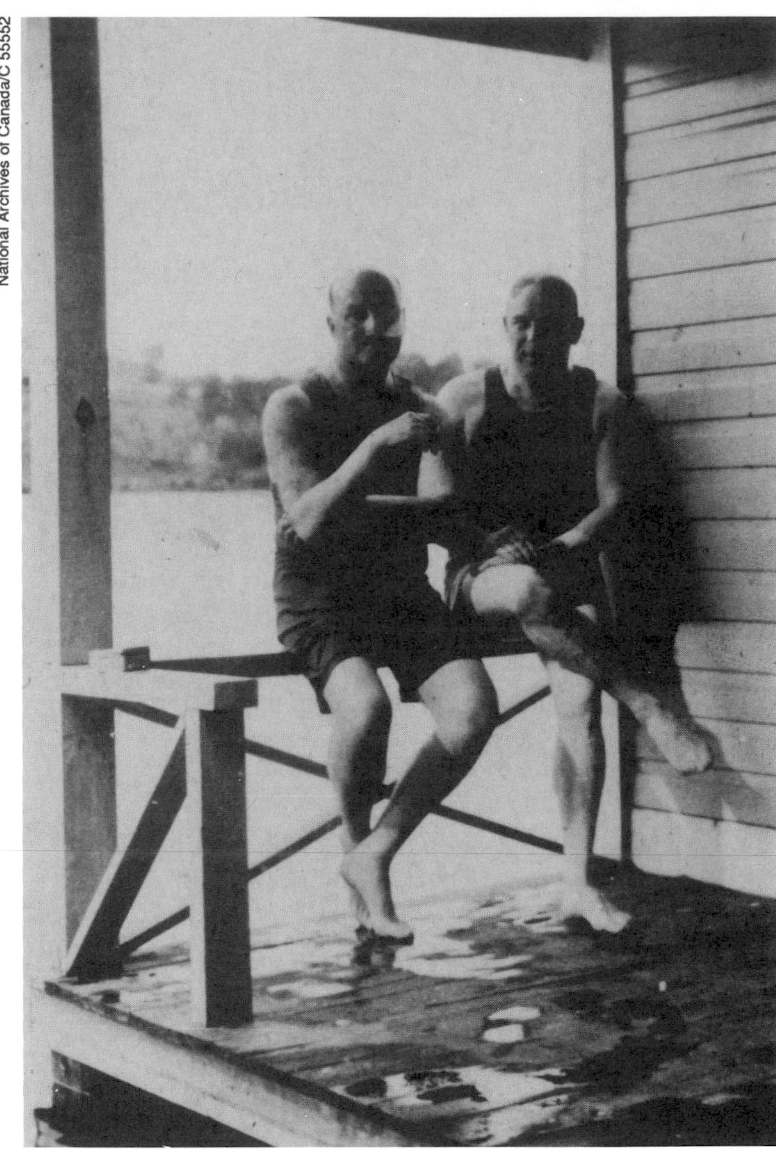

National Archives of Canada/C 55552

King and Godfroy Patteson enjoying the boathouse.

that the property was only worth $3,000. A few days later he commented in his diary that his friends, the Pattesons, would probably buy it. Over the winter King changed his mind. By March 30, 1924, he was negotiating with Reverend Herridge to purchase the property: "I spoke of 2,500 as being what I thought the house & grounds were worth allowing for increase of value in site & decrease in property. He had mentioned a higher figure but evidently was not expecting more than 3,000. I should have agreed to this fig. less what it will take to put it in proper repair" (30 March 1924). After the purchase was completed, Dr. Herridge graciously wrote to King:

> It will be of interest to you to know that you were one of the witnesses of my signature to the original Deed of Sale; & I am rejoiced to think that the property is now passing into the hands of an old friend.[1]

King, thrilled to own Edgmoor, revelled in the beauty of its hilltop views which he said made it the "commanding site in Kingsmere." He was no less pleased that it was prime real estate, close to Ottawa, its value destined to rise. At first it was enough just to own the property, for King did not immediately move into the cottage (too many ambivalent memories of his life with Mrs. Herridge perhaps). Instead he rented Edgmoor to his friends, Joan and Godfroy Patteson, confident that the couple would make "a beautiful spot of it." The Pattesons were to have a significant impact not only on the Moorside landscape, but also on his entire Kingsmere life.

The Pattesons

Toward the end of World War I, while living in the Roxborough Apartments in Ottawa, King met fellow renters, Godfroy and

Joan Patteson. The friendship flourished over cups of tea. From 1918 onwards, the Pattesons, increasingly mentioned in King's diary, slowly became an integral part of his life. Godfroy Patteson, manager of the Ottawa branch of Molson's Bank,[2] evidently was a quiet, accepting fellow, for King's friendship with the couple really focussed on Joan. When they met, Joan was forty-nine and King forty-four. This was a recurring pattern within King's choice of close women friends. Often older, always married, they did not provoke King's apparent fear of personal commitment.

National Archives of Canada/C 14174

Joan Patteson.

By 1920 the Pattesons were calling King, "Rex," (a nickname from his university days used only by his closest friends), and were sharing his Kingsmere life. Was it the Kingsmere air once again which intensified King's relationship with a married woman? Suddenly Joan is fixing King's collar before official dinners, Joan is accompanying him on long hikes at Kingsmere, Joan is joining him for a late supper, and so on. King was soon recording in his diary events similar to his tempestuous days with Marjorie Herridge: "These storms of passion — for that is what they are, are madness and wrong. They 'rock the mind' and must cease" (7 September 1920). The following days of crisis were excised from the diary, as they also were after the Herridge episode.[3] Marjorie Herridge was eventually cast out of his life, but not Joan. They came to an understanding: "Joan and I pledged our lives to united effort and service today. God grant we may be given strength to endure" (14 September 1920). The next year, sheltered by the equilibrium they had attained, King admitted: "...dear little soul — she would have been an ideal wife — if we could have met years ago. Her tender simple loving nature is what mine needs & craves. She has great intellectual forces & infinite charm as well..." (21 May 1921). By 1924 King's relationship with both Pattesons was safe, predictable, and stable. For the rest of his life he enjoyed, without any of the responsibility, the comforts of a home life Joan occasionally provided and sisterly (if not motherly) concern. Joan discussed politics, she read poetry with him, she participated in seances and table-rapping, she lent a willing ear to King's enthusiasms, she helped with the estate planning — she was truly his closest friend. Discounting his mother, Joan was the most important woman in his life, although King often took her for granted.

Paul Horsdal/National Archives of Canada/C55544

King, Pat and Derry.

The Pattesons were also responsible for adding another emotional constant to his life. In 1924 they gave King an Irish terrier named Pat, keeping his litter mate, Derry, for themselves. King's loneliness was often relieved by Pat's companionship. Together they ate (Pat was given his own bowl of coffee), prayed, and roamed the Kingsmere estate. "The little lad" was also mischievous — he was eager to tangle with porcupines and skunks, giving the staff the unenviable job of extracting quills or of giving him a tomato juice bath. He would worry King's livestock or run away and hide, until King and staff were beside themselves. But like Kingsmere, Pat was, in the end, perfect. At the height of his spiritualism, King ascribed qualities to Pat far beyond his dogness: "...dear little soul, he is almost human. I sometimes think he is a comforter dear mother has sent to me, he is filled with her spirit of patience, and tenderness & love" (16 June 1931). The second "Pat" (the first died in 1941 at age seventeen) was granted the ability to understand King's religious discourses. One Christmas eve King talked with Pat as he lay in his basket: "We spoke together of the Christ-child and the animals in the crib" (31 December 1944).

Further Expansion

After the Pattesons were installed at Edgmoor (soon to be renamed Moorside), King began planning to buy more land, seemingly discontented with the amount he owned. To justify the expense, he convinced himself that undesirable neighbours might move in and ruin his view by building too close to the new cottage: "There is always danger of trees being cut down, small lots sold to undesirable people, as campers being given permission to pitch tents nearby, leave tins & papers about etc." (11 August 1924). King paced off adjacent fields, deciding how much more land would "square out the lot" and keep potential neighbours at bay. Buying the additional property, he reasoned, would create "a very fine estate" and would increase its value.

Initially he determined to buy five, perhaps six, more acres from Charles Fleury, then changed his mind. "My walk about today decided me to take in an extra acre or two so as to get in a beautiful pine grove, and some rock which looks like a crystalized waterfall" (13 August 1924). He successfully negotiated buying nine acres (3.6 ha) from Fleury for $1,500, down from his original estimate of $1,850. Immediately upon purchase Paddy Murphy began fencing the borders, tearing down the old barbed wire King found such an eyesore: "The change for the better is indescribable the grounds look like those of a park — a beautiful country estate is what I now have" (10 September 1924). He owned less than 30 acres, but he still had the confidence to write: "...I am sure that some day this will be one of the finest estates *in Canada*..." (14 August 1924). Yet he was not satisfied, he coveted property he could not afford: "I feel I should buy the balance of the moor to the point overlooking the Ottawa valley. Some day I will, in all probability" (10 September 1924).

For the next two years King resisted buying more property until Charles Fleury walked into his Ottawa office one fine spring day in 1926. He offered King 50 acres (20 ha) at $100 an acre "to include bush, creek, moor etc." Evidently King did not get much work done after this meeting, for his mind reeled with land fever:

> I confess I had never allowed myself to even dream of this....I shall take 25 acres at least at that price if I can get it, I believe it will be wise to take 50. It is a better investment for future years than bonds, with rate of taxat'n what it is today on amts of income over a certain point — and it is the best kind of security for all hazards ahead... (20 March 1926).

Despite the preoccupations of leading an election campaign that summer, King frequently considered Fleury's offer. In his free time he repeatedly explored the parcel, discovering views he liked and natural features he wanted to preserve. For four months his thoughts on size and price see-sawed from 50 acres (20 ha) for $5,000, to 66 acres (27 ha) at $40 an acre. At one point he thought he would offer $75 an acre: "It will be worth $1,000 an acre some day & that not 100 years off" (13 May 1926). This internal debate continued into July: "...went for a walk exploring the land by the stream, have decided to buy all that lies on this side of it & over to the fringe of woods beyond so as to keep a fringe of trees on all sides of the outlook from my property. I shall try to get 50 acres for 3,000 — but if need be will go 4,000..."(25 July 1926). The next day he made a final offer of $4,000 for 66.31 acres (27 ha) which was accepted.

Now he really had land fever. In September, while walking an adjoining hundred acre (41 ha) parcel up for sale, he argued with himself to buy the property after discovering "one of the most wonderful vistas to be seen anywhere...I could hardly contain myself, the thought of a place to work & to think & to reflect, to write books, to bring friends to share the joys of nature & to see man & women at their best" (29 September 1926). As King further persuaded himself to buy the land "no matter what the cost (within bounds)," he continued to fantasize over its use: "What I am thinking of most is the walks I can have with public men, ministers, visitors & others thro' my own grounds, & forests & moor" (30 September 1926). Obviously this was the final, powerful stimulus, for that very day he rushed to the seller's solicitor and made an offer of $1,500, for half of the offered land. Within a week, however, he was calculating the cost of buying the entire Lot 19 from Mrs. T. McGillivary. He soon revised his original offer and paid $3,500 for the entire 100 acres. King confided in his diary that he probably could have got the whole parcel for $1,500, but his Christian conscience got the better of his frugality: "felt I wd be taking advantage of a widow" (6 October 1926).

The day after the offer was accepted, King took Governor General Willingdon and his wife for a walk on the new land. They were delighted to be the first to walk there. Impulsively the Governor General's wife took King's cane and used it as her ceremonial sword to proclaim: "...we must call it Freeman's land [after her husband Freeman Thomas, Lord Willingdon]." The Governor General echoed his wife: "Freeman's land it must be called," and King repeated "Freeman's land it shall be" (7 October 1926). Although King never referred to this parcel by that name, he revelled in the little ceremony. The incident became yet another special association with the estate landscape.

When King left Kingsmere soon after to participate in the Imperial Conference of 1926, he felt he was now a "landed proprietor" for he owned over 200 acres (81 ha). Before embarking he ordered Paddy Murphy to install $1,000 of wire fencing along the 2 1/2 mile (four km) boundary. Buoyed up by his recent re-election and his land purchases, King successfully guided the Balfour Declaration through the Conference, ensuring the equality of Commonwealth nations with one another and Britain. Although the Conference entailed long hours of meetings and behind-the-scenes lobbying, King was able to socialize on a number of country estates. During a visit to Lord Beaverbrook's estate, King happily learned that it was the exact size of Kingsmere.

Returning in December, he said he was delighted to be back in Canada: "I seemed to breathe a different air. I have been smothering in England — the environment of wealth & ease is far from a healthy one" (8 December 1926). This aversion, however, did not hinder his dreams of more land — his own form of "wealth & ease" which he defined as healthy and good: "I really believe those hills mean health & strength to me & ultimate salvation of soul as well as body" (27 March 1927).

Although King seemed satisfied with the amount of property he now owned, he was pleasantly plagued by Mrs. McGillivary's offer, made before he left Canada, to sell him the rest of her property, another 100 acres including farm house and outbuildings. Throughout the Imperial Conference he considered the offer. When he returned he wrote Mrs. McGillivary an ambivalent, vacillating letter:

> To tell the truth, I do not know of anyone who I think would wish to take the property in the condition in which it is, for summer purposes...you would be prepared to dispose of the rest of the property at what would have to be a sacrifice. I would be glad to have you write and tell me the lowest price at which you would be willing to make the sale. Please remember I am not in this letter proposing to make a purchase. I am just trying to decide in my own mind whether, seeing that I have already purchased half your property and there is a chance for me to get the balance at a less cost than others would be expected to pay, it might not be better to take over the rest of it at once, provided I can secure it at a figure which would make this worth my while.
>
> Let me impress upon you that I am not in the least anxious to buy and that I am only writing because I recall how anxious you were to dispose of the entire property...[4]

His dithering letter, however, stimulated a lengthy correspondence, visits to solicitors, and agitated diary entries. Mrs. McGillivary did not vacillate, she opened negotiations by noting that there were "bright prospects looming up for Kingsmere in the near future." She saw through King's attempt to negotiate a low price. She tartly observed he was trying to recoup his losses of surveying and fencing the first parcel and reminded him he could have applied it to the entire 200 acres. She reassured him that if he bought the other half, the additional land would enhance the value of his property. She herself would have liked to "...renovate the outbuildings and erect artistic little bungalows, fit up the grounds with winding paths etc. etc. making it — 'Kingsmere the Beautiful.'"[5] This probably was a nightmarish thought for King — all those potential "undesirables" littering the landscape so near his boundaries. The asking price of $8,000 was definitely not to King's liking either. He counter-offered $6,000, stating the land and buildings were not worth much more and reminding *her* of all the trees cut down, small land parcels sold to others, as well as the outstanding litigation on the property.

Stalemated, the correspondence lagged until spring. Then King began negotiating in earnest, offering $3,000 for the parcel plus buildings. His seriousness brought Mrs. McGillivary back to Ottawa from her brother's sickbed in Los Angeles. They met on neutral territory, the Joan of Arc Institute. Mrs. McGillivary held out for $5,000, but King kept offering $3,000. Finally the Mother Superior intervened, suggesting "...when we told her of negotiations, $4,000." King was ready to agree to the higher figure because he was increasingly worried the land might be sold to satisfy the legal claims on it: "...the greatest danger & menace is a sale to Jews, who have a desire to get in at Kingsmere & who would ruin the whole place" (11 April 1927). Her solicitor finally convinced Mrs. McGillivary that $4,000 would be a fair price. By the end of the summer King owned her land, plus a small corner between Mrs. McGillivary's two parcels bought from Willy Murphy. This lot included a cottage, which eventually King rented to the Pattesons.

Two years later King went on another buying spree and bought 100 acres from Michael Mulvihill and two small sections. In 1932 he made his final purchase — a 100 acre parcel from Charles Fleury. King was nagged by misgivings. He worried about possible political repercussions of spending so much on unusable land during the Depression: "It is hard to know what it is best to do, with unemployment, etc. about & need & suffering on the part of many. To increase one's possessions seems unwise. On the other hand it may mean doing more for others in the end, as I believe it will" (7 March 1932). After this soothing defense of his acquisitiveness, King bought the final parcel with hardly a qualm. King was now truly a landed proprietor, owing 497.38 acres (201 ha) at a cumulative cost of $29,650. He was now ready to step into his new role as country squire.

In the traditional British manner, the new country squire decided to name his estate, based on suggestions from his life and reading. In 1924, King renamed Edgmoor, "Moorside" and the Kingsmere Lake section, "Woodside," in honour of his boyhood home in Kitchener, Ontario. However, the last suggestion did not seem quite right. The next year King devised an even more felicitous solution, naming the little cottages Kingswood: "...with Kings*wood* & Moor*side* I have *Woodside* our old home" (30 July 1925). This selection was judged perfect, and within days King had stencils made in order to paint the names on his entrance gates: "The little names painted on the white bar of the gates give the place quite an air — they are really most effective."

Four years later Joan and he spent "quite a little time" choosing a name for the Old Mainguy cottage he had rented to the Pattesons. King pressured Joan to accept "Shady Hill," the name of Professor Charles Eliot Norton's home in Cambridge, Massachusetts. Norton was a famous man of letters in the late 19th century United States, as well as a popular teacher at Harvard. King had tried to become part of his charmed circle while attending graduate school there, and did end up house-sitting at Shady Hill for two months while the family was travelling. To press home his suggestion, King showed Joan Norton's letters and told her of the famous men associated with him. After she capitulated, King remarked smugly, "It fits in beautifully with the situation for that is exactly what the place is" (2 June 1929). His suggestion, however, for the farm house did not succeed, rather Joan's did: "Joan made the happy suggestion two nights ago of calling it The Meadows. (I had thought of green pastures which is lovely but might lead to ridicule as too biblical)" (29 July 1929). This name, however, did not survive, it was usually called The Farm, and the extended estate was always referred to as Kingsmere.

Early Canadian Country Estates

Although the vogue for summering outside the city was well-established in central and Atlantic Canada by the turn of the century, the building of country homes predated the seasonal migration of Canadian Society. In the late 1700s to early 1800s these properties ranged from rustic hunting "boxes" of the avid sportsman, to picturesque log cabins, to substantial villas along the St. Lawrence. Rural estates graced by large, stately homes set within a designed landscape were the epitome of country life in Britain and the standard to be attained in North America. An eighteenth century example was the Governor of Quebec, General Frederick Haldimond's country home. In the early 1780s he built Canada's first villa on the cliffs overlooking Montmorency Falls outside Quebec City. The villa became a focus of Quebec society's summer life.[6] The earliest Upper Canadian example was Lieutenant-Governor Simcoe's country retreat, Castle Frank, built in 1796.

Stamford Park, the summer residence of Sir Peregrine Maitland, yet another Lieutenant-Governor of Upper Canada, was built in the 1820s about six and a half kilometers from Niagara Falls. The house was noted for its extensive grounds, and its panoramic view of the Niagara River, Lake Ontario and the high grounds of Upper Canada. Following the English example, Maitland laid out "...gravel walks, ornamental gardens, and a long driveway while reverently preserving a 'magnificent grove of venerable oaks.'"[7] Anna Jameson, a writer who visited the estate in 1836, wrote she was "enchanted" with it. She claimed Stamford Park combined "our ideas of an elegant, well furnished English villa and ornamented grounds with some of the grandest and wildest features of the forest scene."[8]

As personal wealth increased and country living became fashionable, predictably the number of country estates multiplied. The small cottage, built by a local carpenter to his design or according to a style selected from an architectural "pattern book," gave way to an architect-designed house. As well, the natural landscape was transformed into professionally designed and ornamented spaces. By 1929 the following advertisement epitomized the large eastern Canadian country estate:

> Five acres, lake shore frontage, beautifully landscaped, large house, Stucco Finish, Gardener's Lodge, Double Garage, Poultry House, Two complete Water Systems, Electric Light, all City conveniences, Sandy Beach, Safe Bathing, one hundred foot Pier, good Fishing and Boating, Beautiful Driveway, Ornamental Shade Trees, Shrubberies, Rose Garden, Sunken Garden with Lily Pond, Artificial Waterfall, Miniature Golf Course, Tennis Courts, Kitchen Garden....An ideal country home at a reasonable price.[9]

It is easy to see why a contemporary garden writer said estates "abounded in features" — features which further multiplied with the addition of bowling greens, badminton courts, massive perennial borders, statuary, fountains, flagstone walks, riding stables, grand boathouses filled with mahogany speed boats, and later swimming pools.

Although country house styles and ornamentation varied, the requirements for siting the house changed little over a hundred years. The prospective owner first had to find a good location, accessible by horse, boat, rail, or later car. The site had to have some scenic value such as an impressive view, traditionally overlooking a body of water, or at least the area and the soil to create beautiful surroundings. The house was often built of local materials, generally wood.

The grounds of pre-1914 summer homes were often designed and planted by a hired gardener. After World War I professional landscape architects were frequently employed. In either case, the design usually reflected British styles. For example, the majority of early country "seats" along the St. Lawrence River outside Quebec City were landscaped in the English mode. James MacPherson Le Moine, a social commentator and man of letters, noted that on these Sillery estates "...it would be idle to seek in a certain number for architectural excellence, old-world dimensions, old-world splendor and ancient construction."[10] Although we did not have a Chatsworth nor a Marly, Canadian country houses, Le Moine allowed, "...possess attractions of a higher class, yea, of a nobler order, than brick and mortar, moulded by the genius of man....A kind Providence has surrounded them in spring, summer and autumn with scenery often denied to the turreted castle of the proudest nobleman in England."[11]

National Archives of Canada/C 23553

Rosewood, Sillery, Quebec, ca. 1865. The British influence on the Canadian country estate was quite pervasive.

A British landscape style which translated well onto the shores of the St. Lawrence was the Picturesque. The wild, natural scenery of central Canada was perfect for this style's artful arrangements which tried to emulate the wild, idealized landscapes of such 17th century painters as Salvador Rosa. Dead trees, wild ravines, gushing torrents were part of the language of the Picturesque. Landscape styles, however, were often intermixed on these estates to include the usual components of a gentleman's park — the Picturesque existing side-by-side with the pastoral:

rolling lawns, tree and shrub groupings, and billowing flower beds. Pastoral settings were especially admired in Canada even though the Canadian landscape did not always offer British-style sunlit meadows and roadsides graced by venerable oaks. As well, the legacy of Humphrey Repton, a British landscape gardener of the late 1700s, continued to influence landscape design, even in Canada. His designs harmonized house to garden, while sympathetically incorporating outbuildings, terraces, balustrades, and conservatories into the design.

One example of an English-style estate was established by Anson Dodge. His summer home, Beechcroft, was built at Roches Point on the southern shore of Lake Simcoe, Ontario. The 115 acre (47 ha) gardens and grounds allegedly were designed in 1870 by Frederick Law Olmsted in the style of an English gentleman's estate:

> The expansive grounds were ornamented with rustic arbours, seats and bridges. Close to the house was a widespreading lawn. Nearby were a number of parterres 'glowing with beautiful tints of the most choice flowers of the season'...While the immediate vicinity of the house offered the spectacular horticultural display characteristic of the period, the majority of the property was given over to 'Mr. Dodge's deer park.'[12]

By the turn of the century Beechcroft had become only one of many elaborately landscaped vacation homes found in resorts as well as in the rural areas surrounding our major cities. Land was cheap, servants affordable, and the economy was buoyant. The country home became yet another social yardstick, measuring wealth, social position, and the owner's awareness of the importance of European culture. Size was not as significant a factor in the definition of a Canadian country estate. Estates could stand on less than ten acres, or could encompass hundreds of acres. In the 1930s a Canadian landscape architect noted that three and one-half acres was the minimum size for a country property.[13] Oak Hall, the Niagara Falls estate of Harry Oakes, was an unusual size comprising nearly 6,000 acres (2430 ha).[14]

The summer homes also ranged in size and varied in design and ostentation. Some were built of stone, replicating Loire chateaus: "...towers, turrets, large dormers and bright copper roofs marked by tall chimneys."[15] Others were built in the Georgian Revival style: "red brick enhanced by pediments, pilasters, porticos and doors surmounted by semicircular windows."[16] Another favoured country house design was influenced by the New England Shingle Style: "...totally shingled surfaces ...small-paned windows arranged in series...large bow windows, turrets, gables projecting against the facade, tall chimney..."[17] A few country home owners refrained from outward display and built rustic log houses, reserving luxury treatments for the interiors. The log cabin had a nostalgic appeal and was labelled as part of a "Native Canadian Renaissance." Although its construction appeared simple, do-it-yourselfers were advised to leave design and building to an architect: "You *may* be able to follow such methods, but you may also have some very unexpected results."[18]

Early Canadian Landscape Architects

By the time Mackenzie King was landscaping in the Gatineau Hills, the services of professional landscape architects were increasingly used on a variety of public and private sites. This recognition of the need for professional design was already evident in pre-Confederation Canada. Immigrant Scots, English and merican private gardeners as well as Canadian jobbing gar- ners were hired by Canadian land owners, not only to maintain nsive gardens, but also to design them. William Mundie, a Scotsman, was among the handful of landscape gardeners practi- ing full-time in the Canadas. He came to Canada West in 1850 a time when the pioneering phase was ending, and a profes- sional and mercantile class was establishing itself. At this time there was an increasing need for designed public landscapes — schools, government buildings, etc. Mundie was soon commissioned to design the grounds of the Toronto Normal and Model schools, Trinity College, University Park and College, small cemeteries, and various private projects.[19] Another Scot, George Laing came to Canada in 1856 after working for several aristocratic British employers. He seemed to specialize in designing private estate grounds, the most notable was Dundurn Castle, Hamilton.[20] Edwin Taylor, an Englishman, was active in the Toronto area at this time. He designed a variety of private and public sites, the most well-known was the Toronto Horticultural Society's botanical gardens — later named Allen Gardens.[21]

By the 1890s, due to the increasing emphasis on the "City Beautiful," more landscape architects were lured to Canada. They responded to the call of civic beautifiers for tree-shaded streets, public parks, boulevards and parkways, as well as beautified home gardens in our expanding cities. Beautifying home and public surroundings was defined, in the rhetoric of the time, as a horticultural duty.

Despite the pioneering work of early 19th century landscape gardeners, Linus Woolverton, a prominent Niagara Peninsula fruit grower and the editor of the *Canadian Horticulturist*, could still note in 1911, that landscape architecture was a relatively new profession in Canada. In the United States the first university course for professional training in landscape architecture was not established until 1900. Woolverton said there were two main practitioners in Canada who "have appeared almost before the public was prepared for them...."[22] One of the men he referred to was his son, Charles. He was a graduate of the Ontario Agricultural College's three-year Horticultural program. From 1901 until his death in 1934, Woolverton worked on a variety of landscape projects ranging from parks to country estates to small city gardens. He advertised himself, as was common in the pre World War I landscape profession, variously as a landscape architect, landscape gardener, or landscape engineer. Woolverton worked for landscaping firms in the U.S., and was a consultant, a common practice in Ontario, for a Hamilton nursery.[23]

The other man, Frederick Todd [1876-1948], who had immigrated from the U.S. in 1900, was Woolverton's main competitor. He had apprenticed as a landscape architect at the prestigious Olmsted firm in Brookline, Massachusetts.[24] Todd's commissions ranged from Vancouver to St. John's, from small scale gardens to country house gardens (often for the Montreal architectural firm of the Maxwell Brothers), to parks, garden suburbs and city plans for various municipal clients.[25]

Other landscape architects involved in building country houses and elaborate cottages in Canadian resort areas included Howard and Laurie Dunington-Grubb, who immigrated to Canada in 1911. Their work was to greatly influence our private and public gardens up into the 1950s.

In the Murray Bay area the Olmsted Brothers firm, Frederick Todd, and local gardener Patrick Morgan, were the most frequent landscapers working there during the resort's heyday.[26] It had, by the early 1900s become known for the magnificent homes of its predominantly American summer colony.

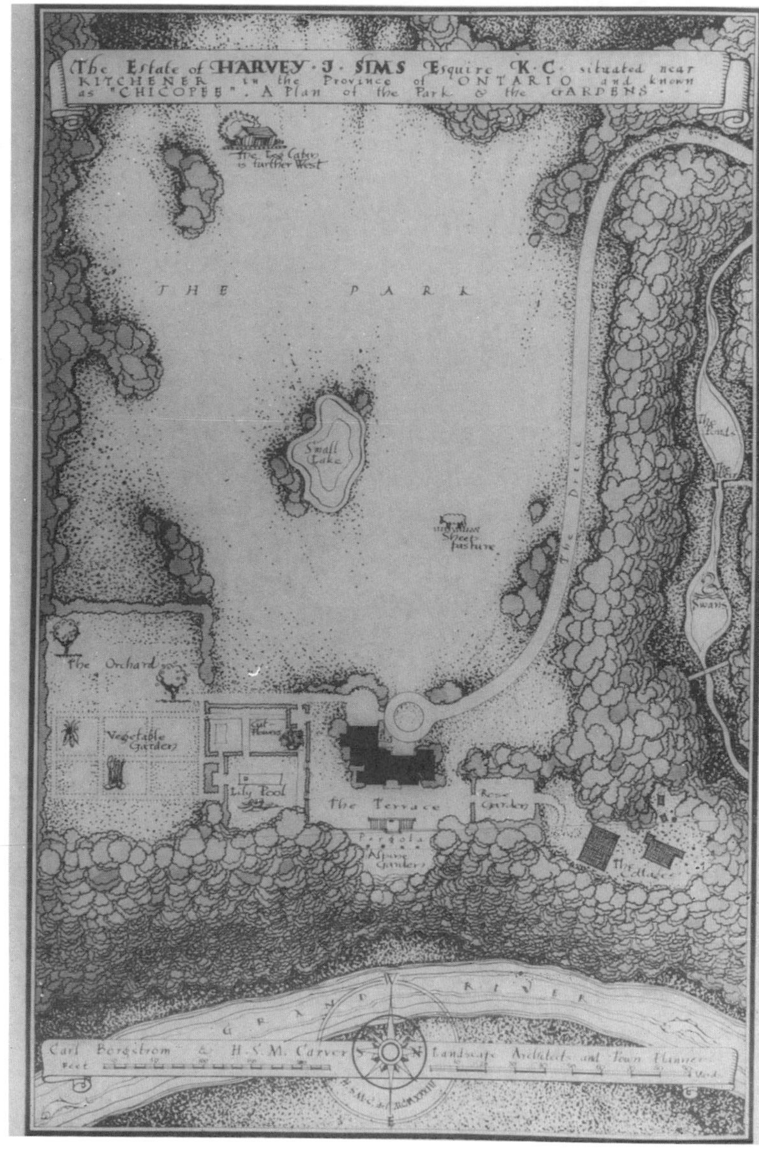

National Library of Canada/NL 16857

A contemporary landscape plan of Harvey J. Sims' Chicopee, published in *Canadian Homes and Gardens.*

Americans lured there by the hint of foreignness and the salubrious climate changed the tenor of Murray Bay life: "The Americans...have greatly raised the scale of living, disturbed the old simplicity of the place, and driven great numbers of Anglo-Canadians who, from motives of taste or purse...to the opposite shores of the little bay..."[27] One impressionable American visitor to Murray Bay wrote: "I was fascinated by the simple life — different from anything I had seen before in America...we went on numerous picnics and informal evening parties, where the habitants sang their native songs and danced their simple, rather awkward dances."[28] Mackenzie King visited Murray Bay a few times to stay at the summer home, Les Falaises, owned by his American society friend, Beatrix Henderson Robb.

After the architects had built their magnificent homes, landscape architects further transformed the wild St. Lawrence River landscape into stylized examples of European gardens. Pre-1930 Murray Bay gardens were a mixture of English, Italian and French formal styles, although the prevailing garden influence was English: "Instead of being in French Canada you might be in Merrie England."[29] Typical Murray Bay country home landscapes were described in 1935:

> Two miles farther on is the residence of Mr. A.E. Francis, of Montreal, a summer home that might be found in any of the country seats of England. The rambling garden that surrounds it is a blending of the work of nature and man. Wild flowers are abundant; Daisies, Buttercups and other familiar flowers creep up to the very edge of the lawn proper, which is trimmed with low hedges and beds of Peonies, Michaelmas Daisies, Iris and Delphiniums. A white frame house, in three sections, partly covered in dense shrubbery and vines, stands in the centre of the lawn, wide verandahs vie with the gardens as invitations

> for outdoor teas. Before the house, on the spreading lawn, are prize Peonies, and leading to the verandah steps is a rustic foot-bridge, passing over a tiny, winding creek. In one corner of the garden is the trout pool, around which are wild flowers in profusion; overlooking the pool are giant twin poplars. Quaint sculptured figures and sundials are placed here and there in the rambling gardens, and in shady nooks are garden benches. Near the house, too, are the open-air swimming pool, with flagstone border, and tennis courts.[30]

In the early days of his estate landscaping, King, unlike his wealthy friends, never considered hiring a professional to unify his designs. His childhood friend, Harvey J. "Peter" Sims, Q.C., of Kitchener, Ontario did. In the 1920s Sims acquired 45 acres (18 ha) in the Chicopee Hills, eight kilometers from Kitchener. Chicopee, a typical example of a central Canadian country place in the 1920s and 30s, had a magnificent view of the Grand River and the surrounding pastoral countryside. Peter Sims confided that he got "...a great kick out of developing my place, putting in gardens, laying out lawns...So interesting & besides so healthy. It keeps me in fine shape."[31]

Although King conceded that Chicopee was beautiful, but "not equal to Kingsmere," he was quite taken with the two ponds Sims built in a picturesque ravine: "...with bridges across... lighted at night with electric lights, and with swan swimming on the water is too lovely for words — like a scene from Lohengrin" (17 June 1933). King also said he was "amazed and delighted" with the final layout of the grounds created by the landscape firm of Carl Borgstrom and H.S.M. Carver: park land, terrace, river view, pergola (this one was spectacularly sited below the house, edging the river bank), rock garden (below the pergola, along the river bank), rose garden, orchard, kitchen garden, lily pond, formal flower gardens, guest cottages, and a park-like expanse of lawn — "Our little bit of England" according to Florence Sims.

The Eclectic Garden

The Sims' landscape had benefited from the broadening of the definition of the English garden to include other styles from beyond the borders of Britain. Beginning in the 1860s, eclecticism had entered the British garden, with an acceptance of the intermixing of gardens representative of different countries and eras: Italian architectonic gardens existed side by side with Elizabethan knot gardens. Some garden designers tried to recreate Medieval gardens based on paintings and illuminations.[32] In reaction to the "glare and vulgarity" of mid-Victorian plantings, other designers promoted the subtler colours of old-fashioned flowers, such as lilies, sunflowers, poppies, standard roses, or hollyhocks.

A favoured component, especially in Edwardian gardens, was the Japanese garden. This interest was stimulated and sustained by the opening up of Japan to the British in 1853, the 1862 International Exhibition featuring a Japanese court, the 1873 Vienna Exhibition including a miniature Japanese village, and books published in the 1890s on the art of Japanese gardens.[33] Wealthy Europeans even imported Japanese gardeners to design and lay out an authentic garden. One of the most publicized gardens was created in 1906 at Tully in County Kildare, Ireland. The garden design and planting was highly symbolic, representing the journey of life from womb to tomb, and decorated with stone lanterns, bonsai, and a miniature Japanese village.[34] Interpretations throughout Britain varied, from miniaturized scale

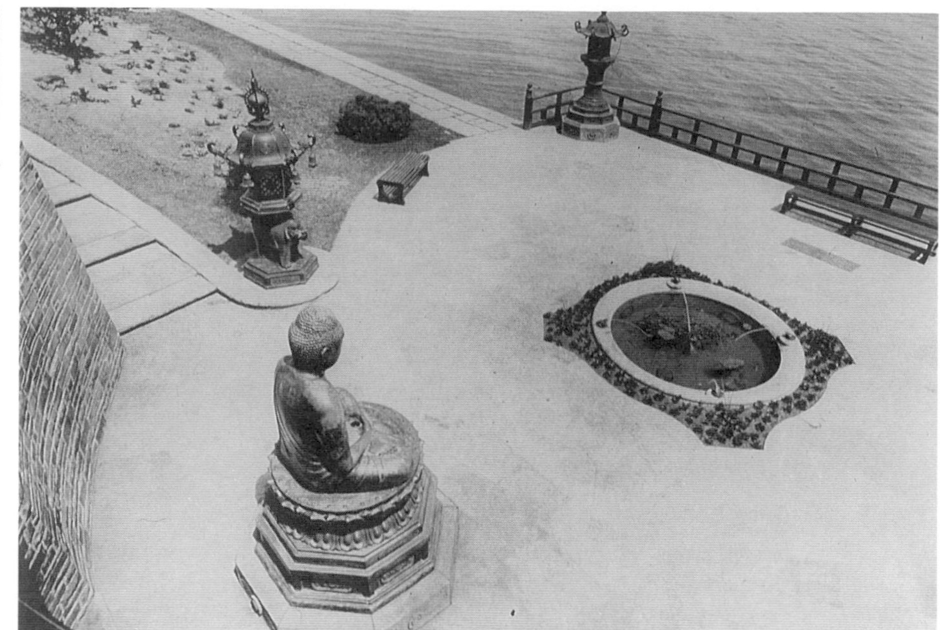

Edgemere — the Japanese garden overlooking Lake Ontario, 1936.

model gardens to incorporation of Japanese elements into an existing garden design: "...ornaments such as stone lanterns, Japanese plants — notably irises — and subdued colour schemes..."[35] Other gardeners briefly acknowledged the fad by growing Japanese plants in a wild garden setting.

Although many estate owners restrained themselves, a bit of Japan crept into many central Canadian gardens, especially in the 1920s and 30s. Shadowbrook, a country estate north of Toronto, was a breathtaking mixture of old and new world, eastern and western cultures. The house was painted a soft salmon pink, trimmed in ivory, and the windows trimmed with turquoise: "Here for the moment you are transplanted, far from your native Canada. You are in Sunny Spain or Sunny Italy.... The place they have built gives the atmosphere of Palm Beach...its sunshine, its glamour and its scintillating picturesqueness."[36] Formal terraces led down into the rose garden, rock garden, and the usual great expanse of lawn. The landscaping, supervised by the Dunington-Grubb firm, took eight years to complete.[37] The owners, the Hamilton B. Wills, had inherited a Japanese garden from former owner, Senator Nicholls, who had originally hired the Dunington-Grubbs to lay it out as a "delightfully quaint retreat"[38] A writer described it as "undeniably, the most pretentious, and the most nearly authentic of any similar garden that I know in Canada..."[39] Seen from the Italianate pink stuccoed house were black, red, blue and gold Japanese-style bridges spanning a tributary of the Don River. The garden visitor wandered through dwarf pines, junipers, imported Japanese shrubs, iris, violas and even asters and zinnas, until reaching the tennis court. There the Japanese theme was further elaborated. A Japanese tea house and huge oriental pottery vases filled with "spikes" and geraniums bordered the court.

Another Japanese garden of note in the late 1920s was on James Ryrie's country estate, Edgemere, later owned by John E. Hammell. Both owners were "intensely interested" in Japanese antiques and works of art, and both owners used the garden as a showcase for their collections. Ryrie alone sent 29,600 pounds (13,430 kg) of bronze and stone ornaments from Yokohama to Oakville.[40] John Hammell preserved the site of the original Japanese garden, but added his own art objects, relandscaping the garden to "give dramatic accents to views and vistas."[41] He also constructed a "Buddha garden" overlooking the distinctly unoriental Lake Ontario: "The Daibutsu Buddha, a Chinese bronze masterpiece weighing three tons, gazes on the medallion of fish pool and Begonias inset in the paving. Ancient lanterns in elephant and lotus-leaf design are placed at intervals. The banks (of the lake) are planted with Japanese Crabs and Ground Roses."[42]

Lady Eaton created an outstanding Japanese garden at her summer home (Villa Fiora) at Eaton Hall Farm near Schomberg, Ontario. When Dorothy Perkins, a Canadian garden writer, visited it in 1927, she found: "stepping stones, tinkling water-falls, pagodas, lanterns and tiny high-arched bridges leading to fairy-like islands."[43] Noting that the Japanese usually have water enter their gardens from the east to leave at the west, following the path of the sun, Miss Perkins archly observed that no such "oriental dictum was heeded" in this garden; however, "no dire catastrophe occurred...."[44] Instead of an authentic backdrop to the garden, Lady Eaton had planted lilacs — "not great statuesque shrubs, but such as would benefit a background for a Japanese garden, compact ones."[45] Recognizing that the climate would not support picturesque Japanese Wisteria, Lady Eaton had planted Spirea Van Houteii to take its place. Miss Perkins gently ridiculed the use of Japanese lanterns to create atmosphere, stating they were useless for anything else in the home garden. However, Japanese lanterns found their way into many Canadian gardens giving these landscapes, in the words of one garden writer, "Japanese touches."[46]

National Library of Canada/NL 16856

Les Groisardieres, the country home of C.E.L. Porteous on the Ile d'Orléans, was predominantly landscaped in the Italian style.

Many Canadian estate gardens had "touches" of Italy as well — the most well-known were Les Groisardieres on the Ile d'Orléans near Quebec City and Parkwood near Oshawa, Ontario. These touches could be as subtle as a marble bird bath or as grandiose as a flagstone and marble sculpture court. Italian style gardens, fashionable in early 19th century Britain, were characterized by terracing, stone staircases and balustrades, statuary, the use of gravel instead of grass, evergreen shrubs and trees, and the use of fountains, pools and cascades. The symmetry and architectonic emphasis of these gardens[47] were punctuated by what the 19th and early 20th century garden designers defined as Italian components — tubbed trees on terraces, flower-filled stone vases on stone walls, paved forecourts. The

Italian influence slowly diminished, but never completely died out, often reappearing as a small component within a larger design.

The Beginnings of Moorside Landscaping

Against this horticultural and stylistic background, Mackenzie King landscaped Kingsmere. His sense of mission and his certainty of a great destiny awaiting him also coloured his landscape ideals. He once wrote at age twenty-one: "I feel that I have a great work to do in this life, I believe that in some sphere I shall rise to be influential and helpful...." (27 August 1895). This professed self-knowledge sustained King through the vicissitudes of university and early Ottawa life, and allowed him to accept the prime ministership as his due. Later his self-confidence, the belief in his progress towards the highest good, was often transferred to his landscaping efforts. Although he fretted, making a landscaping mistake was, in the long run, not serious. King had from the start imbued Kingsmere with a larger-than-life existence — thus, Kingsmere always triumphed. King agonized over every detail, he was not precipitous in his decisions. However if errors occurred, they, in time, would be absorbed and eventually transformed by the goodness, the sublimity, the perfection of the estate.

Kingsmere was also special because it was the first property that was truly his. Until Lady Laurier willed her Ottawa house to him in 1921, King, like his parents, had always rented. But Laurier House was not really his either, he was quite aware of the Lauriers' lingering presence. Also, because the Liberal Party and private benefactors donated money to renovate and furnish it, there was a perception that Laurier House belonged to the Liberal Party and thus Canada. But Kingswood and Moorside and later the Farm were King's as no other property could ever be. Not only was he "lord of all he surveyed," he was also the capricious god who could change the landscape to suit his whims. If he wanted to plant 1,000 trees, he could; if he wanted to cut paths through his forests, he could do that too.

The expanded estate offered a role he was only too happy to play: "There simply is no life in the world like that of a country gentleman," he happily wrote in his diary in 1941. He was creating a sense of tradition, of landedness connected with the family name. Not only was it a sign he had arrived as a man of property, it was also a sign of his class. He did not consider himself *nouveau riche*, but a gentleman within the English mode: loyal, considerate, courageous, honourable, and land owning. Not only was his selfworth aggrandized by his estate and his position in society confirmed, but his well-being, spiritual and physical, was also assured, and his fantasy life given proper scope.

Strongly connected to the connotation of landed proprietorship was duty: to embellish, to preserve, to protect. King felt he was performing a religious duty when he "redeemed" the wilderness. "There is no joy," he wrote in 1924, "comparable to that of redeeming the waste places, asking the desert to blossom like the rose whether it be in the wilds of nature or in the vagaries [?] of human nature" (9 September 1924).

Perhaps his Presbyterian upbringing also had an effect on his land acquisition and landscape projects. One of the forces in Scottish Presbyterianism was the emphasis on the individual's duty to experience God in everything. Allied with this tenet was the concept of stewardship — of using one's talents, wealth, and resources to help and aid humanity.[48] King seemed to interpret this at Kingsmere as a justification for land acquisition or landscape improvements. His forests, he often emoted, were not only preserved for others, but also were a sanctuary where God's voice in the trees could be heard.

It was significant that King brought Emil Ludwig, a famous German biographer, to Kingsmere for two days of interviewing. Ludwig had approached King in the early 1940s for permission to write a short biographical sketch. The resulting portrait was very pleasing to King, for Ludwig had obviously succumbed to the persona King wanted portrayed. We see King, through Ludwig's expressive prose, rambling through the forests with Pat, emoting over his attachment to nature and its restorative qualities. He convinced Ludwig that this attachment allowed him to vigorously discharge his prime ministerial duties. Ludwig characterized Moorside as "...simple and dignified, the home of a man who is deeply connected with European culture and who, in old British manner, prefers privacy to brilliancy."[49] To see photographs of King ambling around the estate in his tweeds, pointing out views with his walking stick, is to fully accept the depth of his belief in this role. Kingsmere was his refuge in more ways than perhaps he would have recognized.

National Archives of Canada/PA 124459

Edgmoor just after King purchased it.

King's urge to enlarge his holdings, to establish an estate, was probably also influenced by his veneration of and identification with William E. Gladstone, considered one of Britain's greatest 19th century statesmen. Gladstone was a passionate moralist who tried, as King thought he was trying, to apply his Christian beliefs to foreign and domestic affairs, and to use them to stimulate social and political reforms. The twenty-five year old King had been so thrilled when reading of Gladstone's work, he said he "sprang from my chair with the words, 'Oh God I want to be like that man,' and my whole nature thirsted for the opportunity to do the work even as he did his, to be strong in my ideals, true to the most real purposes, & firm in the struggle for the right and the true"[50] (12 August 1899).

In his later years he discovered that Gladstone had been greatly attached to his Welsh country estate, Hawarden, a castle located on the English border. Delighted, King read in John Morley's biography that Gladstone also had found relaxation in chopping down trees and supervising landscaping activities. From then on King began comparing the two estates: Hawarden with its huge, turreted stone castle, original ruins, and magnificent

King visited many American country homes, such as John D. Rockefeller, Jr.'s Seal Harbor, Maine estate.

lawns and vistas, to Moorside's truncated grounds and clapboard house. By the 1930s King was quite happy to have the public associate the estates with one another, and, uncharacteristically, for he usually abhorred Kingsmere publicity, drew attention to the association in a Parliamentary speech. When Gustave Lanctot of the Public Archives submitted a draft of Kingsmere area history King had requested, he immediately corrected the first paragraph:

> The great distinction of Kingsmere lies in the fact that it is a kind of Canadian Chequers when the Liberal party is in power, as the Prime Minister of Canada, Mr. W.L. Mackenzie King, has a country house there. And there he goes either for rest, meditation or consultation, according to circumstances, so that Kingsmere has become one of the by-words of Canadian politics.

to read,

> The great distinction of Kingsmere lies in the fact that it is a kind of Canadian Hawarden where the Liberal Leader, Mr. W.L. Mackenzie King, now the Prime Minister of Canada, has his country home. There he goes, as Gladstone went to his home in Wales at the week-ends, and in the summer, either for rest, meditation or consultation, and so Kingsmere has come to have its associations with Canadian politics.[51]

During the Depression, King was quite pleased when one of his secretaries found a reference to Gladstone's hiring of unemployed Lancashire factory workers to work on his estate "for the purposes of relief."[52] King, perhaps to salve his conscience, saw himself as offering employment and "salvation" at Kingsmere: "As I looked at Jack going to work with a manly stride & new look on his face, I felt there was a lad 'saved' perhaps from going to pieces by employment & position given him" (31 July 1937).

Although proud of his estate and all its associations, King tried to maintain a low public profile for Kingsmere. King was occasionally attacked within the Liberal Party and in the press for secluding himself at the estate. King worried about the political repercussions of bad Kingsmere press:

> I felt distressed today when I learned the *Citizen* & *Montreal Gazette* & other papers had mention of my having purchased an estate at Kingsmere — said to be four miles (?) in all....This is calculated to do great harm in circles that have been helping me with Laurier House & in creating suspicion in minds of public of graft, etc. I think it best to let it pass unnoticed but may have to say something later. It takes the pleasure a little out of what I am attempting (26 April 1927).

Later that year he was rebuked in the *Ottawa Journal*: "Now, human nature being what it is, and there being a common notion that premiers, having a supposedly hard job, are presumed to be occasionally in their offices....We're envious of a man who can run a whole party, and a country, and appease people who want senatorships, and judgeships, and breakwaters, and a host of other things — all from a cottage."[53] King was furious: "The *Journal* has a mean article on my being at Kingsmere so much. I intend to hold on here & get all of health I can this year at least. It is the one real chance to get into shape not only for the year but the years ahead" (30 September 1927). In 1928 he tried to downplay his expanding estate, calling it "a sort of diversion." However, this did not deter journalistic curiosity or comment. A year later he had misgivings when Senator Raoul Dandurand, after a tour of his property, asked King where he "had amassed the fortune to have such an estate." King did not note his response to the senator, but commented in his diary: "That is a question which many I assume will ask" (26 July 1929). In the mid 1930s his distaste of Kingsmere publicity finally provoked him, after yet another damning article, to ask the editors of the *Ottawa Citizen* and *Ottawa Journal* to safeguard his privacy at Kingsmere. Both editors agreed to keep Kingsmere out of the news.

The Patteson's Gardening Efforts

Despite threats to his privacy, King thoroughly enjoyed his estate activities. During the early Moorside years, King's many and varied horticultural diversions were focussed on landscaping Kingswood, as well as altering the little cottages. The Pattesons, who rented Moorside from King in 1924, initiated landscape alterations at Moorside with the help of King's handymen. They laid out flower beds in a square (the four corners filled with flowers, and the centre with grass), culled trees, cut grass, and began underbrushing. By July 1925 King remarked: "...the garden beautiful in morning sun. Several trees & shrubs have been cut away and improvement is great...the place looks very pretty, large sweeps of lawn and beautiful vistas. With long grass cut it is fine" (30 July 1925). King himself cut down trees, pruned branches and donated a bird bath for the middle of the quadrant garden. By 1927 Godfroy had extended the lawn (i.e. scythed the wild grass) below the cottage, down toward the forest edge. No matter how much love, effort, and planning was expended, the Pattesons were never allowed to forget it was King's estate. One fall when the Pattesons were away, King cleared trees, shrubs and underbrush on the approach road leading from the house to the entrance gate. The effect, which King greatly admired, had the opposite effect on the Pattesons: "Joan upset me terribly by remarking I had 'taken away their front door.'...I had so looked forward to their delight in the work which I meant as a surprise that I did not get over the shock of her words all day" (2 October 1927).

The shocks and disappointments were not one-sided. One of the Patteson's early projects was a rock garden: "...went up to see progress Joan making on rock garden at foot of Moorside,

National Archives of Canada/PA 124699

The Moorside ornamental garden was begun by the Pattesons in 1928.

became a favourite feature proudly pointed out to guests touring the estate.

After a long history as an elitist, upper-class feature of English gardens, the rock garden became, by the 1920s, a common component of fashionable Canadian gardens. Canadians would not have recognized its earliest British form. Emerging as a decorative element in the 1830s, it was a rockwork garden with a decided emphasis on the rocks. From the 1840s up into the early 1900s, rock gardens went through various changes. By the late 1800s, the rock garden was treated in two ways. One treatment emphasized rock constructions which mirrored the natural occurrence of rocks in the landscape. An outstanding example, built in 1871 at Stancliffe Hall, featured an excavated cliff — a massive arrangement of boulders and outcropping stones planted with

the clearing being made is most effective" (28 August 1925). Joan, with the help of King's gardeners and handymen, had the soil mounded up and rocks and boulders placed on a rise at the bottom of the formal gardens, away from the house. King noted a few weeks later: "It is really a marvellous achievement most imposing and will be lovely when aglow with flowers" (13 September 1925). What he did not admit to Joan, however, was his distress. She had removed trees to provide a clearing for the garden, which King said left "a great open gap & exposure of rock," which "...for quite a while made me distressed indeed" (24 May 1926). A year later he acknowledged that he was nearly reconciled to the change. Later he was so reconciled, as the Patteson's finally were to their "doorway," that the rock garden

conifers.[54] The second type of rock garden imitated exotic nature or well-known scenes. This led to some superb gardens as well as some rather amazing ones, such as: "the Khyber Pass in East Park, Hull...in artificial stone; the thirty-fool scale model of the Matterhorn at Friar Park, Henley-on-Thames; Mount Fuji in the Japanese garden at Fanhams Hall, Ware; and...the Mappin Terraces in the Regent's Park Zoo, modelled in concrete after the Atlas Mountains of Morocco.... "[55]

A third type, the form we are most familiar with, emerged in the 1870s when interest in growing alpines in rock gardens rose significantly, deflecting attention from the rocks themselves. Rock gardens were increasingly designed to show off alpines and other dwarf plants discovered by avid late 19th century plant hunters.

Herbaceous borders were thought inadequate to display these tiny plants. Upper class enthusiasts went into the mountains (the fad of mountaineering also stimulated interest in these flowers) to gather specimens for their spacious rock gardens. Also, the promotional writings of the plant explorer and gardener Reginald Farrer, including his seminal work *The English Rock Garden*, were instrumental in popularizing this style of gardening. The difficulties and mystique of cultivating many of these new arrivals elevated rock gardening, in the words of one historian, to a cult.[56] It was definitely a passport into the league of "real" gardeners if one had a rock garden filled with rare species intimately known by their Latin names.

National Archives of Canada/PA 124712

The rock garden was Joan Patteson's special project.

The true home of the "show-place" rock garden in Canada was on country estates. There considerable space could be devoted to a British-style rock garden, where money was available for specialized collections and for employment of gardeners to cultivate this labour-intensive component. These rock gardens, where the plant was supreme, were designed to appear as if they had always been in place. In 1929 Sheridan Nurseries, Toronto, characterized the estate rock garden as suitable for "...terraces, banks, and ravine slopes," and as an attractive feature due to "the informality of design, variety of plants that can be grown in a restricted area, and the masses of colour to be obtained..."[57]

F. Cleveland Morgan, a wealthy Montrealer and enthusiastic gardener, maintained a large rock garden on his country estate, Le Sabot. On ten acres (4 ha), described as "...a Lilliputian affair calling, therefore, for imagination and also for intensive cultivation"[58] he managed to squeeze in a bowling green, tennis court, rose gardens, formal gardens, lawn, various shrubberies, an orchard, flower borders, walks, woodland garden, bog garden, as well as an impressive house and outbuildings, and, of course, the rock garden.

The main rock garden was sited on the lakeside where the ground dipped steeply to the water. Stratified limestone slabs, gathered from the surrounding district, formed a series of ledges. The slabs, following British practice, were large enough so that one could "...hop nimbly from ledge to ledge and use deft fingers to advantage without leaving a footmark, and without inflicting injury on tender growths.[59] The garden, at one time, contained 500 species, for Morgan heretically defined a suitable rock garden plant as one that did not look uncomfortable and out of place in his rock garden. According to Morgan, a rock garden could be anything except a perennial border.[60] *Iris cristata* grew alongside mossy Saxifrages and the common dwarf Phlox. He also prided himself on the successful cultivation of exotic, imported alpines such as a number of European Gentians.

Jenny Butchart, a contemporary of Morgan's, created an internationally acclaimed garden at her residence, Benvenuto, at Tod Inlet near Victoria. Jennie Butchart, Morgan, and Elsie Reford (who had an award-winning garden at Grand Métis, Quebec) were among the handful of pre-World War II Canadian gardeners who achieved international fame (i.e. recognition from the British and its Royal Horticultural Society). Mrs. Butchart evidently did not know a daisy from a rose when she first began gardening. From these humble beginnings, however, she created Butchart Gardens, which slowly expanded into a 30 acre (52 ha) designed landscape. Its main feature was a limestone quarry her husband's cement company had abandoned. Rock gardening in abandoned quarries was not novel in the annals of British horticulture, but was quite rare in Canada. She planted the walls as well as the quarry floor with rare alpines, ivy and native British Columbia flora: "We've made it ugly. Now let's try to make it beautiful again."[61] Mackenzie King found much to praise there in 1920: "...saw the most beautiful grounds & residence I have been in — for sheer beauty & taste" (26 September 1920).

In fact, King saw a variety of rock gardens during his lifetime. Not only did many of his estate-owning friends in Canada and Britain have rock gardens, but closer to home, King observed the handiwork of Lady Byng, the wife of Governor General Byng. Lady Byng's rock garden was not as extensive as Morgan's or Butchart's. She said she built it mainly as an object lesson: "...I hoped my neighbours would realize that they could get more amusement out of something of that kind than out of sweating over the mowing of a small grass plot all summer through."[62]

The Rideau Hall rock garden presented some problems: "...where I needed rock slabs I had to put up with boulders, and where a northwest aspect was best, I had to content myself with a fiercely hot southern one."[63] She gathered stones from nearby Rockcliffe Park and within three years, she had created a garden which normally would have taken five years to finish. A showplace of choice exotics as well as a home for the plants and seeds she collected on various vice-regal trips across Canada, Lady Byng happily grew Canadian orchids alongside imports such as *Daphne cneorum*.

Another nearby rock garden was on the summer estate, Laurentian Lodge, of the J.A. Ruddicks, located near Wake-field, Quebec, north of Kingsmere. Ruddick was the Cold Storage and Dairy Commissioner for Canada and a renowned dairy expert. His wife was an enthusiastic and knowledgeable gardener who created, beginning in 1915, a rock garden on an immense outcropping of Canadian Shield in the Gatineau Hills. The rock formed the greater part of the estate, in a "...flow from the verandah like a stretch of giant corduroy...a glacial immensity of solid proportions." Her first task was not to plant flowers but to find the suitable "nooks and fissures" into which to plant. Mrs. Ruddick mixed wild flowers (saxifragas, anemones, orchids) with perennials and annuals such as delphiniums and hollyhocks. She used every portion of available growing space: "Use every bit of rock, don't be afraid of it. Plant between, atop or along side. Presently, you will be convinced that flowers need near them the harsh stability of stone."[64] King, impressed by the site in 1934, wrote that it "...commanded fine views and a most attractive interior" (19 July 1934).

The Moorside rock garden, in comparison with these grandiose gardens, was quite unpretentious. The original plantings are not known, but plant lists in the 1930s indicate that Joan and King did not cultivate rare alpines, nor did they mix special soils for difficult plants. By 1932 Joan, in King's words, had "done over" the rock garden — perhaps following Cleveland Morgan's advice. He felt this was the only way to keep the rock garden at its finest. It is also known that King especially liked to see lily-of-the-valley blooming there, a flower he strongly identified with his mother. As one of her favourite flowers, it had an "association" with King's early childhood. King was delighted to discover they were also the favourite of his good friend's wife, Mrs. John D. Rockefeller, Jr. After she died King sent lily-of-the-valley to Rockefeller, noting: "I am as certain as I am living that dear Mrs. Rockefeller and my dear mother have already shared many hours together where lilies-of-the-valley have continued to gladden their sight, and to speak to them of you and me."[65]

If a 1934 list Joan drew up for King was typical, the rock garden plant choice was quite prosaic: lobelia, verbena, dwarf zinnia, dwarf nasturtium, annual phlox, Shirley poppy, ferns, candytuft, and portulaca. Five perennials were also added to the 1934 garden: dwarf hardy aster, saxifraga, *Campanula rotundifolia*, viola, and *Daphne cneorum*. Daphnes were very expensive, so Joan cautioned King to buy only one plant.[66] According to alpine flower experts, this variety was easy to grow, prolific, and loaded with vivid pink, fragrant flowers.[67] But like so many other speciality plants noted in King's papers, the plant was never mentioned again.

Edwinna von Baeyer

The restored Moorside rock garden.

In 1933 King received from L.W. Brockington, city solicitor for Calgary and an enthusiastic gardener, seed collected from nearly 180 different varieties of alpines and regular garden plants, ranging from *Aquilegia transylvanica* to *Linaria alpina* to *Verbascum phoeniceum*. When writing King that the seeds were on their way, he obviously had second thoughts about their reception by someone who did not know plants. Brockington added in a postscript: "If you are bewildered about these seeds probably your neighbour Mrs. Patteson will know what to do with most of them."[68] If she did, King never commented on the seeds or on their subsequent growth. Although King regarded his rock garden as a notable feature of the ornamental gardens, the difficulties of obtaining labour during the war forced King to allow the rock garden to deteriorate. In 1948 King sadly remarked in his diary how overgrown it had become.[69]

Moorside Renovations and Moving In

Coinciding with the Patteson's horticultural activity, King began renovating the Moorside cottage. In early May 1928, reflecting the change in his social and political position, he transformed the one and a half storey wood-frame building into something much grander: "I think the changes will completely transform it and that I will have there a very lovely country residence and grounds, simple but beautiful & appropriate" (14 May 1928). The small cottage was converted into a large, rambling summer home on the scale of a modest English country home. Some elements of the architectural British Picturesque tradition were incorporated to create a low-lying profile which blended into the landscape. As well, other Picturesque elements were added to the structure: french windows leading out onto a balustraded terrace, a vine-covered pergola, wide verandah, and balconies.[70] The extensive renovations King shrugged off as "...bits of reconstruction and possible changes and additions.[71]

King immersed himself in the details of the job, directing Paddy Murphy, drawing floor plans and choosing window and door styles. He consulted his files of articles and pictures of house features and furnishings culled from Canadian and American periodicals, as well as his small library of architectural books.[72] To produce a desired visual effect, he experimented by drawing different arrangements of house components.

King had the small verandahs torn off ("they were too small & mean"), and replaced by a porch which wrapped around three sides of the house. A low, stone and concrete wall was built along the verandah from the kitchen door to the sunroom. King later erected a pergola on top of this wall. The new verandah was broad and deep, large enough to hold furniture for warm-weather living and dining. A large addition was built, to accommodate servant's rooms, offices, entrance hall, and extra bathrooms. In fact, King replaced the original bathroom fixtures which had been installed for the Pattesons in 1924 when the Kingswood plumbing system was first modernized. Stairs were moved from the old hall to a new position. A stone chimney and fireplace were built. Still enjoying little ceremonies, King and Joan marked the inauguration of the hearth by inserting into a specially-built box in the fireplace a "...little statement of the fire place being built by Paddy & Willy Murphy & Paddy Dean, of Paddy's friendship & mine...Joan wanted a note about what I had done to save the forests round about etc...." (12 July 1928). Afterwards the house was painted in King's favourite colour combination: pale yellow clapboarding, white trim and dark green trim on the screens.

After the renovations had been underway for two weeks,

King experienced his usual qualms: "I am really getting alarmed at the proportions of the house it is more pretentious than I had imagined it wd be" (1 June 1928). He also had misgivings about the amount of time he was spending at Kingsmere: "I feel sometimes I am getting out of touch with colleagues, members & country in giving too much time & thought to Kingsmere & not enough to the policies etc. of Govt. Must concentrate on these" (25 July 1928). These fears, however, were overridden by King's relish in supervising the activities:

> ...all classes of artisans were at work. The plumbers were busy, making the most important connections....The electricians were out doing more in the way of wiring & making real headway. The roofers were out & completed the job of putting tar on the roof of the sun room & the little verandah over the living room. Ahearn's men were out did more blasting & digging for the flag pole & have hole in readiness for construction of base, the carpenters were about finished the clapboarding on the outside, & almost finished the first large room fir sheeting inside. Paddy is at work on the fire place the last indoor masonry job (20 June 1928).

By the late 1920s electrification, an urban enhancement, had become standard in the country home. Upgrading Moorside through electrification and indoor plumbing was a significant indication of King's desire to transform his cottage into a summer home. In the midst of the work, King mentioned to Thomas Ahearn, industrialist, entrepreneur and president of the Ottawa Electric Company, that he had wired his summer home, but had been put on the International Power Company's waiting list for the power hook-up. Ahearn, who had received a Privy Councillorship earlier that year from King as well as the chairmanship of the Ottawa Improvement Commission, said he would fix King up. King noted that night in his diary:

> I almost jumped I was so delighted. I do not recall ever feeling greater delight at anything. He said he wd install the necessary equipment. This is what I have been most hoping for — or rather not daring to hope for — but waiting the day — fearing the expense of anything of the kind, now it has come as a gift which I can easily accept. It will be a real joy to Ahearn to do it... (30 June 1928).

King delightedly watched the line of electric poles advance slowly towards Moorside, overjoyed to save so much money: "The expense of putting up poles etc. must be great, being prime minister I am getting all this done for me without any cost. I might have to wait for years were I out of office, "Unto him that hath shall be given," what a world!" (1 August 1928).

He fussed over the path of the electrical poles, altering the line so that it did not intrude into his view over the moors. However, he did not spend additional money to bury the cables and wires, as did Alfred Rogers on his Lake Simcoe estate, Uplands. On this estate there were "...no unsightly poles in evidence. Electric light and telephone wires are underground. Nothing is allowed to be seen that detracts from the natural beauties of the place."[73]

In addition to the renovations, King built an ice house, tool shed and garage. Although he never learned to drive, King decided to buy a car of his own, making him more "independent in feeling & in reality," instead of relying on government issue. Designing these small buildings was aesthetically challenging: "...I changed the site of the shed which I thought should be indented a little more to destroy a straight front line, the broken effects are the prettiest when there are buildings of different sizes combined" (28 July 1928). In all, the renovations and car cost King nearly

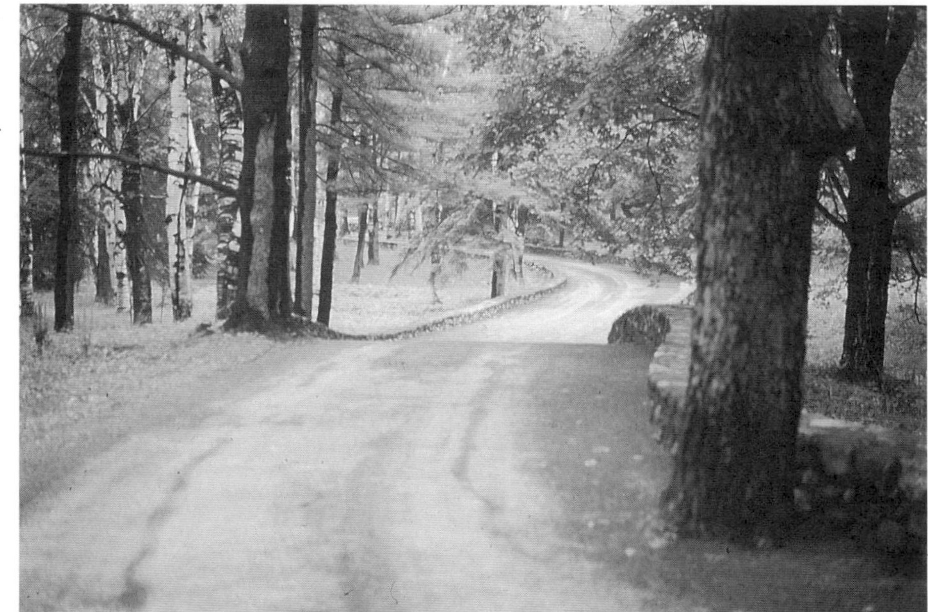

The Moorside drive.

$6,000. Unfortunately King could not immediately enjoy his new home, for he left Canada in late August to attend an international conference in Paris. His thoughts were often of Kingsmere — while visiting a French castle, all he could comment in his diary was: "...I thought much of Kingsmere & what with a few paths of white gravel [what] the whole place can be made to look like" (28 August 1928).

But what of the Pattesons in the midst of these changes — the good friends who had laboured over four years to beautify Moorside — what happened to them? For some time King kept his own counsel on their Kingsmere future, and only after a month of renovations did he mention to Joan that it might be better for the Pattesons to move into the farm house which he would make over for them. Joan felt badly about leaving Moorside, but this did not stop King from "evicting" them.

King had an ambivalent relationship with the Pattesons. He often took them for granted, dropped into their house at all hours, had them look after small details of running the estate, and depended on them to relieve his often unadmitted loneliness. When Joan was in hospital in 1930, he did wonder, "...what I would do with this place if anything were to happen to Joan...she is the life of the place to me & without her Nature would lose its glory" (31 August 1930). Yet King could criticize a new dress of Joan's so severely that she left Laurier House in tears: "I simply cannot understand women in the manner of dress" (16 October 1927). And he could also write in exasperation "...Godfroy is a very stupid man, & is not the least helpful in cooperating to make matters pleasanter for others" (23 September 1930). He occasionally chafed against his dependance upon them:

> ...I must do things more and more myself, and not seek too greatly to share everything, to read more to myself, to work more alone, to decide things, even re gardens, dinners, etc., alone & carry them out and wholly free from unnecessary contacts or consideration of personal relations with Joan & Godfroy. Each going our own way more & more will be better in the end, with days or hours shared now & then" (20 April 1938).

Near the end of his life, he finally admitted their great place in his affections: "I have had no friends as close as she and Godfroy have been over the past thirty years" (15 October 1948). And, "I owe much to them of the happiness & help I have had from them in my active years" (12 June 1949).

That admission, however, was twenty years away. For the remainder of the Moorside renovations, King lent the Pattesons the Kingswood guest cottage, where they reluctantly accepted the idea to move to the farm house. King and Joan spent the last months of 1928 planning the move and house alterations. However, King noted in April the next year that he had decided instead to renovate the "old Mainguy cottage" (on land he bought in 1927) for them: "I decided to have the roof covered with the roofing material instead of reshingling...to put on a new verandah floor, add a back wing about 20' x 10' so as to have a servants' bedroom downstairs, and to have the house painted white & yellow outside & to be lined with fir inside. The house has a good situation and will make into a very pretty summer cottage" (21 April 1929). Joan admitted she was ready to move as she "...said very truly that she hesitated to alter anything in my cottages (Kingswood) & that also she felt I did not like anyone else living there which is true. This is better in every way and I am immensely relieved in feeling. It avoids the intimacy in the relationship which is certain to occasion comment" (26 May 1929).

National Archives of Canada/PA 129818

Shady Hill.

King's conscience may have been appeased, but the Pattesons were initially unhappy in the new cottage and felt "shut in" — Shady Hill was a little too shady. Joan poignantly remarked one evening, as King and she admired the view from Moorside's second floor balcony: "'This to me is the most beautiful place in all the world. You have travelled & seen many places but I have seen nothing equal to this' & her eyes filled with tears" (6 July 1929). King's brief feeling of contrition was followed by the usual justifications: "I can see wherein I have perhaps seemed selfish in 'evicting' Joan & Godfroy after they had worked so hard on the place, — but I am sure it was right & in my present position necessary" (6 July 1929).

King and the Pattesons shared Moorside during the Shady Hill renovations. When King spent his first night alone in the cottage in early July, he complained about the wind, a complaint he would voice for the rest of his years at Moorside: "The wind was *very* high. It blew gales all evening. I almost fear the wind is going to be too much for me up here, that it will get on my nerves" (2 July 1929). The effect of the moonlight through the willow branches outside his Moorside bedroom consoled him: "beautiful as anything in Italy or Greece" (3 August 1928). Later in the summer when he slept once more at Kingswood, he remarked: "I wondered a little how I had had so great comfort in other years, never realizing discomforts" (6 August 1929). Although he would not live there again, he preserved and maintained the buildings as guest houses for relatives, staff quarters, and rental properties.

The architectural phase completed, King settled into his new cottage. He was now ready to step out into the garden. In the following ten years King substantially altered the Moorside landscape, modelling his design on the ideals of the English country home landscape. The preliminaries were behind him, the foundations laid for the next stage — the enhancement of his estate, and through it, his self image.

CHAPTER FOUR

The Moorside Gardens

"THERE IS GREAT JOY IN LANDSCAPE GARDENING"

WHEN HIS GOVERNMENT WAS DEFEATED IN THE JULY 1930 ELECTION, Mackenzie King took refuge on his estate, healing his political wounds through a variety of landscape projects. During the six years King was in opposition, he enjoyed supervising tree planting, plant selection and brush clearing — more so than overseeing his political duties. For King the 1930s were a time of experiment, creation and exploration, as he defied the barriers to landscaping on the Canadian Shield.

The challenge of gardening on the harshness of the primeval rock was relished by King even though he grudgingly admitted there were limitations to landscaping Moorside. For example, while admiring the extensive lawns, flower beds and rock garden of Fulford Place, King noted: "All the time my thoughts were of Kingsmere and the beautiful country home it can be made. There is not the [chance] for flowers etc. that there is here, too much rock, but it has its own natural beauty..." (22 July 1928). It was this natural beauty he sought to enhance and then to alter in favour of an English pastoral effect.

King was probably guided in developing his landscape by a mental model of a British country estate — he never drew up an actual master plan. Whenever he thought he had realized his intent, King exulted: "...greatly enjoying the beauty of the views after the rain. They were really like the most lovely of old country garden scenes. The softness of the twilight and the moisture of the trees and grass produced the lovely effects" (19 August 1934). King's landscaping consisted of carrying out a series of related projects which slowly formed a design, rather than implementing an organic, integrated landscape plan. He incorporated contemporary and traditional design elements, featuring a formal/informal mix of components — formal gardens near the house, expansive lawn leading to informal elements, bordered by a forest, accessible by woodland paths.

Edwinna von Baeyer

The Moorside garden.

Lawn

Creating an extensive lawn on the Canadian Shield was one of King's primary horticultural concerns, a recognition of the lawn's status as the main component on a country house landscape. In the 1920s a Canadian landscape architect archly noted: "One of the first needs to be arranged for is an ample lawn on which garden parties can be held."[1] Annie Jack, a turn-of-the-century Canadian garden writer, expressed a more traditional view that the lawn was "...the canvas, and on it you paint with flower and shrub the picture that your fancy desires or your purse can gratify."[2] Evidently King's purse could gratify quite a lot, especially when his delight was involved. In 1924 when visiting Sir William Mulock's country estate, The Elms, King was greatly impressed by Mulock's great expanse of tree-bordered lawn: "..everything looked very beautiful, grass green, great open stretches, trees....Naturally I thought of what Moorside can be made with stretches of lawn down to the trees & white fence — nothing more restful or beautiful than lawn and trees" (17 August 1924).

In 1927 King began creating the lawn of his dreams with the help of the Pattesons. Long grass was burned and stones and boulders were removed. Then in the following years he turned to the Department of Agriculture for advice. By 1929 the first stages of lawn preparation had been accomplished. At that point W.T. Macoun, the Dominion horticulturist, came out to extensively survey the various lawn areas — some of which were composed only of wild grass and weeds. He did not encourage the use of sod for the large, thin-soiled expanses. Instead, King was advised to top dress the soil with black muck obtained from a cedar swamp on his property, then fertilize and seed with a mixture of Kentucky Blue grass and white Dutch clover.[3] These instructions were so successful, King continued sowing lawn up into the late 1930s. Each phase was supported by professional advice which was then paraphrased and typed by King's Parliament Hill staff for his Kingsmere caretakers to follow.

Despite surmounting the challenges of creating and maintaining the lawn, King did not regularly host garden parties on it. In the 1930s garden parties were held for a variety of purposes — political, charitable, social and fund raising. King attended quite a few, always fussing over whether to wear the grey or the black suit, the top hat or the felt hat. His sister gave garden parties in his honour whenever he visited her Barrie, Ontario home. King, however, held only one recorded garden party at Kingsmere, on September 9, 1937. Joan supervised the food, furniture and flower arranging, and police managed the traffic and parking. King shook hands with all 170 guests, and then retreated to do office work — entertaining on this scale was too nerve-wracking.

National Archives of Canada/C 84093

King's gardeners found it difficult to mow the rock-strewn lawns King had created.

The Balustrade

After the main lawn areas were established, King concentrated on ornamenting them. A major project was the design and placement of a wooden balustrade on the west side of the house. King said he had had this structure in mind ever since he realized that something was needed to give "proportion to the front of the house" and to "centre" the garden. Now he had the leisure to energetically pursue the idea. King would have seen balustrades (the railings on the edge of terraces and stairways) when thumbing through issues of *Canadian Homes and Gardens* and other garden magazines, on visits to friends' estates in Canada, and on visits to English country homes where they were common. For example, in 1926, during the Imperial Conference, King visited Lord Astor at Cliveden. There he must have seen Astor's "Italian Garden" which was ornamented by a balustrade from the Villa Borghese Astor had brought back from an Italian holiday.[4]

With great zest and his usual perfectionism, King began planning a Kingsmere version of the balustrade. He spent nearly an entire day going through old copies of garden magazines searching for a suitable design. Finally he found just what he wanted in an issue of *Country Life*, a British publication devoted to promoting the virtues of country living, gardening and landscaping. Once the design was chosen, King, Joan, and the carpenters spent an entire afternoon taking measurements:

> It was amusing to see the many optical illusions as we worked on the different levels of the lawn, and tried to centre the garden from the oblique position of the verandah. The large stone in the centre of the lawn & the elm tree were the deciding factors...first the place was — then it changed to — and next to —. We took a good deal of time to guess at heights — & levels & putting up white furniture, tape measures, pickets etc. (28 August 1931).

National Archives of Canada/PA 124734

The carpenter had difficulty making the exact shape King wanted for the balustrade supports, which he said should look "like a vase on a stand."

& the tree" (11 September 1931). After the workmen laid the concrete foundation, King decided another entrance into the lower ornamental flower beds was needed. The next day, he moved things again: "Oddly enough I came back in the final adjustment to just the spots I had decided upon before placing the order..." (12 September 1931).

All the effort, delays and frustrations were forgotten in an instant when King saw the first two sections in place: "The morning sunlight was very beautiful on the new balustrade, and throughout the day with shadow & sunshine chasing each other over the lawn and the forests and fields beyond the effect was too beautiful for words" (6 September 1931). After the balustrade was painted white, King was speechless once again when he saw it in the moonlight. Sited atop a stone retaining wall, the balustrade was broken by two entrances. Stone steps at one opening and a low boulder at another led into the gardens below. The balustrade bordered the newly created upper terrace — flagstone next to the house and grass beyond. His boyhood friend, Peter Sims, remarked when looking at photos of the Moorside grounds, that King's balustrade looked exactly like his at Chicopee, his summer home. King was not embarrassed to copy or to be influenced by other gardens, for he always believed his design to be unique and special.

This pleasant afternoon's work, however, was not conclusive. Later additional measurements were taken and decisions were again made and unmade: "It is a difficult business to arrange to centre a garden obliquely from a house but that has been the task. I think I have succeeded very well, but have had to trust my eyes more than follow rules, save as to preserving proportion" (2 September 1931). King enjoyed readjusting the siting, but it must have been frustrating for his employees. One day King congratulated himself on securing "just the right dimensions," then a few days later he moved the lines nearly two meters closer to the house: "...it was too far into the garden, it lost the intimate touch with the house and crowded over too much towards the garden

Ornamental Gardens

King's careful placement of the balustrade was deliberate. He wanted to align the openings with the axis of the flower gardens on the west lawn. The flower gardens, as noted earlier, were begun by the Pattesons in 1924. They laid this first section out as a square — the four corners filled with a mixture of annuals and perennials and the centre with lawn. At the height of the Moorside landscape development, the quadrant was somewhat enlarged, and a double row of perennial beds was created further on, leading down to the forest edge. Below the perennial borders, just within the forest, was a spot King called "the Hidden Garden." Here Joan made the rock garden, and King placed flower beds and a lily pond. By the late 1930s the horticultural improvements also included a rose garden on the southwest side of the house, and plantings of shrubs and vines around its foundation. At the front of the house the entrance drive swung around a circular flower bed. It was an uncomplicated design, a typical mix of formal and informal elements — all anchored on the extensive, rolling lawn.

Although King's gardens included a number of common design features, his versions were often scaled-down translations of contemporary and traditional garden styles and components. His balustrade was wood, not marble; his perennial borders were small, not extensive. A garden writer might have described his ornamental gardens as average given the surroundings and the materials King could have worked with. Even though his ornamental gardens were not typical for such a large estate, in King's eyes they were, of course, the most beautiful gardens he had seen. He continually measured them against others, and always found his flower beds comparable or superior.

The estate grounds of his contemporaries, however, were much more elaborate and often were professionally designed. For example, a common early 20th century innovation in British garden design occasionally found on North American estates,

The lily pond at Batterwood House, the country home of Vincent Massey near Port Hope, Ontario.

National Archives of Canada/PA 124706

The Moorside ornamental gardens in the late 1930s.

was a landscape designed as a series of "rooms." The rooms, linked into a unified plan, could be devoted to a particular colour, such as Vita Sackville-West's famous White Garden at Sissinghurst Castle in England — all silver, white and green. Or a section could contain only a single species (such as roses), or a single growing medium (such as a bog garden), and so on. King could have, given the size of his property, designed his gardens this way, but he did not. No high hedging separated his rose garden from the terrace. His flower beds were not sequestered, but drifted on a sea of lawn.

King enjoyed visiting gardens designed as "rooms." Vincent Massey's Batterwood House near Port Hope, Ontario, was described as having the harmonious architecture of Georgian England (what King once called a " charming cottage"), and the landscape of contemporary Britain: "Here are the gardens...panels of colour between backdrops of evergreens, stretches of green turf to carry the eye to distant groups, little intimate gardens dropping gently down a slope, each separate as a room, yet bound together by the ribbon of water that flows through."[5] On 350 acres (142 ha) the Masseys installed a bog garden ("...where Mrs. Massey is experimenting with such fragile, lovely things as the pink Lady's Slipper and the Wild Iris"), flower gardens, water lily pools, rose garden, and perennial borders. A planting of a double row of lime trees, their branches interwoven (a very British touch), led down to the swimming pool. A vine-covered pergola, tea-house, badminton court, vegetable garden, greenhouse, terrace and balustrade were also blended "conveniently yet unobtrusively" into the overall scheme. Although King enjoyed rambling around the Masseys' garden, he silently compared it with Kingsmere, noting that Kingsmere views were finer and nature grander and even Joan's flower borders at Shady Hill were more beautiful than the Masseys'. King thought his judgments were verified when he took the Masseys on a walk around Moorside. He was quite gratified to hear Vincent say he was "much taken with the variety of trees, & of scene, the valleys, mountain, brook, moor, etc....He thinks the place 'perfectly lovely' & rightly treated" (8 July 1933).

King frequently visited Fulford Place, a Brockville, Ontario "show-place...and a mecca for annual pilgrimages of horticulturists..."[6] Fulford Place, with its magnificent stone house and formal gardens designed by the American Olmsted Brothers landscape firm, was said to be inspired by the sumptuous Newport "cottages." Built at the turn of the century by Senator George T. Fulford, it overlooked a section of the Thousand Islands area on the St. Lawrence River. After the senator's death, his widow and son maintained the estate in its Edwardian splendor. King found the estate's "lawns, flowers, river bank, rock gardens, etc... lovely," but never mentioned the magnificent waterfall in the rockery, nor the dramatically-placed gazebo on the cliff-high river bank. Prime ministers and royalty were entertained there, including the Prince of Wales in 1927. In 1932 King was invited by Mrs. Fulford to participate in a seance led by the famous American medium, Etta Wriedt, who would later play a further role in his life.

National Archives of Canada/PA 124733

View of landscaping at the side of the Moorside cottage.

To maintain the high standard King thought his gardens deserved, he often intervened in the planning as he did on other estate projects. His gardeners did the labour — there is little evidence that King participated in double-digging the perennial borders or dead-heading the flowers. On one occasion King did note in his diary that he helped the gardener plant a box of perennials. He studied flower catalogues, compiling, with Joan who seemed to have quite a free hand with the flowers, lists of plants and seeds for the coming year. King also read gardening books for inspiration: "...read afterwards from a book on Herbaceous Borders — arranged for more planting of perennials" (19 May 1934). King also experimented with a flower planting theory popularized by the influential British garden writer, Gertrude Jekyll. She advocated grouping plants by colour, then artistically blending the clumps as if painting a watercolour. King wrote that he "Spent some time studying the effect of different colours & of high & low flowers at the foot of the garden — see that what is needed is yellow & gold, white and blue — these effects, especially the first and last are very fine" (19 September 1931).

King was deeply touched when a Scottish gardener once remarked that King must be "a man of understanding and kind heart" because of his love of flowers (8 July 1937). King truly did love flowers. In early June, for example, he rhapsodized: "The Iris in the garden at different points are most lovely at present. They are in full bloom, and quite joyous & glorious in spots" (14 June 1933). He once characterized flowers as "the silent voices of God...part of the vocabulary of Heaven" (16 October 1901).

National Archives of Canada/C 83998

King and Joan agreed that white alyssum was a perfect border plant for the perennial beds.

After nearly forty years of gardening and reading flower catalogues, he could still marvel:

> When I came into the sitting room and saw beautiful red, pink and white hollyhocks in a vase, flowers and ferns in the other part, I almost broke down at the beauty of the scene. Nothing has impressed me so much this summer as the new varieties of flowers each week end, as though God with His own hand, had arranged to disclose how bounteous and varied His gifts are as weeks and seasons pass by (25 July 1943).

Finding religious symbolism in the garden and its products was not unique to the religious Mackenzie King. Nineteenth and early twentieth-century religious moralists drew parallels and metaphors from the garden's cycle of growth, renewal and decay. A favourite observation was to say that one felt a closeness to God in the garden. Canadians were thus urged by religious leaders to garden, not only for aesthetic and healthful reasons, but also for the sake of their spiritual health.

King was not upset if he could not identify every flower he grew. Flowers were a manifestation of God; by appreciating them, named or not, he participated in the miracle of life and recognized God's underlying power. In the late 1940s King tried to console Flora Scrim, who had suddenly lost her brother, her co-worker in the family florist company: "I do hope you will not feel too greatly alone. Fortunately, flowers have their own message at all times, and they will speak to you I know of the love and beauty that lie at the heart of the universe and will help to keep your faith strong."[7]

King especially loved flowers and plants with personal associations. For King these associations raised his gardens above the mundane "house and gardens" landscape and into the realm of the beautiful. Flowers coul be associated with friends who sent the plants. For example, after receiving a *Polygonum baldschaunicum* (a vining knotweed) he had praised in a Toronto admirer's garden, King responded: "I have taken it to Kingsmere, and have selected the spot which will, I trust, afford it space in which to breathe...I cannot thank you too warmly for adding in the way you have to the charm and beauty of Kingsmere and its many associations."[8]

Plants and flowers given to King on significant occasions were also enjoyed for their associations. King nurtured a white cyclamen given to his mother during her final illness. Auspiciously it lost its last flower only after she had died. When it bloomed the following year, King happily wrote in his diary: "I spoke to it as though it were the spirit of my mother speaking to me, so pure and white & beautiful, who will say that it was not her expression of joy & blessing to me from the invisible world about. At any rate I like to believe it was and enjoyed the beautiful sight as such" (13 February 1918). In later years, he would not doubt such "signs," but would accept them as a confirmation of the presence of his dear departed ones.

National Archives of Canada/PA 124456

The upper garden.

Plants collected from meaningful locations were given special treatment and placement. In 1937 he received a selection of plants and bulbs from Ladysford, Scotland ("a wonderful assortment...beautifully packed and labelled, a marvelously generous gift" (12 July 1937), a year after he had visited the "home of his ancestors." King planted the material in a "memorial" garden, where each year he delightedly saw the violets, lily-of-the-valley, hepatica, and crocus bloom. He enjoyed this spot so much, he planted material from other sentimental sites there as well. He was overjoyed one spring day to see in his memorial garden "...a beautiful flower like a star, pure white, and six petals in full bloom," transplanted from his boyhood home, Woodside. This unnamed flower was more than a pretty thing: "I could not but think of how it symbolised our family as we were all together there, six in number..." (7 May 1939).

He was thrilled to receive seeds gathered from the locust trees planted by his grandfather, William Lyon Mackenzie, at Queenston near Niagara Falls. Joan and he immediately walked the property to find just the right spot to plant them. King mused happily on the coincidence of receiving the seeds on the very day he read Mackenzie's letter written after he had returned from exile and was revisiting Queenston. He saw "...how [the locusts] had grown into great trees, the locust seeds which he had himself planted to commemorate the day on which he gave up the idea of following personal pursuits which might have brought him great wealth and ease" (7 May 1939). Following in his grandfather's footsteps, in more ways than one, greatly pleased his namesake.

By 1928 King's plant purchases were sizable, for he did not rely solely on floral gifts to ornament his gardens. One year, King had his gardener and Joan estimate how many annuals were needed to fill the flower gardens. The result amazed him: 400 ageratum (for edging), 300 petunias, 120 blue salvia and 50 red salvia, 100 nicotiana, 250 salpiglossis, 300 double and single asters, 100 small flowered zinnias, 250 large flowered zinnias, 150 verbena, 150 pansies, 40 heliotrope, 40 annual chrysanthemums, 150 snapdragons, 100 stocks, 100 dwarf and 200 tall African marigolds and 225 lobelia.[9] Worried that his substantial order might fall into the wrong hands, King had his secretaries check on two major Ottawa seed and nurserymen, with this result: "Mr. Chevrier says that both Kenneth MacDonald & Sons, and Graham Brothers are all right politically. He therefore suggests that whichever gives you the better service should be patronized."[10]

Rather than seeking unusual or rare plants or specific colours, King selected common varieties from whatever was in a nursery's stock. However King was not immune from occasional horticultural bragging — often common among gardeners. In 1931 he initiated a short correspondence with Frank E. Bennett, a St. Thomas nurseryman. Bennett, an energetic horticultural "evangelist," was a dentist by training, and a horticulturist by avocation. He supervised the horticultural society's trial gardens where exotic and new varieties were introduced, bred gladiolus, served as an officer in horticultural organizations, and in his later years, was a florist and nurseryman.[11] Not surprisingly, Bennett enthusiastically responded to King's request for a Dreamland Gardens catalogue. In a closely typed two-page letter, Bennett recommended specific varieties suitable for Kingsmere conditions, including Bennett's own "splendid" delphiniums.

Although King kept the local horticultural economy humming, he also gratefully accepted "surplus" stock from government greenhouses, including those of the Central Experimental Farm and the Federal District Commission. Davis, head gardener of the Parliament Hill greenhouses, often sent out left-over "odds and ends." King noted that Davis "was most appreciative of what had been done in the way of providing new conservatories" (15 June 1929). Other government gardeners were just as amenable. In 1947 A.E. Challis, head gardener of Rideau Hall, sent out 10 boxes of petunias, 5 boxes of verbenas, 10 boxes of zinnias, 7 boxes of dwarf marigolds, 5 boxes of pansies, and 100 potted salvias.[12]

Prime ministers are subject to opportuning letters — King's experience was not exceptional. However, in his case the opportuning was occasionally horticultural. In 1928 Arthur Miles, an avid Ottawa gardener, offered King plants propagated from a stray seedling of a yellow-flowered euphorbia he had discovered: "It was so interesting that I cultivated it not knowing what it was. Happy the day when I did so. It has taken possession of me and of everyone who has seen it."[13] Miles wanted King to champion its planting throughout Ottawa. It was simple to cultivate, not subject to disease or insects, withstood dryness and dampness, and grew happily in any soil. King was circumspect about helping Miles "promote" the plant — he praised him for his public-spiritedness, saying he would pass the letter on to the chairman of the Federal District Commission. He then gave Miles permission to plant a few bushes at Laurier House as well as Kingsmere. Unfortunately we hear nothing more of this bold experiment.

Another horticulturist, although a much more famous one, Frank Skinner of Dropmore, Manitoba, offered King horticultural immortality. He wanted to name a new lilac hybrid after Mackenzie King, to honour the part King had "...played in maintaining and developing to a new high point the goodwill and understanding between Canada and the United States..."[14] King replied saying he was greatly honoured, but he would be even more pleased if Skinner would name the new lilac after his mother, Grace Mackenzie,[15] which Skinner did.

National Archives of Canada/PA 134767

Joan Patteson and her granddaughters in the Moorside rose garden.

Roses

Of all his flowers, King especially loved his roses. King enjoyed seeing his houses filled with vases of Kingsmere flowers (twenty-five at the Farmhouse alone). Roses were his favourite cut flowers, especially when arranged by Isabelle Kelly, wife of the last caretaker/gardener, who King said had a green thumb. King particularly liked his roses displayed in a gold and glass bowl placed on a mirror.[16]

King's rose garden was separated from the other garden sections — a common arrangement. This practice of cultivating roses in their own plot, supposedly was invented by Napoleon's horticulturally-inclined wife, Josephine. Her rose garden in the early 1800s at the Château de Malmaison evidently contained all the species and varieties then known.[17] This way of growing roses persisted. In fact, to further set off the plot, twentieth century garden commentators urged rose fanciers to construct enclosures around the rose garden. Brick or stone walls, latticework and hedging were to be used as striking backdrops for the beauty of the rose in full flower, and as screens when the roses were not at their best. Although necessary, paths in the rose garden were to be kept to a minimum. The favoured design was symmetrical and formal, the centre ornamented by a garden pool, sundial (the sentimental favourite), statuary, or grass. Only after the rosarian had designed the framework of the rose garden, was plant selection and colour coordination to be considered.

The Canadian rose gardener had to surmount a number of obstacles to successfully cultivate roses: the short growing season, the extremes of winter temperatures, and the ever-present menace of disease and insects. In addition the rose grower was challenged by contemporary garden designers who charged that the average rose garden was not "living up to its highest traditions." "The rosarian's path is not thornless," Dorothy Perkins in

The Canadian Garden Book archly commented. Certainly King's greatest "thorn" was the annual mortality rate of his roses.

Perhaps seduced by pictures of climbing roses smothering picturesque English cottages, or by glowing descriptions of hybrid tea roses, King began ordering roses in 1929, but did not seem to have a well-developed rose garden until 1931, even though *Rosa rugosa* was mentioned growing at Kingswood. Included in King's papers was a list, titled "12 good roses," written (not in King's handwriting) on the back of a Toronto florist's tag. The varieties ranged from 'Frau Karl Druschki' to 'Mme Butterfly' to 'Mrs. J. Laing.'[18] However there is no evidence that King grew any of these varieties. We know King ordered 100 bushes (no variety names survive) from a Scottish rose grower, R.C. Ferguson of Dunfermline, Fife. Attached to his order and the import certificate was a note from King, thrilled to add yet another association to his plants: "I am looking forward with great pleasure to having in my garden in Canada roses from the land of my ancestors."[19] Evidently King was encouraged to order from this Scottish grower after a horticultural chat with his dentist, George Gow, during an appointment.

From this year onwards a steady supply of roses came and went in the Moorside garden. Aided by typed, detailed instructions from the Fulford's head gardener, King hoped his roses would be properly cultivated and protected by his gardeners. In 1936 he obtained dozens of rose bushes from the Bedford Park Floral Company in Richmond Hill, Ontario through an intermediary, Norman Scrim, a prominent Ottawa florist. If King did not know the general manager, Paul E. Angle, was a Tory, the thank you note he received from Angle left him in no doubt:

> I am particularly pleased to acknowledge this letter, because any correspondence I have had with you in the past has been more or less contentious, and I think there are very few people who like being contentious, certainly I do not. To me it is one of the unpleasant obligations which democracy places upon it's [sic] citizens; and so it is pleasant to respond to the appeal of flowers which knows no division of race, creed, or politics.[20]

King continued to order from Ferguson in Scotland, as well as from various Ontario growers, including his brother-in-law who ran (after his retirement) Boulderfel Greenhouse in Barrie, Ontario. King was also given free roses. The Scrims in 1936 not only gave King twenty-five Polyanthus roses when they cleared their Eastview greenhouses, but also loaned one of their gardeners to plant the bushes.[21] Flora Scrim sent along instructions on how to cultivate th and how to best keep cut roses. In the same year, King received nine roses originated at the Central Experimental Farm — seven hybridized by Miss Preston. The Dominion Horticulturist, M.B. Davis, noted that the roses (mainly *Rosa rugosa* hybrids) were "not to be compared with the Hybrid Perpetual or Tea roses, they are all hardy material which do not require winter protection and are more useful as specimen shrubs or bushes than for cut flower purposes."[22] The C.E.F. was continuing the fiction that King should treat any plant material from the Farm as trial material and would submit a report to the Horticultural Division on their success. On King's request, Dr. Gow, the gardening dentist, was sent a "duplicate set."

Exact details of the dimensions, plant varieties, or colour combinations of King's rose garden are non-existent. But photographs do show that King acknowledged some design rules and ignored others. In the quadrant garden below the house, he planted roses intermixed with perennials and annuals. The centre of the quadrant was further ornamented by a bird bath and small statue. His main rose garden, isolated on the side of the upper grass terrace, was not overly formal, nor was it offset by hedging or walls. Crazy-paving pathways led through informal plantings which had a bird bath as the focal point.

Despite the anguish of the annual winterkill, King loved to walk among his roses as well as admire them from afar: "It was a beautiful morning out of doors and I was enchanted by the sight of the roses, thro' the white rungs[?] of the balustrade....Joan came over with Jack & Molly [Patteson] & the three little girls. I saw them all coming towards the hosue from the rose garden, and it was as lovely a sight as I have ever beheld" (2 July 1933).

He also received "spiritual" insight from watching his gardener working in the roses. King said the gardener looked like a "grave digger" as he dug winter trenches for the roses to lie in. When the gardener explained what he was doing for the roses, King happily thought: "The new and larger & more beautiful life after winter....So the summer ends in promise of a fuller life" (23 September 1929).

Greenhouse Plans and Other Construction

Although King lavished attention and money on his ever-changing rose collection, his plant expenses, by the 1930s, began to alarm him. He had his political and custodial staff gather information to explain and tabulate the difference, over a two year span, between buying potted plants or growing garden plants from seed. Despite the "surplus" plants and gifts from well-wishers, King was amazed to learn that he spent nearly ten times more on plants: $104 for plants in 1933 and $10.43 for seeds in 1934.[23] Perhaps influenced by these statistics, King considered buying a small greenhouse.

Greenhouses by the 1930s were often seen in the back yards of enthusiastic gardeners. From the late 1800s, Lord & Burnham, a major North American supplier of pre-fabricated greenhouses offered a full range of structures suitable for the small grower or for the large commercial nursery. Before the advent of cheaper units, conservatories and greenhouses were common features on prestigious city and country properties. Greenhouses were not only decorative appendages there, but also useful structures, providing bedding plants as well as indoor plants, cut flowers and out-of-season fruit. King spent a few pleasant hours considering the addition of a conservatory onto Laurier House, after Sir William Mulock (who, unfortunately for King, lived to be 100), confided that he planned to leave him a $20,000 bequest. King thought he could sit there "amid flowers & ferns in reading & talking with friends, & perhaps keep a bird or two....It would be a remembrance of the finest side of Mulock's nature..." (8 June 1934). He never fully pursued the notion, thinking it too great an expense. The idea of having a small greenhouse at Moorside, however, persisted over a three year period.

King corresponded with Lord & Burnham's Toronto representative from 1933 to 1936. As usual during his bouts of enthusiasm, many letters went to and fro. King advised the sales manager that what he had in mind was a "quite small" greenhouse sufficient to "...start seeds a little earlier in the spring..."[24] He noted that his brother-in-law, H.M. Lay, had bought a greenhouse range from the company. Before the sales manager saw dollar signs dance before his eyes, King hastened to add: "...Mr. Lay's requirements, however, are quite different than mine, he being in the business for a profit, and I being at a loss for pretty much everything I undertake in association with my country home, whenever I permit myself the luxury of indulging in fancies associated with rural pursuits..."[25] King studied the catalogues this letter elicited, then wrote Lord & Burnham a more informed letter detailing his requirements: a small, "pipe-form" construction, sixteen by twenty-five foot greenhouse, mainly sun-heated, but to include a small stove.[26]

Meanwhile, King had a local Ottawa florist, Charles Craig, accompany him to evaluate a small greenhouse range on a city estate: "...saw the 3 splendid houses there. The equipment is a very expensive one; it cost 10,000 to put these buildings up...a fabulous price — tho everything, iron, glass, road egress, plumbing...etc. the best" (18 September 1933). Craig then drove King to his own range as a comparison, but King was appalled at the outlay: "I can see that to buy an up to date equipment would be a very considerable expense" (18 September 1933).

As King cooled off on the idea, Lord & Burnham accelerated their sales approach. They sent King a set of blueprints for a small greenhouse (known in the trade as a forcing house) that the company felt ideally suited his needs. These houses, designed in conjunction with the C.E.F.'s horticultural division, were popular with the small commercial grower who wanted to begin business modestly. King, however, thought the cost ($142) too high. In his last letter to the firm in 1933, he resisted further eager suggestions and offers to send a company representative to Kingsmere: "...with the number of things to be done before the season is over, it would be better to defer to another year any new work of construction."[27]

Surprisingly, King, after continually demurring, suddenly re-opened correspondence with Lord & Burnham and other companies for another round of estimates the next year. However, these inquiries once again failed to materialize into a greenhouse. In a final attempt to find the cheapest structure, King and a contractor inspected a city greenhouse for sale. The contractor advised King it would be foolhardy to move the greenhouse to Kingsmere: "the extra cost of changes would amount to more than a new one" (5 June 1935). Although he dithered a bit in early 1936, King's dream of horticultural self-sufficiency was mentioned no more.

However, not all of his Moorside construction ideas went unrealized. In 1934 King built a pergola on the side porch of the Moorside house, atop the stone side wall. Porch pergolas had become popular before World War I. Even after the war, the structure was popularized as part of the increasing vogue for "outdoor living," and was said to be "...fast supplanting the old covered porches of yesterday."[28] The porch pergola gave "added charm" while furnishing shade and privacy without the drawback of a permanent roof darkening the interior.

King enjoyed observing the patterns of light and shadow as the sun filtered through the pergola's spaces between cross beams and vines. "The effect," King wrote, "is very pleasing and quite Italian. This sort of thing gives me an infinite delight" (18 August 1934). The vines (probably Virginia creeper) took a few years to flourish, but by the 1940s covered the pergola. The porch was very inviting, shaded on one side by the vine-covered pergola, surrounded by low foundation plantings softening the transition between landscape and house, and ornamented by lush flower-filled cement urns placed on the stone walls. King certainly enjoyed dining on his porch at a linen-covered table seated on a cushioned chair upon an Oriental rug.

Another successful project was the construction of an impressive approach drive, a further enhancement of the entrance to the Moorside cottage. Curving up from the entrance gate, the drive ended in a circle in front of the house. An extension branched off to the garage. The drive, covered in crushed white stone ("most effective with the white of the house"), was raked and weeded by the gardeners. As at Kingswood, King built stone walls to demarcate property lines and to provide transitions from one precinct to another. The "drive" wall, as King termed it, extended along one side of the road from the entrance to the garage, twenty inches (51 cm) high, "...dividing the residential from other parts of the grounds" (16 August 1928). King also had his favourite white-washed, three-plank fencing and gates installed on visible sections of the Moorside boundaries. King conscientiously maintained these fences and gates. In 1938 while on holiday, King wrote Joan asking if Godfroy would speak to King's employees about white-washing the fences: "As there is just a possibility the King or Queen or both might come out to the country, it would be well, I think that this should be done."[29]

Trees

Fencing, roads and plant material were minor projects compared to King's tree planting. King simply loved trees, they had great emotional significance for him. Trees "spoke" to him as no other form of vegetation ever did. During a lonely stay in Germany in 1900 he said he found "a companionship in the trees." After pruning a pine tree at Kingswood, King confided in his diary that he missed "the companionship of a bough that was very close." Trees could remind him of loved ones. He compared his mother to an elm tree at Kingswood: "The one near the gate in its graceful purity & aristocratic bearing makes me think of dear Mother" (3 October 1922). A maple tree he had planted at Moorside evoked sentimental musings about Joan: "We looked later at one of the most graceful, spiritual of all the trees, a tall slender maple — It made me think of Joan herself in her spiritual beauty — so full of grace and tenderness & radiance" (13 October 1943). King even compared his family friend and mentor, Sir William Mulock, to a black walnut tree planted to commemorate his 100th birthday: "With its soundness of heart, its buffetings in the open that test and make the sinews of a man no less than the fibres of a tree, it will become increasingly a fitting symbol of his life. Through time to come, Canadians will think of Sir William as of some mighty tree which has helped to shelter the generations that have rested beneath its boughs."[30]

Tree worship and association of trees with individuals was not unique to the impressionable Mackenzie King. Tree worship is nearly as old as humanity — the idea of the sacred grove is present in our symbolic life from classical up into modern times.[31] In late 18th, early 19th century Britain, trees were venerated. Some artists specialized in painting portraits of trees, while poets used trees as symbols of their ancestors. Books depicting handsome trees, famous trees, ancient trees and how to draw them were widely published. Travellers in Europe were often shown venerable trees planted by saints and national heroes.[32] A British historian noted that: "English gentlemen...spent hours discussing the shape and beauty of individual trees, as if they were statues or horses; and in Victorian landscape photography the trees often have greater individuality than the figures standing beside them."[33]

Even so, the forests could still engender feelings of superstitious awe and fear within otherwise enlightened people. In Europe some feared the malevolent spirits, demons and outlaws inhabiting the dark wood. Endless Canadian forests were frightening in themselves, but the settlers also feared lurking Indians, bears and wolves. Early Canadian pioneers certainly cleared as much dark and dangerous forest as possible. In the 1930s a Canadian landscape architect bemoaned this wholesale clearing — but not on environmental grounds. Ontario had too much open space, he said, which made it difficult to find a pleasingly wooded property close enough to the city for easy commuting.[34]

Mackenzie King venerated his trees, but could atavistically feel a shiver of apprehension and almost superstitious awe when walking through the forest. King generally did not fear hiking in his forest, although he preferred following a path: "...Joan and I went for a long walk...lost our way before getting back and had an anxious half hour trying to find a path which would lead us home. It was a welcome sight when it came" (24 May 1934). He shivered when reading "The Man Whom the Trees Loved," a short story by Algernon Blackwood. This rather chilling story, written by one of England's master storytellers of mystery and the supernatural, described the victory of the unholy, but not evil, force of the forest trees over a man's life and his wife's futile fight to save him:

> And in trees...behind a great forest, for instance...may stand a rather splendid Entity that manifests through all the thousand individual trees — some huge collective life, quite as minutely and delicately organised as our own. It might merge and blend with ours under certain conditions, so that we could understand it by *being* it, for a time at least. It might even engulf human vitality into the immense whirlpool of its own vast dreaming life. The pull of a big forest on a man can be tremendous and utterly overwhelming.[35]

After reading the story, King commented in his diary: "Though exaggerated am inclined to agree with its view of the influence of trees as semi- or quasi-conscious entities upon men. The companionship of the forest & plant life is a real thing & must be based on something vital" (11 January 1914). Evidently he never relinquished this belief. Near the end of his life, distressed when workers removed too many trees in one clearing, King declared: "One can no longer hear voices in the trees" (17 June 1949).

Trees certainly provided King with an imaginative focus. Not only could trees personify loved ones, or provoke superstitious fear, they could also demonstrate God's love for King and provide signs of God's presence. While debating where to plant seeds collected from the locust trees his grandfather planted at Queenston, King walked along one of his favourite paths, past the Bethel Stone, a massive boulder where King and Pat, his dog, would often pray:

> As I walked along the path, I thought of that being the best place to plant them, a sort of memorial to what has become an almost sacred way...some day they might be tall & great & would be a reminder to others of my walks there where I have communed with God and received the strength to make all important decisions & to hold to them. So when I came back to the garden, I counted the number and found there were 12 in all...What was most significant of all was that when I was praying very earnestly for a 'closer walk with God,' something seem[ed] to say, that is what you will be commemorating if you plant the trees there, where you had your morning walk with God. It was as if I was being told this must be done (31 October 1943).

In 1934 King was given the chance to plant hundreds of trees — a pleasure shared by many other central Canadian estate owners at the time. A Quebec provincial forester came out to Kingsmere to check King's white pines threatened by white pine blister rust — a fungal disease. During the inspection, the forester happened to mention that the Quebec government was offering trees to large land owners at low cost to stimulate reforestation. King was thrilled. With the assistance of the Quebec government he felt he could create a "real" forest on his estate. The information also had an other-worldly impact. King had been reading a collection of Laurier's letters that very day. After the forester's visit, King was amazed to recall that in one letter, Laurier mentioned trees sent to him at Arthabaskaville for planting. King rejoiced at this "sign" and noted in his diary that obviously the forester was "inspired to come by Sir Wilfrid himself" (16 August 1934). King immediately dictated a letter to Honoré Mercier, Quebec Minister of Lands and Forests, requesting further information on the reforesting scheme:

National Archives of Canada/PA 124717

King greatly enjoyed participating in the massive tree planting on the estate in 1934.

> I have done a good deal in the way of developing the property to make it one of the most beautiful spots in the Gatineau region, and any assistance which I could get by way of counsel or advice from members of your forestry staff, to preserve the trees already growing and to do something in the way of reforesting, would be most welcome...of course I would not expect any favours from the Government, but simply to be treated in this matter in the same way as other residents of the province....As an elector and tax payer in the Province of Quebec, I have a special interest in all that pertains to the province, and I am particularly anxious that my summer home shall be in every detail worthy of the great natural beauty for which the Province and the Laurentians are so justly famed.[36]

King agreed to fulfill the Department of Lands and Forests' requirement that the reforested area measure at least five acres (2 ha), and that one acre would be reforested annually with a minimum of 1,000 trees. King waived the cash bonus for planting them and was told he would be given his trees free. With all this free material at hand, King excitedly sent in an order for 200 hard maples, 400 white spruce, 50 white cedar, 25 mountain pine, 100 red pine, 100 white oak, 100 white elm, 25 mountain ash, 25 European tamarack, and 25 Engelman spruce.[37]

At this time Sandy Stewart, superintendent of the Federal District Commission, was working with King replanting the Laurier House grounds. King asked him, as well, to come out to

Kingsmere and give him "helpful pointers:" "Most important of all was the decision in which his view & mine were the same to make a plantation of green at foot of the large field, as a shield from the road, instead of planting shrubbery near the house. He suggested something much larger than anything I had thought of, a wavy border formation, while I had thought only of a double avenue of trees" (4 May 1935).

It was a great day when the partial shipment of trees arrived from the Berthierville provincial nursery. King was almost beside himself with excitement as he directed the twelve men planting the new trees: "It was quite a sight to see the group at work, like a bee hive" (9 May 1935). The trees were hardly in the ground when King began speaking of them as mature trees — he could actually see them thriving, shielding the cottage from the public road, enclosing the front field and providing "an ornamental finish to the end of the grounds."

Six days later they were all at it again when the remainder of the trees were delivered. Not even the cold, which made him feel rheumatic, dampened his excitement. King spent the day planting oaks (which he said gave him particular joy), mountain pine, spruce and cedar. Near the south-east corner of the house he lavished trees: "I marked out places for a row of elms — a tree I am very fond of — two groups of ash in front, then a row of ash (with red berries) then spruce & evergreen in between..." (15 May 1935). He put in a row of maples along the east side of the stone wall along the entrance drive, as well as in the field between the Farm and Moorside. King also planted a few trees near a haunted house (since demolished) where a doctor once lived. King legitimized this planting, as he did for many of his landscape projects, with references to the past and the spirit world: "It was making good at all events the efforts of others long ago. I felt the old doctor's spirit was somewhere not far away, and grateful at what was being done" (15 May 1935). King was delighted with the entire plantation, which cost only $132.49 for transportation and the services of the department's men.

From 1937 to 1939 King's reforesting enthusiasm seemed to vanish. The Federal District Commission supplied a few trees and the labour for sporadic tree planting. Only in late 1939 did King reveal the reason for the abrupt decline. He confided to his diary that he did not order more free trees from the Quebec government because he would not have "wished to have secured this from Duplessis even as part of the government's policy" (31 October 1939).

However his delight in reforestation and in sentimental memorializations could be easily rekindled by smaller plantings. In 1937 he was characteristically thrilled to participate in planting acorns to mark the coronation of King George VI. The program was sponsored by Canadian representatives of the "Men of the Trees," an international organization of tree lovers who worked "to create a universal tree sense and encourage all to plant, protect and love trees everywhere." They certainly picked the right man to participate in their Ottawa ceremony. King was given the first two acorns, out of a shipment of ten thousand, to plant on Parliament Hill and at Kingsmere — the rest were to be planted by school children across Canada. As patron of the society, King arranged the Parliament Hill ceremony for July 12, 1937 as "a climax to their [Men of the Trees] work that day." The Kingsmere acorn was planted the next year during a private ceremony King thoroughly enjoyed. A representative of the organization came out to Kingsmere and chose a site near the Farm:

We all assembled together, Nichol digging out a suitable

> spot, Mr. Keith doing the planting, his wife & Joan standing to my right looking on, — Keith and I facing each other with tree between — my back to the old oak, Lay to one side my left looking on & the two little dogs Pat and Derry running about & watching with curiosity & interest, most beautiful of all "as a sign" — the bluebirds have made a nest in the large Canadian Oak — the male bird first flew about & watch us — then the female looked out of the nest eyeing us with curiosity & interest & finally sat on a bough near by as the tree was planted — Keith made a little address....& read a little poem... It was a lovely ceremony....The beauty of the open — the blue of the skies the green of the grass & the fields — kind & loving and true friends — the Spring of the year — associations many and dear... (15 May 1938).

King treated his trees with reverence, tender feeling and a sensitivity rarely displayed towards other landscape components. Once when watching his men prune a few trees, King remarked: "I dislike to see a single tree barked or the bark scratched, or leaves torn off & branches left ragged. Fortunately nature has a happy way of healing wounds & making scars look well" (1 August 1929). He consciously studied the effects of tree placement, of high or low pruning, and of tree removal. In the 1930s King spent considerable time working on the wooded part of the estate, culling, planting, pruning and underbrushing — always with a view to improving the design of his landscape. In 1931 King noted: "...mustered up enough courage to take out a good sized iron-wood tree on the lawn that was obscuring a distant view, also some juniper bushes beautifully shaped but which did not look well from a distance" (19 September 1931). His sensitivity to the use of space was also exercised: "Up at Moorside, the cutting out of a thorn tree has made a great improvement, has quite changed the view from the front verandah, given space

National Library of Canada/NL 16862

Tree planting was not unique to Mackenzie King. Other estate owners, such as his mentor, Sir William Mulock, planted hundreds of trees on their country estates. Above: The Elms, Mulock's country estate.

in foreground. That I think is most desirable...." (25 October 1925). These decisions were not easily reached, King hated to cut down trees: "...witnessed the cutting down of a large pine tree to the left centre of the lawn. I have debated a long time about it, and to take it down in its prime was a painful process — a kind of murder it seemed, — however it was blocking a long-range view" (14 August 1939).

Views were very important to King, their enhancement a strong tenet in his loosely articulated landscaping philosophy. To create or enhance Kingsmere views usually entailed considerable underbrushing and tree culling. In fall 1940 King had a large pine tree near the Moorside verandah removed, a decision he debated all summer. But as soon as it began to topple, King knew he had made the right choice: "...I saw [a] tree with larger trunk immediately behind it stand out in fine relief, I saw that the taking away of the other one in the foreground was a great improvement, and felt really quite delighted. It also, from another point, opened up a fine view of the mountain" (28 September 1940). With the tremendous amount of activity occurring at the estate during the 1930s, however, it is not surprising that some mistakes did occur:

> Was terribly distressed to find when I went out to the lawn that the men had cut the branches of the trees far too high up & taken out too many trees....It was heart-breaking....There was nothing to be done but to make the best of it....I went out & lay on my back on the lawn gazing at the splendour of the Heavens for half an hour to seek to gain some of their calmness and to become like them "untroubled and impassionate" (5 August 1931).

Trails

Another of Mackenzie King's major landscaping projects was the creation of walking, later driving, trails throughout his property — another common feature of the country home landscape. King had, from the beginnings of his residence at Kingsmere, greatly enjoyed creating paths. He would have observed, in his garden readings, the variety of trails, paths, rides and allées depicted in landscape plans, engravings, and paintings. These pre-20th century trails, mainly designed for horseback riding and carriage travel, facilitated access to far-flung portions of an estate. Mackenzie King's trails connected features of interest (vistas, garden structures, natural formations, etc.), as well as permitted access into the distant sections of his property. He also used the paths as "fitness trails:" "We went as far as the falls and the lookout, and came back by the lower field and across the far field to the opening in the path and back" (10 October 1931).

As King added to his holdings, the path system expanded. New trails were cut and old ones extended. Although he was very impressed with Rockefeller's walking paths on his summer property ("very smooth & nicely gravelled [with] fine small stones..." 12 September 1927), King did not groom his paths so expensively.

Walking his property not only gave King a chance to meditate and commune with nature, but he also saw the walks as places to bring visiting dignitaries and other visitors, to discuss ideas and problems completely isolated from officials and duties, and "...to share the joys of nature & to see men & women at their best" (29 September 1926). He also enjoyed, on these walks, pointing out landscape features he had discovered or created.

In the early years, he himself underbrushed and cleared, to advance the trails. But the expanded estate demanded the work of others. King created three main paths on the estate, as well as many small ones: "My desire is to get the whole property linked up with a series of walks and drives, through the woods, the fields, by the streams etc...I find an intense joy and excitement in this work and could revel in it if all my time could be given to it" (20 July 1928). He hired Paddy and Willy Murphy to supervise the leveling, under-brushing and tree removal. King loved watching the Murphys sculpt a path outline with a plough: "Merely outlining a path thro' long grass lends a sort of beauty to the entire environment" (14 June 1931).

National Capital Commission

King loved to create trails through his property.

One of the main Moorside paths led south from the Abbey ruin, over a stream, through fields, past an inactive mica mine, through a portion of forest, finally arriving at Mountain Road. To beautify this stretch King had his workers clear the scrub, build a bridge with cedar railings over the stream and construct a low stone wall between two fields. His men tore down the decrepit buildings on the mica mine site: house, blacksmith shop, stable and bunk-house. King's frugal soul rejoiced in the useable lumber that was retrieved. Later a second main trail, "a very lovely path," was constructed which branched off the Mica Mine trail and led over the moor to the farm.

His favourite walking, later driving, trail was one he named the "Waterfall Trail." After buying the initial Moorside lot, King explored the land around the parcel. He was overjoyed to discover a waterfall and stream further down the valley adjoining his property. From that time on King determined to purchase this "entrancing spot...without fail. It is just what the place needs, a stream of fresh water, a wonderful spot to walk to, beautiful as beautiful can be" (16 September 1924). During the six years it took to acquire the necessary portions, King was continually encouraged by the thought of making a beautiful walk there, an inspirational trail, one that would be "a joy all my life & a joy to others after" (16 September 1924). Paddy Murphy was again hired to supervise the improvements. King thought the completed trail was the "showplace" of the estate.

This path, a favoured walk with guests, started just beyond the "hidden garden" area at the foot of the Moorside ornamental gardens. One of the first spots of interest King invariably

G.B.P./National Archives of Canada/PA 124693

King had his employees clear brush, plant trees, and construct a stone wall near one of his main paths.

pointed out was a small cave ("quite a feature") he discovered below the rock garden. In 1933 he highlighted it by building a protective cedar railing around the entrance. A little further on, a lookout, marked by a low stone wall, invited the walker to pause and enjoy the vista of the wooded valley. Low stone walls, constructed by Paddy Murphy, followed the path. The next portion curved through magnificent groves of birch and beech, an area King named the "Valley of the Kings." Perhaps this was where he once remarked: "One hears the voice of God in the woods — It is one's salvation in political life" (24 July 1926). Beyond this grove, jutting out of the hillside, was a striking rock face King found particularly beautiful. All along the path his labourers created small clearings to further enhance the views.

King's greatest enjoyment of the trail involved landscaping the stream and waterfall area. In 1929 aided by Department of Interior engineers, King had the stream diverted here and there by a series of small dams creating a picturesque meandering stream. Winston Churchill, on a tramp around the grounds in 1929, evidently was greatly impressed by the dams. The diversion also created small pools and cascades. At one time King considered blocking the stream to create a deep pond — his own lake to be used for swimming, fishing and small boating, but the financial outlay and fear of "seepage" problems halted his mounting enthusiasm for the project.

This was only a minor disappointment disturbing King's intense enjoyment and excitement during this phase of development. For he was soon at work landscaping the stream path, especially two exquisite spots he thought could be made into "a sort of paradise." Adding to the rustic picturesqueness, King had Paddy Murphy construct five wooden plank bridges across the stream in 1929: "...it was intensely interesting seeing first the large timbers put in place parallel to the stream then the 'stringers' 4 across [?] & finally the planking, a bridge ten feet wide & about twenty feet long...was the making of the walk" (2 August 1929). Garden designers had decreed that artificial plantings or showy bridge construction would mar the natural beauty of woodsy sites. Instead wooden planks, rough logs, and wooden railings were advocated, — design advice King followed. His railings were of cedar, rather than stone, which he felt "produced a better effect." Wild flowers, native vines, weeping willows, or even flag iris were advised plantings for these sites, but it seems King did not alter the original flora. Nor is it certain that he had the bridges placed for artistic effect, to be partly obscured by groups of trees or shrubs.[38] He enjoyed their effect on the landscape, but their real function was to further his intention to link all sections of the estate. In honour of the current Governor General, King named one of the structures, the "Willingdon Bridge."

The final portion of the trail steeply descended the escarpment, overlooking the Ottawa Valley, to the falls. The falls were usually the last stop on King's tour, unless King or his guests wanted to follow a westerly trail leading to King Mountain, an old path which crossed his property. The falls, especially in spring, were spectacular. King once remarked that he could hear them from the Abbey ruin sounding "...like a train of railway cars rushing at full speed" (23 June 1935). When King saw white foam hanging over the rocks "like a veil twisted around a forehead and face," he named it the "Bridal Veil Falls." A stone wall with protective cedar railing was built as a lookout, where King and his guests would sit, admiring the view while gathering strength for the uphill trek back to Moorside.

By 1930, the major work on this trail was complete. King contentedly noted: "The paths made last year are in perfect shape and a real delight. The bridges and stream too splendid for words, the waterfall a thing of great beauty. The whole investment has been well worthwhile....It is a great joy not having to begin more work of construction, clearing etc....There is now a note of rest and repose" (27 April 1930). All during the thirties King walked the various trails alone, with Joan, or other guests, continually delighting in what he had created. The advent of World War II and increasing infirmity finally curtailed his hiking on the paths.[39]

The Last Years: Professional Help

When Canada entered World War II, King's large landscaping projects were severely reduced by labour shortages and his available time. Minimal maintenance, vegetable gardening, and some flower planting was done. Once the war ended, King began to make up for lost time. As he neared retirement, landscaping Kingsmere became an important element in his need for activity. This landscaping phase of the late 1940s involved the hitherto unwanted help of landscape architects. King's health was failing which undoubtedly increased his receptivity to include outsiders in his landscape planning.

King did not often like the handiwork of landscape architects. After touring southern Ontario in 1933, visiting a number of professionally-designed country estates, he remarked: "Of one thing I am certain, Nature herself knows best what to do & we produce the best effects by not trying to improve on her" (25 June 1933). A lofty thought on designed landscapes, but a rule not always followed by King himself. King's dislike may have been financial — he was reluctant to pay for something he enjoyed doing himself, something he felt he was good at. In fact, near the end of his life he remarked during a short speech to the Canadian Society of Landscape Architects, that if he had his life to live over, he still would have liked politics, but he would have also enjoyed being a professor of landscape architecture.

King was convinced to speak to the Society by Edward I. Wood, a landscape architect who worked for the Federal District Commission [later the National Capital Commission] from 1934 up into the 1960s. Wood guided King's first foray into professional landscape planning. He had approached King in 1942 asking if he could write a history of the estate. Wood had been involved in restoring the grounds of Monticello, the country estate of the American president and ardent horticulturist, Thomas Jefferson, as part of his post graduate studies at Harvard. Because Kingsmere would undoubtedly share the same prominence in Canada, Wood urged that its history and landscape design be recorded "...as a valuable contribution to the future."[40] King demurred, citing his need for privacy. Wood then re-entered King's life in 1947 when he supervised a team of F.D.C. employees who were engaged to thin out King's ten-year-old tree plantings. King was amazed how the small alterations improved vistas and enhanced landscape effects. Wood praised King's trees and talked of possible additions to the landscape, heightening King's enthusiasm to further improve his property.

In September 1947 W. Ormiston Roy of Montreal, a landscape architect and contemporary of King's, came to Kingsmere. He was invited by J.W. McConnell, owner of the *Montreal Star* and prominent Liberal, to study Kingsmere, as a gift to King, for possible landscape improvements. Roy was a man of many enthusiasms. In addition to his landscape practice, he was a leading Canadian authority on collie dogs, publicly advocated certain health foods as cures for heart disease, and promoted the peony from the 1920s up into the late 1940s as the national flower of Canada. At one time he cultivated peonies for cut flower sales in Quebec, Alabama, New York and England.[41] From their first meeting, King felt Roy was a kindred spirit: "He is a man after my own heart; a great lover of Nature and strong believer in planning landscape" (26 September 1947). Roy said he learned many of his landscaping ideas from the eminent Scottish gardener and horticultural "revolutionary," William Robinson [1838-1935]. Roy had designed landscapes (or as he phrased it "passed on his ideas") for various prominent Americans: John Burroughs, Thomas Edison, Henry Ford, Dr. George Washington Carver, and Canadians: J.W. McConnell, F.N. Southam, and Howard Stewart.[42]

Roy proudly told King that the eminent naturalist John Burroughs had once characterized him as a "landscape naturalist," a title Roy preferred to landscape architect. Roy believed in making full use of a garden's natural features and deplored "the tendency toward formalism" in British and American landscape designs. His congenial ideas and evident enthusiasm for the Kingsmere estate found an appreciative ear. King was enthralled by their first ramble through the grounds:

> What had impressed him was the enormous beauty of the properties in Kingsmere and what could be made of them through having let Nature develop matters as she had. He showed me what was needed in the way of taking away certain classes of trees. Trees that stood in the foreground, to make possible a long view....He said I was the one man he had met in the class he termed "great" who really had seen the importance of this before he, himself, had said a word, and had pointed out where mistakes had been made through too much underbrushing. He told me that was one of the most fatal of all mistakes of landscape (26 September 1947).

Roy, however, did not like some of King's landscape embellishments. He disliked how the Moorside lawn was split up by flower beds and perennial borders. He also wanted to eliminate King's beloved balustrade, because "it was something imported from abroad" (26 September 1947). Yet, this criticism did not dampen King's enthusiasm for Roy's suggestions, nor for the possibility of Roy's free services. McConnell, a noted philanthropist, said he kept a "little fund" for landscape work for which he retained Roy and offered to pay for Roy's services. King agonized over the decision for a month, finally deciding in May 1948 to go ahead:

> ...I would not be under obligation to him personally but that payments to Roy would be from this fund which he regards as being in the nature of public service work. He had understood I was thinking of Kingsmere going some day to the nation.... Anything that might be done this way might be a contribution toward some national improvement....As it is now known that I am leaving office altogether, within a few months, I do not feel that accepting this through Mr. McConnell's kindness will put me under obligation of a character which would, in any way, affect my attitude in public life toward which he might be concerned. It is a matter of personal friendship and very generous friendship at that (17 May 1948).

He was reassured to hear that Edward Wood shared Roy's views on natural landscaping. Also King was further heartened after visiting McConnell's country property Roy had landscaped:

> I don't know when I have enjoyed a walk more, looking at the beautiful landscaping carried out at Mr. Roy's direction. It seemed to me quite perfect, wide open spaces of lawn. Distant vistas surrounding the trees with their branches down to the ground. Little by little, other parts of the estate revealed which were hidden behind shrubs, lilac bushes, etc. such as garage, kitchen garden, swimming pool. The flower garden was off by itself. A single garden for the roses. Very lovely (13 June 1948).

National Archives of Canada/PA 124430

King and Ormiston Roy.

Their friendship deepened as letters were exchanged filled with flowery rhetoric and quotes from Roy's favourite poet, Robert Burns. Subsequent rambles around the estate further cemented the bond:

> ...Roy said he had not seen any place anywhere that seemed to him to be as beautiful as what was to be seen in Kingsmere — of natural beauty unspoiled. He thought it had possibilities greater than he had seen at any other place....He thought I had a much finer property than McConnell in what it made possible of natural beauty. Certainly to me, it was much more beautiful than any

thing Mr. Rockefeller has at Williamsburg or elsewhere. Indeed I was amazed at the wealth of the beauty revealed as I saw it today… (24 May 1948).

King rejoiced in Roy's approval of what he had done at Kingsmere: "I have experienced exceptional pleasure in discovering how closely my own untutored mind has been in accord with your own on some of the problems of landscaping…"[43]

Inspired by his association with Roy and a recent tour of the various paths and gardens, King was determined to "redeem" his landscape. His old enthusiasm rekindled as he assessed the amount and type of work to be done: "…one saw in a moment the possibilities there were for replanting" (24 May 1948). On the Waterfall Trail, "One or two days work would do about all the clearing that needs to be done," King concluded. Along this path King continually sized up "…the trees it might be best to cut down to get a better view of the exquisite and distant woods, with their large trees, and yet not destroy the 'intimacy' of the path" (14 September 1949).

In June 1949 Roy began supervising tree removal to open up distant views, to improve existing vistas, and to enlarge some paths to admit King's car. On a recent trip to Rockefeller's Seal Harbor estate, King was impressed with Rockefeller's woodland drives. King felt it was just the thing to have for his aging friends and himself, to permit greater access to the beauty of the Kingsmere forest, the stream, and the inspiring vistas. However, as this construction proceeded, King became uneasy. He thought Roy's men were clearing too much on the main path, destroying the charm and intimacy King so loved. He urged caution and a slower pace:

> He [Roy] was most decided about all trees, maples — as well as cherry trees and poplars and hawthorn being taken out clear up to the top. I was against taking out too many Maples, but yielded…but I really think we have made a great mistake, destroyed the charm — which lay in the intimacy of the path. I feel very badly about this misfortune. It was the pride of all my walks. One can no longer hear voices in the trees (17 June 1949).

Roy further upset him by suggesting King's beloved artificial ruin, built on a Moorside hilltop in the late 1930s, should be removed. King only noted: "… it will take time before effecting that change" (30 June 1949). King felt there were too many men at work, causing too many hasty mistakes. He did not want a repetition of a recent over-clearing, a mistake causing a "glare of a wide expanse, instead of a series of vistas." King unhappily noted that he "…could not bear to go near to the place.…It is a kind of desecration" (18 June 1949). Yet, other changes were heartily approved:

> Went to the seat overlooking the distance, and watched while the pin-cherries were cut down & an opening made to the horizon. Later an opening to the ruins in the distance, finally, an opening to a large clearing at the junction of the paths, quite awe inspiring, large trees in a circle surround a sort of amphitheatre which one looked "down upon," a real discovery, something quite exceptional (13 July 1949).

Replacing the ten-year-old, rotten, neglected wooden bridges, on the Waterfall Trail was the next project. Roy convinced King to rebuild them on a Scottish model — resting on boulders with tile drains for the stream to course through — which would not only enhance the landscape, but also support a car. The rustic wood railings were to be replaced by stone which King now decided added significantly to the perfection of the site. At first King excitedly watched the bulldozer (auspiciously rented from the King Engineering Co.): "It was a thrilling sight to all this 'Massive' work being done, and all rapidly...the scenery grandeur itself. It brought back all the thrills and happiness of bygone years to both Joan and myself" (24 August 1949). This happiness soon changed to shocked dismay when he saw the "heartbreaking" damage the bulldozer did to the surrounding forest, especially around the Willingdon bridge. King halted the work, banished the bulldozer, and allowed only a tractor and horse-drawn implements to finish the project. King told Roy of his "brutal disappointment" over the destruction at the Willingdon bridge. Roy admitted he had made a mistake and outlined how he would rectify it:

> We examined with care what it was best to do — a circle for turning cars to be made, a large gate to be put in — fence line to [be] adjusted, side of ravine to be filled up, stone or two dynamited, & stone wall moved in part to make ravine path safe...went over the several culverts and discussed what has to be done in the way of making them into bridges by putting safe guarding railings of cedar or other wood on either side a 14 foot road way. There are about 8 or 10 of such 'bridges' required and some filling in 'and up' along the road way it can be made very beautiful (21 September 1949).

Unfortunately at the same time King discovered his neighbour, Basil Mulvihill, had dammed the stream at an upper point, creating a small lake on his property. This action reduced King's section of the stream to a trickle: "It was heartbreaking to see the beautiful gorge-like shaped openings where formerly there were limped and beautiful pools, having fine fish, all completely dried up" (24 August 1949). He only took legal action against Mulvihill after much anxious deliberation, and a visit to the dam. The lawsuit never came to a conclusion as King died early the next summer.[44]

As for the day-to-day maintenance on the developing estate, King preferred to rely on a variety of seasonal gardeners, rather than landscape professionals. They ranged from farm hands to trained gardeners, reflecting the usual choice of available garden help. These gardeners were not often mentioned in the diaries, but when they were, King usually did not remember how to spell their names. They were, however, the unsung heroes of the King estate. Without them, King could not have successfully played his chosen role as country squire, gentleman landscaper or, in the late 1930s, builder of ruins.

King's pieces of statuary may have been small in scale, but his imagination magnified them in size and importance.

CHAPTER FIVE

The Faun Among the Ruins

MACKENZIE KING'S FASCINATION WITH STATUARY AND RUINS

MACKENZIE KING'S FANTASY LIFE DEEPENED AND INTENSIFIED IN THE 1930s. Despite his suppers with Joan, political activities and occasional entertaining, King was a lonely man. By now his immediate family had shrunk to one sister and her family and the sons of his deceased brother — none of whom King attempted to see very often. He did little to alleviate his solitude and at times aggravated it by isolating himself at Kingsmere. Paradoxically he had a deep need for affection, and was often hurt by slights others might not feel, such as when his political colleagues failed to send Christmas cards. As well, King needed to reassure himself of his worth not only as a private person, but also as a public figure, a statesman whose career would assure him a place in history. One of the ways he immediately gratified these needs was by contacting the spirit world.[1] King did not seek advice on governing the country or what policies to follow, rather he sought comforting messages from the dead, especially his family, that he was loved and guided from above. One commentator noted that King's spiritualism was "best regarded as a defence mechanism directed to easing the tensions and anxieties aroused in the public world."[2]

His increasing involvement in spiritualism characterized his years in Opposition. Part of his, as he termed it, psychical explorations included contact with mediums, an enthusiasm shared by many early 20th century North Americans. Some of his friends were believers and arranged sittings for King at their homes. King also consulted spiritualists and mediums on trips to England, visited the Society for Psychical Research and corresponded with the Countess of Aberdeen about his bits of "psychical research." Mrs. Etta Wreidt,[3] a famous American medium, was invited to Kingsmere for private consultations after

King met her at Mrs. Fulford's home. King, however, was not always comfortable with the mediums' communications. His uneasiness was not only aggravated by worry over the political risks if his enthusiasm became widely known, but also by the sometimes faulty messages conveyed by these intermediaries. After one session King was unhappy and suspicious when his father was presented as an "authoritarian businessman" and his mother was said to be absent. It was unthinkable that her spirit was not ever-present and he suspected from then on that some mediums were unreliable.[4]

Ultimately more satisfying were the immediate, direct, controllable signs and messages from above. In 1933 Dr. Arthur Doughty, the Dominion Archivist, introduced King to the popular parlour game of table-rapping: "It was an amazing evening. The first time I have seen table-rapping and having messages come thro' to me from father, mother, Max and Bella. There can be no shadow of doubt as to their genuineness."[5] Was Doughty amazed by King's instant elevation of the game into a serious pursuit? One wonders.

King was so taken with this direct line to the "other side" that for the next six years King and Joan often sat at the "little table," sending and receiving messages from departed loved ones, political mentors, and even figures from the distant past. In late 1934 Lorenzo di Medici, belying his rather sinister and bellicose reputation, sweetly counselled King to go to bed early and conserve his strength, for he would be elected prime minister the next year. More often the messages from his family, notably his mother, were full of encouragement, praise, or reassurance that King was on the right course in decision-making, speech-giving, etc.

Sometimes reassurance originated outside the family circle. One night after an important speech, Laurier came to the little table praising King's delivery. In another instance, with almost indecent haste, King rushed to the table after hearing of Lord Byng's death in 1935. After contacting Byng, King was overjoyed with Byng's message: "I have not forgotten...you advised to be granted dissolution. You were right and I was wrong" (9 June 1935). Communicating with the "other world" also had its hazards and upsets. In spring 1934 when King and Joan were at the little table, messages from an unidentified source spoke of "earthly" love. The messages were so personal and so direct King refused to write them down and quickly ended the session. King and Joan said they were very upset, but the next night they were right back at the table. Both were quite relieved when a message appeared, correcting the previous night's communication, noting it was in "praise of spiritual rather than physical love."[6]

By the end of the 1930s, King's enthusiasm for table-rapping had waned. The solace of the little table was not always available when King needed it. As well, King was now relying more and more on "signs from above." These heaven-sent signals could be anything from a bird landing on his windowsill, to a chance meeting with someone he had just thought about. Or he inferred heavenly guidance when he opened a magazine and saw a picture of a planned Kingsmere garden improvement, or when picking a Bible verse at random and finding in it a pertinent message for his past or future. He even studied theatre programs underlining cast and character names to form the first and last names of his departed friends and family — when successful, King knew it was yet another sign that he was being watched over.

By the 1940s, his favourite sign of heavenly approval was the aligning of his watch hands at auspicious times, either together, at right angles or in a straight line across the dial. After giving important speeches in the House of Commons he would often glance down at his watch to see if the hands were in an auspicious position.

No matter how different the signs, they had a common theme. King believed all were evidence of the constant monitoring by the spirits, if not by God himself, of his life and destiny: "As I looked out a little bird flew and settled on the sun-dial. I thought to myself, a little messenger from God, to shew me the significance of time, — one step at a time — the future unknown only the immediate present & the near approach being shewn. It was all very satisfying to my mind and comforting to my heart" (6 July 1934). At one time he attempted to formulate a theory to unite the signs: "All these are evidences of a 'something round about' which not only makes all things work together, but brings together all visible & invisible what is kindred to itself" (17 May 1935).

Everything became grist for his spiritual mill. He interpreted his shaving lather blobs every morning, searching for hidden messages. When the outline of his dead dog, Pat, appeared in the lather, he understood it to be a sign from Pat of his continued presence in King's life. Tea leaves were also "read" by King, who often called in one of the servants to confirm his interpretation: "...the third was distinctly (McLeod [the butler] saw it perfectly) a man in bed, head propped up on pillow..." (17 April 1934). Not surprisingly, the servants always verified King's reading. He also "read" clouds. One day when he saw clouds shaped like his beloved Pat, he immediately believed they were additional evidence of "invisible hands," manifestations of "continued presence, tenderness and love," of his family and other friendly spirits. Not surprisingly, King often interpreted his dreams, which he called

National Archives of Canada/PA 178407

Mrs. Etta Wreidt, a famous American medium, in the Moorside garden.

"visions." They became yet another conduit to his family and the "world beyond." One morning he dreamed he was walking with a group of people across moors and farmland:

> I was left to bring up the party with Miss Lily Snowball. I saw there was not room for her to get past a bit of the shore between the fence & the water without getting wet, so I swung her round to the farm land, that we might go thro' the fence, it seemed to me the scene instantly changed. I was in what looked like a court yard with rooms opening out on to it from the right and left. Seated on a horse in sort of royal fashion was a lady about to start out in style, horse in trappings etc. as I approached in front of her she said 'You are Mackenzie King are you not' — I said Yes, she then said she wanted to help me...dear mother had helped her, that she owed much to mother and wanted in turn to help me....Later the lady on the horse seemed to be serving us with afternoon tea in the other adjoining room...Joan was in a very jovial mood...& I had difficulty keeping her quiet....Water is always a sign of tribulation — a house... a good sign & one of shelter. The dream may have symbolized the beauty & shelter of Kingsmere as against the social life etc., but what I think the real significance of the dream to be, is that dear mother is letting me know that she is helping me, and is helping thro' others, that we are again closely in touch (10 June 1933).

During the last twenty years of his life, Mackenzie King was eagerly receptive to echoes from the past, to the reverberations of the spirit world. His rich fantasy life spilled over into and was reinforced by the Kingsmere gardens and landscape. Increasingly his landscape was animated by the presence of God, the spirits of the dearly departed, and the multitude of auspicious signs from Heaven. The estate reverberated with spiritual emanations understood only by King. Within his enchanted garden, the acquisition of statuary and the building of ruins were concrete expressions of King's other-worldly pre-occupations, physical projections of his fantasy life.

Statuary

King first attempted to acquire suitable statuary for his Kingsmere property in 1929, the year he moved into the Moorside cottage. He had noticed the disappearance of four stone statues ("...whether Grecian or Roman I cannot say, symbolical, I think, of the Seasons or of the Fine Arts, or representative of some of the deities of ancient mythology...")[7] from the Normal School grounds a few blocks from Parliament. He wrote as prime minister to the premier of Ontario who was also minister of Education, G.H. Ferguson, asking if he could buy the statues, "...to be placed here and there in the pine groves which are a feature"[8] of his Kingsmere estate. Undoubtedly King thought he could get them for a pittance for he pointedly wrote that he had heard the statues were stored, damaged, in the school's basement. The Premier replied that unfortunately the scantily clad ladies, actually representing the four seasons, were not for sale. It was true they had been damaged during a Halloween prank, but they were soon to be repaired and then, following the style of the day, repainted white and replaced on the school lawn. King wrote back rather cheekily that he was delighted that the four ladies would reappear and that "...their confinement during the past two or three years has not been due to any improper behaviour on their part."[9] King also noted that he "...had not a little fun out of giving the idea of their presence a place in my imagination..."[10]

By the late 1800s and early 1900s placing statuary in pine groves or elsewhere in fashionable North American gardens was not unusual. Statuary, it was believed, not only highlighted garden design, but its presence also created a tasteful conjunction of nature and art, while quietly asserting the refined sensibilities of its owners. Statuary also signalled permanence and echoed Old World values and fashion in the relatively new gardens of North America.

National Capital Commission

This ceramic donkey was only one of King's collection of garden ornaments including a rooster, rabbits, a deer and a gazing globe.

In Great Britain, meanwhile, interest in garden statuary was, in part, stimulated by a revived interest in the Italian garden. The design theories and practices resulting from this interest affected North American garden design as well as attitudes towards garden statuary. Edith Wharton, writing in *Italian Villas and Their Gardens*, noted in 1904 that "the cult of the Italian garden has spread from England to America, and there is a general feeling that by placing a marble bench here and a sun-dial there, Italian 'effects' may be achieved."[11] The Italian garden was further characterized by 20th century theorists as a garden of paving, stone vases, fountains, flowing water, stone balustrades, terraces, and above all, statuary.

North Americans had already defined emulating their cultural "standard bearers" as a social necessity. Not surprisingly, after seeing or reading of the new European garden fashion, North American gardens began to change. By the late 1800s and early 1900s, the clutter of Victorian gardens was cleared, and gardens of ample lawns and perennial beds became the fashion. The designs provided ample room for statuary.[12] In the years before World War I, garden statuary was collected on trips to Europe: "Many wealthy Americans, freshly returned from their Grand Tour of Italy, found an agreeable and tempting simile between the Italian merchant prince of the fifteenth century and the rising American industrialist of the nineteenth century."[13] Fountains were especially favoured by the wealthy. Also acquired were urns, vases, and statues of classical gods and goddesses, as well as the favoured Pan and assorted fauns. Perhaps this fashion was also influenced by one garden commentator's belief that all gardens whatever their size should have a "...presiding genius, its Nymph of flower-garden or grove or woodland or Naiad of the well...to give a personal interpretation to the forces of Nature."[14] However, Gertrude Jekyll, a famous arbitrator of British garden design, advised a restrained use of statuary, because an "undue liberality in their use calls up visions of the mason's yard."[15]

By the turn of the century some North American manufacturers provided less costly outdoor ornaments for the middle-class gardener who, aware of current garden design, desired to emulate fashionable gardens. The improvement of cast-iron production promoted the proliferation of mass-produced, more affordable fountain fixtures, cast iron dogs, deer, lions, rabbits, and similar objects. Cast iron rabbits were popular with gardeners on a limited budget. Mackenzie King, at Joan's suggestion, in 1933 bought six rabbits and a deer from an Ottawa hardware merchant named Bedard. Rustic-work baskets, stands and vases also continued to find a place in the less affluent garden.[16]

By the 1920s, when King began collecting his bits of statuary, Canadian sculptors were enjoying increased patronage, partly as a result of war memorial commissions. Sculptors also benefited from rising Canadian economic prosperity, and increased home-building which was accompanied by a greater interest in ornamenting interiors and grounds. Undoubtedly the majority of home owners continued to order mass-produced statuary and garden ornaments, but there were also discriminating art patrons who had the money to commission original works. Garden sculpture was included in this upsurge of patronage. Fountains were the most popular available garden sculptures. By the 1920s Canadians could choose from a variety of styles and materials. Indeed, fountains were noticed "springing up" everywhere from the home yard to the city park.[17] Fountain design was said to be "progressive," a favourite watchword of the early 1900s. One did not have to settle for a three-tiered basin or a bevy of toga-clad ladies, but could choose among children, fauns, nymphs and small animals: "A solemn or pedantic fountain figure will defeat its own end, for the mood of dripping or wind-tossed water needs a joyous, or, at least, a high-spirited motif. Pan should be the god of gardens, and he likes small, humorous water animals — frogs or tortoises..."[18]

The promotion of garden sculpture in Canada was championed by Laurie Dunington-Grubb, the noted landscape architect, who often incorporated commissioned pieces into her firm's landscape designs. She remarked in 1927 that abundant and good garden sculpture was difficult to obtain in Canada, therefore Canadian sculptors should be encouraged to create more of it. She especially promoted the work of Florence Wyle and Frances Loring,[19] prolific Canadian sculptors who also created garden pieces.

Sculpture and Garden Decoration at Moorside

Mackenzie King's admiration for statuary-filled gardens began in his twenties, stimulated by his first European trip. In 1900 he toured Italy visiting the usual churches and museums, as well as castle and villa gardens. When he began landscaping in earnest in the 1930s, he enjoyed creating what he called Italian "touches" on his estate. In 1934 when again visiting Italy, he wrote in his ever-present diary:

> The Russi has a café looking out on a beautiful garden rising up a high slope — bits of statuary walks — ivy — old statuary — stone seats & balustrade, all most effective — a small circular pool with a fountain figure in the

centre gave me a good idea for Kingsmere — in the hidden garden. I will try to make that into an Italian garden with Sylvia [sic], geraniums, foliage leaves, Aduratum [sic]...fountains etc. — I love the Italian gardens & villas (6 November 1934).

The effect of the vine-covered Moorside porch King found most pleasing and "quite Italian" (13 August 1934). When visitors commented on how "Italian" his composition of flower beds, statuary and balustrade looked he was, not surprisingly, delighted.

In 1935 King and the Pattesons took a short holiday on Long Island. Joan and King went on long walks around the Southampton estates, visiting private gardens, evaluating them, seeking translatable ideas for Kingsmere. Their favourites were Italian-inspired gardens: a "beautiful reproduction of Pompeian gardens, long cloisters of pergolas, ornaments in centre of enclosed lawns — the latter in series, some beautiful statuary" (25 April 1935). Another was praised for the "...many fine heads at top of large marble mounts — sundial beautifully placed..." (27 April 1935).

King amassed an eclectic collection of classically-inspired pieces (urns, sundials, vases and figures) which he intermixed with ceramic and cast iron animals, a gazing globe, gargoyles from Westminster, and bits and pieces of dismantled buildings. King frequently imbued even the smallest of these objects with associations to the past or special events or to the friends who gave them. King certainly would have agreed with a Canadian horticultural journalist who said that "nothing was so suggestive of garden magic as an ideal marble figure against a dark green background of trees or holly hedges."[20] As well, he would have also endorsed Francis Loring's opinion that sculpture was the heart of the garden and not just a finishing touch — that it raised a garden "out of the realm of the horticultural display."[21]

National Archives of Canada/PA 178401

King was quite impressed with the statuary collection in the gardens of The Orchard, a Southampton estate he visited on Long Island, New York.

One of his earliest acquisitions, a stone faun, was ordered from a Parisian firm, La Decoration Ancienne. The firm certified the figure to be over 150 years old. Although King felt the small figure "required a grove," King and Joan spent an enjoyable time finding just the right place for the faun in the lower garden. King was completely taken with the little statue: it was "...really marvellous — full of pain, sadness & equally a sort of slyness and downright wickedness, but mostly a noble nature arising out of the beast. The eyes are quite wonderful" (16 May 1935). Later on that evening after Joan had phoned to recount the day's delights and to say goodnight, King returned to the book he had been reading. When he saw that it had fallen open to a picture of a dancing faun, King exulted: "This is not 'coincidence' it is 'evidence'" (16 May 1935). The next day King reinforced his belief in the spirit world's continuing interest in him by asserting that the faun had "come" to help him "understand the mixture in man of idealism, brute instincts & sadness & joy etc." (17 May 1935).

King did not have statues of nymphs, driads, or classical gods in his collection, but he did have three "Pan" figures. Pan, a human figure with the legs, ears and horns of a goat, piping his merry songs, was a popular garden ornament, lending, it was thought, an Old World Arcadian flavour to the North American garden. King also amassed a collection of Italian and Venetian stone vases and urns ornamented with garlands of stone flowers.

His collection was usually placed along the balustrade railing and on top of the low stone walls of the Moorside verandah. This collection did not have an auspicious beginning. King's first attempt to have antique vases sent from a Venetian firm in 1928 ended in disaster. The vases arrived in Canada heavily damaged. Correspondence detailing cause and blame continued for two years, only to end when the firm of Candiani and Sommer went out of business. King, however, over the years managed to collect others. His acquisitiveness prompted him to shamelessly pursue two stone vases the Lauriers' nephew, within the terms of Lady Laurier's will, had taken from the Laurier House steps. Because King thought the vases completed "its appearance," he convinced himself they should never have been removed from the front steps, and should have been left as a "memorial." He phoned, then wrote Robert Laurier, offering to pay for the vases if he would consider selling them. In a never ending sentence, King, rather unfeelingly, told Robert:

> It is just possible, however, that some garden ornament of a different size or shape could be substituted for them in the location in which they now are, which might be even more suitable than they themselves may be thus located, while, on the other hand, it is certain that nothing could be found which would be more suitable for the front of Laurier House than the vases which were there in Sir Wilfrid's and Lady Laurier's day, and which were always a feature of the front entrance of the house.[22]

Robert Laurier graciously replied that he would be delighted to give them to King as "a token of my admiration and our friendly sentiments."[23]

Over the next ten years King added pieces of varying sentiment and association. He continued to collect sun dials and bird baths. In 1934 he bought a stone bird bath bowl decorated with rose garlands and a goat head from the same Parisian company where he had bought the stone faun. At one time King had at least two sundials and perhaps five bird baths — two of them sandstone, another blue ceramic. One sundial, bought in Toronto on Centenary Day, came from a monastery. It was appropriately ornamented with a carving of a monk holding a bell. King with typical hyperbole noted: "...the dial symbolical of Time — the bell of eternity — the glad tidings from the high heavens" (6 April 1934). All these pieces were among the first objects to be set out on the grounds each spring.

King scattered bird baths around the Moorside, Shady Hill and Farm grounds. One was placed in the centre of the quadrant garden at Moorside. A small statue, perhaps a pint-sized Pan, was placed in the centre of the bowl — a common combination. In the late 1930s at Joan's suggestion, King erected a bird bath within the Abbey ruin as a memorial to Mother's Day. He felt it symbolized Kingsmere as a sanctuary for himself and for the birds. After it was permanently placed, King was thrilled to see a little bird sitting on the entrance to the ruins "as if to greet me and thank me for the bird bath — who will say it was not a divine messenger greeting me" (18 July 1939). In 1941, King placed a bird bath on the very spot he had laid Pat, his beloved first dog, after the trauma of his death. This bird bath, visible from the Farm house window, reminded King of Pat's "continued guidance by the example of his life and fidelity" (19 April 1942).

Other people helped King's quest for interesting garden ornaments. Joan and Godfroy's son was European manager of the Canadian Pacific Railway Company in London. During his years there, Jack Patteson was instrumental in securing and shipping many architectural stones to King. While checking, at King's request, the salvage yard at Westminster Hall for appropriate stones and statues, he discovered four gargoyles which had been taken from Big Ben. Jack described them as a "type of prehistoric dog, and are about the size of a very much doubled up fox terrier...They have nasty faces, and nasty tongues, and sell for 2 guineas each."[24] Unfortunately by the time King wrote that he would be delighted to secure them, the gargoyles were gone.

King's disappointment encouraged Jack and his wife, Molly, to hunt for more. Success did not come until the following year when they found another pair taken from Big Ben: "They are not exactly the same, but as they are both equally ugly I thought they would prove very acceptable!"[25] After opening the crate, King mused: "This is a great bringing together of the old world & the new. The Pagan & the Christian" (23 August 1937). King at first placed the small gargoyles on the Moorside steps to "guard" the cottage. Within two weeks he moved them to the base of one of his ruins (called the Arc de Triomphe) noting that they had been "ill omens" in the house: "...symbolical of the evil spirit that was here while they were at the door, now they are surmounted by the Arc de Triomphe & will be kept in their place at its base — a symbol of necessity of passing through evil to the highest good" (2 September 1937).

The evil spirit infecting Moorside had a domestic, as well as an international, aspect. A "sordid story," according to the abstemious King, had been revealed about his butler McLeod. King learned that not only had he been drinking at Kingsmere in the company of one of the Mounted Police security guards while King was away, but McLeod had also narrowly escaped arrest in Ottawa for public drunkenness. King, greatly disheartened by McLeod's behaviour, wanted to save him from ruin. His solution was to strongly lecture McLeod and his wife, who, under King's questioning, admitted she had occasionally joined her husband for a drink. In addition to his household troubles, King was growing increasingly worried about world events — Japan and China were at war and Hitler and Mussolini were meeting that same week. King greatly feared he was witnessing the coming of another world war.

The crate sent from the London salvage yard yielded even more treasures. King's architect, J.A. Ewart, who helped design the Abbey ruin, whetted King's appetite for found objects. In spring 1936 Ewart sent King a clipping from *Country Life*, explaining that damaged gargoyles and other carvings taken from the old Westminster Parliament buildings, were often cleaned and sold to the general public. "How about a small piece for Kingsmere," Ewart wrote.[26] In the fall, when King was in London, he hastened to the fabled salvage yard and bought two carvings — one of which was the arms of the speaker of the House of Commons. The shipment, overseen by Jack Patteson, did not reach Kingsmere until 1937. In the crates were the carvings, two gargoyles found by Jack and two stone angels. It is not clear if Jack or another well-wisher found the angels.

Unpacking the crate, King was absolutely astounded when he uncovered the angels: "As I stood beside it, & removed the wool...from the face, & saw the beauty of the face and the curls, I was startled for a moment, the resemblance was so like that of dear mother. It was as if she were lying there quietly resting" (21 August 1937). Before this revelation King thought he would use the angels as garden ornaments. Now he could not bear the thought of them buffeted by the forces of nature. No mortal, however, would place them, God would choose the site. Not surprisingly their final resting place was soon revealed:

> ...as I walked in the front door and looked at the large bench in the small hall beyond I said there is the place for them on either side of this seat — the mercy seat came into my mind & with its Grace — God's Grace — Mother's power — God's mercy & His Grace...that seat is carved with figures symbolical of celestial harmonies...It will be a daily inspiration to see these figures there — a note to the house — the guardian angels (21 August 1937).

King also actively searched for garden ornaments, especially for those which "spoke" to him. One of his more protracted quests was his search for the original street lights he had loved as a child in Berlin [now Kitchener], Ontario. King said it had always been his dream to light the path from his cottage "by the light that guided me in childhood's days" (19 July 1932). He obviously had ample time on his hands during his years in opposition, for the amount of effort and time he invested in securing them was significant.

Decorative lanterns were a feature in many gardens of note. Garden commentators pleaded that the home landscaper harmonize the style of lights to the house and landscape design. Lamps were not only picturesque elements on the landscape, but also useful adjuncts to the design, especially when they illuminated a choice piece of statuary or a beautiful shrub.

In 1924 King had already received "six rustic lanterns" compliments of the Hotel Department of the Canadian National Railway. However, these once-prized lanterns were instantly devalued in King's eyes six years later when he heard from his friend, Peter Sims, that the coal oil street lamps of their youth had been replaced and the old ones were to be sold. Nostalgically King remembered the old lamplighter "who went his rounds ere the close of day,"[27] lighting the oil lamps inside their four-sided glass enclosures. Unfortunately Sims could not find any, but King did not give up. In another attempt to secure the lamps, King wrote two years later in 1932 to the mayor of Kitchener, Mortimer Bezeau, noting, "What I want is the genuine article to which I can point and say it came from my own home town, and which, as long as life itself continues, will evoke many cherished memories."[28] Then King added a note of subtle, sentimental flattery: "I need scarcely say that the association of your own term of office with the acquisition of this souvenir of childhood days would be a feature of added interest and satisfaction to myself."[29]

Well, this certainly was an incentive. Letters between the participants flew thick and furious detailing the progress of the hunt, history of the lamps, and stories about the lamplighter. News of the project was even reported in the newspapers. King thrilled to the stories. He wrote Bezeau he would delightedly tell them to all his estate visitors. Within six weeks the mayor had found two lamps, which a local hardware merchant refurbished free of charge. The mayor then wrote on how everyone who was approached eagerly supplied labour and information.

King, determined to be historically accurate, rejected the offer of iron support posts. The hardware merchant found someone to draw up a sketch and the specifications to replicate the original wooden support posts and the ladder used by the lamplighter to reach the wicks. An Ottawa artisan used the sketches to duplicate the objects. Finally the lamps were installed, one at the entrance gate to Kingswood and the other in the centre of his grounds at Moorside, in time to light the way of King's Imperial Conference guests that summer. King said they brought "their note of joy to my heart each time that I pass them by."[30]

National Archives of Canada/PA 126202

King thought this Canadian ship's bell looked like the one which hung in a Mount Sinai monastery.

Not quite as sentimentally exciting but quite as thrilling in its own way, was his acquisition of a ship's bell in 1934. When Godfroy saw the bell in Sachs Brothers Ottawa salvage yard, he hastened to tell King. After a visit to the yard, King thought he would buy the 100 pound brass bell. Through a series of amazing coincidences that same day, King's moderate acquisitiveness was transformed into a spiritual quest. On opening a newly-arrived issue of the *Illustrated London News*, he saw a short article on the British Museum's recent acquisition of the Codex Sinaiticus, a fourth century Greek manuscript of the Bible. The article was illustrated by photographs of St. Catharine's monastery where the Codex was discovered in a waste-bin, waiting to be burned. King excitedly noticed a bell hanging from the monastery wall the exact shape of the one he was thinking of buying. He was further intoxicated when he read that the monastery was at the foot of the mount in Sinai where Moses was said to have received the Ten Commandments. King reeled with the significance of it all. King immediately felt a great urgency to save the bell at all costs because of its symbolic representation of sacred themes and associations. His bell was transformed into the monastery's bell, allying it with one of Christendom's most sacred manuscripts. King's rescue of the bell from a Jewish merchant's waste yard, he felt, paralleled the Codex's history — saved from the waste-bin, and sold by the godless Soviet government to the British.

Later on that day as King sorted his mail, he rather anti-climatically discovered less resonant, but still confirmatory evidence of the sacredness of the bell: a letter from Egypt, a postcard with a picture of a monastery to which Lady Laurier had given money, and a card from Jerusalem: "All these associations indicate the directing power behind all this is in the highest heaven..." (3 April 1934). A final note was struck late that night when King realized it was also the anniversary of his sister Bella's death.

Soon after King bought the bell, he had it engraved with the inscription, "Spes tutissima Caelis" which could be translated "The most secure hope is in reaching Heaven." He thought he would hang it in a building he planned to build at Kingsmere in memory of his revered grandfather, William Lyon Mackenzie. This plan assumed greater significance and force a few days later when he dreamed of a bell in a ruin which looked like his grandfather's Queenston printing office. However, his grandfather's memorial was never built; instead King hung the bell, at Joan's suggestion, at the far end of the Moorside porch pergola. Soon after he had a British admiral, who had come to dinner, ring "eight bells with his own hand." Always the Anglophile, King happily noted in his diary that "it was most delightful to have it performed by a British Admiral..." (18 August 1934).

By the end of the 1930s King had quite a "little collection," as he termed it, of various carvings and stones. In addition to the fauns, Pan, angels, and lanterns, King also owned two small "Venetian" lions which guarded the entrance to the Moorside porch, a lead boot scraper, ornamented with reclining dog-like lions, a "Greek" figure placed near the rustic gate at the entrance to the Hidden Garden, and various carved stones from the remains of the Centre Block on Parliament Hill which burned down in 1916. He also collected ornaments of a less exalted nature: lead rabbits, a lead deer, a gazing globe, a ceramic coq and a ceramic donkey. King used the donkey to play gentle jokes on visitors to the estate. "If you're very careful and very quiet, you're going to see a donkey,"[31] King would caution his victim. His nephew's wife remembered her first Moorside walk with King: "He said, 'Oh, there's that little boy with his donkey. He comes there every morning.' And I bit properly. And he never let me forget it."[32]

Ruin-Making, Memorials and the Picturesque

Building his ruins, however, was no laughing matter. Although foreign to contemporary Canadian landscape design, artificial ruins were perfect vehicles for King to express his various preoccupations. In one neat package King could combine his romanticism, love of antiquity, psychical interests, and his religiosity. Building ruins was also motivated by his enjoyment in enhancing his landscape with picturesque elements, his love of all things British and his concern with his legacy, his memorial to the nation.

In his drive to establish himself, to prove his *bona fides*, to exalt his past, King collected memorabilia, family papers, objects of historical significance and sentimental pieces such as the gold-headed cane presented to him by the Liberal Women of Vancouver. By owning and displaying such objects King established a strong tangible connection with the past, a continuity between the past and the present. For example, visitors to Laurier House were often shown a table which once belonged to Matthew Arnold, one of King's favourite poets, or the poster offering £1,000 reward for the capture of his grandfather.[33] His houses were full of knick-knacks, political souvenirs, old furniture, family portraits, and paintings of a distinctly 18th century style.

On his European trips, in between political meetings and other duties, King revelled in the past by visiting churches and museums. In November 1934, for example, he took a true holiday, indulging his veneration of the European past. While visiting Rome, Florence, and Naples he visited every antiquity possible. He also shopped for chair coverings, draperies, and commissioned marble busts of his mother and father from the sculptor, Guisppe Guastalla. With an eye firmly on posterity, he also commissioned a bust of himself: "...were I to die something of the kind might some day be attempted & that if there were a good portrait of myself, I would be grateful — I disliked leaving it to chance in the future..." (5 November 1934). However, he decided to "hide it away for awhile," keep it secret. Other souvenirs of his trip included pieces of purloined antiquity. His guide through the Catacombs of St. Callistus obtained two "lamps" from the tomb of St. Cecilia. Another guide, at King's suggestion, pried up some pieces of pavement from the ruins of Pompeii.

The trip was a success, King felt he had truly communed with the spirit of antiquity. When he returned to Canada, he had a session at the "little table" with Joan. He was thrilled to speak to Leonardo di Vinci and Lorenzo di Medici. Their interest, he wrote, was a prevailing influence in his life. He read of Michel-

E.H. Hodge/National Archives of Canada/PA 178402

The ruin-like printing office at Queenston, Ontario, where King's grandfather, William Lyon Mackenzie, once worked.

angelo that night: "But in nature, as in Art and as in love, it was God for whom he was seeking and to whom he daily drew nearer...Oh it is to this school that my soul longs to belong, to dwell in such a spiritual home as these men who true greatness belonged to" (25 November 1934).

King viewed the past (at least his romanticized, rather sanitized version) as sacred, worthy of study and preservation. As well, delving into his own past gave him a sense of rootedness. Collecting a stone from an English ruin or visiting a Scottish village connected King's North American self with the antiquity of Europe. This sense of continuity not only enhanced his feelings of self-worth, but also fulfilled his need to feel loved, to be comforted and to not be alone. As well, King reached out to connect the past to the present through his spiritualistic encounters. The past lived in the present when King talked to his mother at the "little table," or when he communicated with his grandfather's spirit while rereading family letters.

To enhance these connections, King thought of building memorials to family members. Soon these thoughts extended to his own memorial — he began viewing his estate as his legacy, a memorial for future generations to remember him by. However, before he seriously began planning his own legacy, King had a trial run creating a memorial. Motivated by his increasing interest in Kingsmere area history, King decided something was needed on the summit of King Mountain to mark the site of the Geodetic Survey of Canada's first triangulation station. This surveying system, spanning the entire country, was established by W.F. King, the Director of the Geodetic Survey, but no relation to Mackenzie King. Rather aptly named, the King Eccentric Station, was marked only by a copper bolt. To convince the National Parks Historic Sites Branch of the need for a memorial, Mackenzie King corresponded with the Branch by telephone and letter during 1930. King then greatly expanded the Branch's intentions by negotiating successfully for a stone cairn on the site. King, who had final word on the design, wrote the Parks commissioner, J.B. Harkin, that the cairn should be set back far enough on the rock face for proper visitor circulation.[34] King further suggested that the cairn should be ornamented with a bronze commemorative plaque and a wall sun dial: "If this could be done...you would have a monument worth while."[35]

Four years later King planned a more ambitious memorial. Unlike the cairn, it was never built, but it was a prelude to King's future architectural projects. In April 1934 King heard that his grandfather Mackenzie's house in Toronto was to be demolished. King did not intend to write his grandfather's biography nor compose a suitable historic plaque to him; rather he decided to build a memorial building at Kingsmere. King thought this would give him the opportunity to memorialize the past in an evocative form. He constantly felt Mackenzie's legacy of political activism and social reform on his shoulders, firmly placed there by his mother and his overweening ambition. Only he himself remained, he thought, to keep the past alive and to honour it. However, this building in the form of a monastery or ruin, King could not quite decide, was never built.

A year earlier, in 1933, King had already embarked on a romantic, sentimental project. He decided a forge was needed at Moorside — perhaps due to the summer's reading of Wordsworth's poetry and biography, or his boredom in opposition. This project was part of King's dream of self-sufficiency on one level (it was begun during King's greenhouse research), and, on another level, was part of his landscaping ideals. He also planned a woodshed and carpenter's shop nearby. The forge, originally planned as a simple structure, was greatly expanded by King's enthusiasm to create an actual blacksmith's forge. He visited a local one gathering authentic details and memorizing the layout. He bought a used forge, anvil and other equipment for $25. King, caught up in his crescendo of building, expanded the forge to include a dovecote (a romantic, Victorian structure), and a carpenter shop. Characteristically he altered the plan after the workmen began building. The carpenter shop was transformed into a gardener's tool house and potting shed and the carpenter's shop was moved to another site.

The dovecote by Victorian times had lost its utilitarian character, for pigeons were no longer a staple meat source. Instead it had become a sentimental, picturesque object. In Scotland, home of his ancestors as King enjoyed noting, the dovecote was "almost the badge of a gentleman." The young pigeons were regarded as a food delicacy.[36] King installed four pigeons (one of which he thought looked like the one that appeared at Noah's arc) in the dovecote. Less than a month later they had all disappeared — eaten by hawks and owls. King grieved for "the little creatures" especially the one that reminded him of his sister Bella.

Two weeks later King invited a local blacksmith to inaugurate the forge. King had a photograph taken — the blacksmith forging a horseshoe, and King briefly working on the anvil. King, thrilled with the realization of his planning, became nearly incomprehensible when he strained to explain what it all meant:

> The little carpenter shop as well — gave one a thought of the scene at Nazareth — having the pidgeons [sic] (doves) about as well is all a part of what unconsciously has been effected in a symbolical way. The incinerator is at hand, to cast into the ovens that which encumbereth the earth, and ought to be destroyed (9 October 1933).

The initial excitement and novelty of the forge, unlike his attachments to other projects, soon wore off. In 1938 King admitted in a letter to J.A. Ruddick that he had only been in the forge once in the last two years.

Another element, perhaps one more complementary to the Canadian setting, was added to the estate in 1934. King was given a tepee by a western political admirer. After it was set up, King was amazed to see how large it was. When Joan and he entered the tepee, King said to Pat, his dog, "...Look at Big Chief and squaw." And then that night he mused in his diary that "the significance of this will be seen later" (16 July 1934).

Mackenzie King's Ruins

King's landscaping, statuary, and ruins were the props on his Kingsmere stage set. King actively created the scenery he needed to enhance his fantasies and complement his activities as a country squire. Even as a passive observer, King enjoyed the spontaneous "pictures" on his landscape, the frozen tableaus of country life, activities divorced from his political life. Unselfconsciously he wrote after watching the gathering of his hay:

> A neighbouring farmer was gathering the hay which has recently been mown. It was a beautiful sight to see the hay wagon with the farmer's children helping in the loading of the hay, one of the boys holding a dog with a rope. It would be difficult to describe the loveliness of this rural scene on one's own grounds. Nothing gives me quite the same pleasure as these glimpses of rural life particularly where they are associated with one's own gardening (11 July 1945).

Ruins perfectly complemented King's desire to create pictures on the landscape. However, building ruins was not unique

National Archives of Canada/PA 124441

The teepee on a Moorside field.

to him, not an isolated product of his over-active imagination. In 18th century England these romantic, fantastic additions to the landscape were quite fashionable, and were a major component of the Picturesque Landscape Style. Garden design was to be based on the observation of nature, often raw, wild nature, and the study of painting. The ideal Picturesque garden should resemble a landscape painting, especially those of 17th century artists Claude Lorrain, Gaspard Poussin, or Salvador Rosa. These artists were praised in 18th century Britain for their depictions of rural classical landscapes, an idealized antiquity characterized by untouched nature, cascading waterfalls, wild ravines, crags, grottos, hills, and ruined temples, suffused by an atmosphere of an Arcadian peace and innocence of the pre-industrial past. Although by the 19th century the Picturesque style was on the wane, ruins still exerted a fascination for garden designers.

Building a ruin necessitated "money and security and peace"[37] all of which King had in abundance by the mid-thirties. Blessed with such a volatile imagination and, at times, intense emotionalism, King was naturally attracted to ruins — overwhelmingly romantic symbols of the past. Ruins, artificial or real, were emblems of decay, reminders of mortality and the transcendence of Nature. As Barbara Jones, a keen observer of follies and ruins, noted "more mood and emotion are built into follies than into any other kind of architecture...."[38]

Although King patriotically praised the Canadianness of the Gatineau Hills, his love of things British dominated his landscape improvements and designs. It is not surprising that his study — often first hand — of British estates, fueled King's ambition to build ruins. King sought inspiration in such British estates as Abbotsford, which Sir Walter Scott had landscaped according to Picturesque principles. King confessed that all during the summer of 1932 he had "a desire to make Kingsmere like Abbotsford."

In early 1935 after the Mackenzie house fiasco, King tried once again to find "material" for ruins. When Joan mentioned that Godfroy's father's home near Woodstock, Ontario had been sold, he was interested to also hear that the new owners might be willing to sell the stone entrance posts and gates. Godfroy's father had salvaged them from a building demolished on Toronto's University Avenue. The octagonal carved pillars, five feet high (1 1/2 m), were surmounted by wrought iron posts from which lanterns were hung. King wrote to the owner, stretching the truth a bit, by noting that Godfroy was the object of the sale: "...my friend Mr. Godfroy Patteson would greatly welcome seeing the posts put up somewhere on the grounds, which we share more or less in common."[39] King thought he had done everything possible to secure them. After sending many, many letters, he received confirmation from the owner that he could purchase the gate and posts for $50. Unfortunately the story was carried in the newspapers, which upset King. However, he persevered and tried to find someone to remove and deliver the posts. After a stone contractor submitted a substantial estimate for their removal and delivery to Kingsmere, King stopped all negotiations while he searched for a cheaper estimate. He stalled too long and another collector, no doubt attracted by the press notices, agreed to all costs and won the pillars.

National Archives of Canada/PA 136610

Ruins, such as the one at William Gladstone's Hawarden, were fashionable on the English estate in the 18th and early 19th centuries.

A month later, his desire to build a ruin, strengthened by his thwarted plans for a Mackenzie memorial and the Woodstock pillars, was finally fulfilled. Driving along Daly Avenue in Sandy Hill, a prestigious area of Ottawa, King was in a receptive frame of mind when he suddenly came upon a stone house being demolished. His romanticism was immediately aroused by the sight of a beautiful, now free-standing, bay window. King rhapsodized that it looked like "the front of some old great Temple." If he "...could secure it at a fair price," King thought it would make a wonderful ruin on a Kingsmere hilltop (8 May 1935).

After a feverish night of vivid fantasizing, he transformed the bay window into the Acropolis. He now determined to have it whatever the cost. Luckily the contractor, Wolf Shenkman, submitted a low quote: $50 for the stone and $100 for transport to Kingsmere and $100 to re-erect it. King was delighted for he had prepared himself for a much higher estimate. He reasoned that the costs of the materials and the architect's specifications for a comparable, original structure, as beautiful and inspiring as the window, would be at least $1,000. After the decision had been made and the estimate accepted, King wrote Peter Sims. Not mentioning his fantasy of Grecian temples, he told Sims that the project would relieve his mind of "...political anxieties and

King often enjoyed visiting the Kingsmere hermit, Miles Barnes.

strain, and to get it objectively interested in something that stimulates the imagination in a wholesome way."[40]

Stimulated he certainly was. It was an event-filled week when the stone, numbered for easy reassembly, was delivered to Kingsmere. Not only had King acquired his heart's desire, he had also planted a thousand trees acquired from the Quebec government, and purchased several new garden ornaments. King and Joan wandered the Moorside grounds, seeking just the right spot for the window. Traditionally ruins were strategically sited on a hilltop, in a secluded valley, or on a path turning. This placing was to surprise the garden visitor, pleasantly shocking them into contemplation of the ruin and its symbolism.

King, guided by tradition, finally chose a high hill overlooking a valley, in this case facing King Mountain. The next morning his delight was unbounded, he had received a "sign" confirming his choice of site in his daily Bible reading: "The words that caught my eye at the outset were 'the bay that looketh southward' — It has been my purpose to have the bay window being put up to face exactly south...to the top of the mountain that lieth before the valley of Hinnom westward' — King's mountain so lies, 'from the top of the hill unto the fountain.' I have thought of a fountain in the lower garden..." (15 May 1935). The verse ended on a high note ("this is the inheritance") which King interpreted as referring to his dear mother's presence as well as the presence of God.

Every detail of construction inspired and excited King — an interest which occasionally gave the contractor, Alex Garvock, and his men headaches. First King fussed over placement. Then when the foundation was nearly finished, King decided that an additional six inches would give "...a better appearance from front, and making possible addition to the sides later on...also by raising earth inside the 'look out' can be made the most convenient height" (19 May 1935). A long Sunday afternoon phone call, however, was needed to convince the contractor. When more money was promised, Garvock finally agreed, warning King that each additional inch added to the trouble and danger of hoisting the heavy top stones.

But all went well, no accidents marred the completion of the folly. As the last stone was hoisted into place, Joan urged King to act on his deep desire to complete the ruin, to create a building.

National Archives of Canada/PA 9020

The original Daly Avenue house with its bay window intact.

King was certainly tempted. A stone house at Kingsmere, incorporating a library and music room where he could write books in the winter, he thought would be perfect (13 March 1932). Three years later, however, King told Joan he did not dare "to entertain it for the present."

God, however, was working in mysterious ways, for that very afternoon Mr. and Mrs. Shenkman appeared unannounced at Kingsmere. They delighted King by saying they were overwhelmed by the beauty of the window on the hilltop. Then Shenkman spontaneously suggested that the window should be completed. He offered all the stone salvaged from the Sandy Hill house which King would need to construct a building, as well as the wooden front door, the best carved stones for steps, and lumber — all free of charge. Now it was King's turn to be overwhelmed. As soon as the Shenkmans left, King's amazement over his great fortune was soon replaced by an intense excitement. King and Joan feverishly began planning, drawing up plans and consulting books on mythology and architecture for inspiration. By the end of the day, King decided he would erect "...something in the nature of a chapel or library, or hall, or all combined, which could be made an art room, with piano moved there, bits of statuary, a vaulted ceiling, etc." (24 May 1935).

That night he excitedly tossed and turned, anticipating the marvels to come. Early the next morning ("...to lose no time") he rang up the contractor to tell him of the great change of plans. The contractor wisely advised King to use the services of an architect, recommending, J. Albert Ewart [1872-1964]. King called him at once, and Ewart came to Kingsmere that very afternoon.

Ewart designed high schools, churches, libraries and homes, as well as some of Ottawa's finest buildings such as the Ottawa Masonic Temple, Ottawa Civic Hospital, and the Protestant Children's Village. Probably appointed by King, he was a member of the Federal District Commission and, later, a member of the National Planning Committee which advised Jacques Gréber on the plan for the national capital. One wonders, however, if during his long practice, he was quite prepared for the Leader of the opposition's grand conception for a lonely hill in the Gatineaus.

King certainly thought Ewart was a kindred soul, perhaps due to his special interest in church architecture. King remarked that he had "caught the vision at once." They staked out the building according to King's specifications: fireplace, long windows on each side, and vaulted ceiling ("not steep incline but like leaves of a book pressed open"). Then King told Ewart what he really wanted was a "combination of the Parthenon at Athens — a cathedral or Abbey (Westminster) — Westminster Hall..." (25 May 1935). To further illustrate his heart's desire, King showed Ewart pictures of the interior of Westminster Hall: "its notes are what I would hold to." King did not record Ewart's reaction.

Ewart's reply probably would not have mattered, King was completely enthralled by the idea. His imagination was in a joyful turmoil, bolstered perhaps by his conviction that he was being guided in his decisions by the remote past: "There is an association in my life with Prince Charlie & that period which I must yet discover & which may explain much — some Jacobean blood — as well as Cromwellian spirit — these forces are all exerting their influence I am sure" (25 May 1935). That night, further stimulating an already overworked imagination, King browsed through "English Homes Vol. III — Period late Tudor & early Stuart 1558-1649....Also a volume on American Homes & Houses of Stone & Bullfinch's Mythology — also life of Michael Angelo & the 'glory that was Greece'" (25 May 1935). He joyfully noted that the books and the day's events gave him an incomparable interest, stimulating "a desire to know the best of the past — their civilization, and to carry on their influence to the present" (25 May 1935).

In the small hours of the night, King finally sobered up, the day's euphoria vanished, replaced by his habitual financial nervousness. Ewart's estimate of $2,000 to construct the hybrid building had finally penetrated. King now decided it was more relevant economically to invest the money in renovations of the farm house. His decision not to build a miniature Westminster Abbey was also political. He feared that Canadians would be extremely critical and suspicious of such an extravagance during those hard economic times. Then he consoled himself: "...the public mind can be prepared for its completion later on" (26 May 1935).

Instead of a building, King now planned a smaller, less ambitious, construction — he just could not forgo the free stone. Near the bay window he designed a corner wall broken by a doorway and window, and sited to appear as if it and the bay window were fragments of the same building. King's efforts to site the wall perfectly were continually frustrated. Finally King climbed an opposite hill to get another viewpoint. His frustration immediately vanished, for he could now see exactly where the wall should be placed. He later joyfully wrote that he had prevented a fatal error of placement. After construction began, King closely supervised every phase. He felt he was continually improving the ideas of the architect and the contractor. He found this work "quite entrancing," and often explained his vision of the structure to them. For example he told the work crew how to make the construction more ruin-like: "...by having walls extended 6 feet at bottom on either side of 'porch' and also by adding a ragged edge, instead of a straight course...I was able too by the distant door view, and for the window view...to get a 'battlement' effect on the side of the porch" (30 May 1935).

Until the wall was finished, King could not shake an uneasiness that he had cluttered up the site. However, once completed he pronounced it perfect. He immediately instructed the gardener to plant vines, traditional on ruins, along the new wall to soften and obscure the addition. He felt this planting further enhanced the window, his "Greek temple on a hill." King, proud of his achievement, was especially pleased with the beautiful vistas he had created: "Nothing could be more exquisite than the pictures that are framed by the doorway and the window of the landscape beyond, and, particularly, of individuals approaching either side of the open spaces. My mind was immensely relieved in seeing the realization of what I had hoped for as nearly as possible to what I had conceived" (11 June 1935). Inspired he named the view from the bay window L'Infini. King owned a small reproduction of a similarly named European scene, resembling the view from "the Temple" of encircling, distant hills and valley. He had the original copied and gave it as a special gift only to close friends.

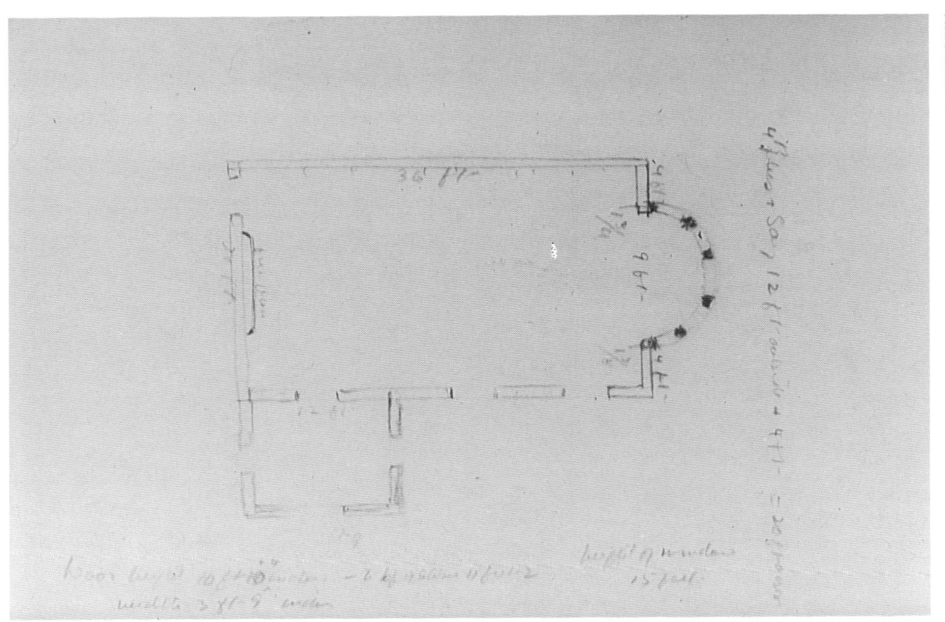

National Archives of Canada/C 136611

King's drawing of his conception of his ruin: a combination of the Parthenon and Westminster Hall.

Soon after completing the ruin, King received a sign that, with the addition of a few stones, this Moorside hilltop had become sacred ground. One morning he read a Bible verse confirming the rightness of his ruin building. King, deeply moved, lay face down on the hill near the bay window, fervently affirming that it was "...truly holy ground & prayed with my heart as my heart's prayer that God's will might be done on earth as it is in Heaven" (2 June 1935). Later King and Joan read Thomas Gray's "Elegy Written in a Country Church-Yard" to inaugurate the ruin. They thrilled to the lines: "Save that from yonder ivy-mantled tower/The moping owl does to the moon complain..." "The whole setting," King noted in his diary, "added immensely to the feeling of the poem" (11 June 1935). His thoughts then turned to the pictures of the famous British ruins, Melrose Abbey and Tintern Abbey, his father had hung in his student quarters and had later passed onto King. Instantly he was inspired to name his ruins "The Abbey," a name of great resonance: "The Abbey brings in the religious note, as well as that of a place of residence. It speaks of an order of things which was prevalent in the Middle Ages, and which gave a distinctive note to the life and architecture of Britain, as well as of Europe" (12 June 1935).

That evening after his hillside inspiration, King was delighted to receive further confirmation of the ruin's significance. When

The ruins in 1946.

ground...[is] increasingly the most sacred spot in the whole of the Kingsmere area" (12 June 1935).

This belief was soon confirmed by an outsider. When Canon Heeney, a clergyman King respected, visited the estate, he was taken on a tour to see the grounds. The Canon proclaimed, in a vocabulary dear to King's heart, that the ruins had a "redemptive quality." He elaborated: The ruin seemed to "redeem the whole landscape round about and gave it new meaning and significance" (29 June 1935). To reinforce this heightened significance, King took Joan out to the ruin and, in a little ceremony, made her swear in the moonlight that they "...must keep it always a very sacred place — let no word or thought enter there which was not the holiest and best" (5 July 1935).

he opened a new book, *Homes and Gardens,* at random, he was amazed that the first picture he saw was a building with the same battlement design as his ruin. Later when Joan opened the same book, she immediately saw a picture of a window similar to the one King had preserved. Then after turning to a picture of a ruined temple dedicated to the goddess Diana at Ephesus, an ancient Greek city, Joan pointed out how similar it was to King's ruin. If these coincidences were not enough, King received a copy of the annual report of the Chapel of the Order of St. Michael and St. George. This King treated with great significance — it was, he proclaimed, the deciding factor in naming the ruin: "It should be regarded as one of a chapel, and really as affording, under the temple of Heaven, the outline of a chapel. That bit of

By the next spring King was prime minister once again and embroiled in the pressures and activities of the office. Despite the increased demands on his time, his enthusiasm for building ruins was quickly rekindled when he heard that the British North American Bank Note Company building in downtown Ottawa was being torn down. As soon as he saw the building, King was immediately entranced by the entrance pillars — "a crime not to salvage it." King quickly phoned Ewart and then Cummings, an Ottawa contractor, to see if the pillars could be secured and re-erected at Kingsmere as a ruin. King was so excited he was not even annoyed when Ewart corrected his identification of the entrance columns as Corinthian, when they were Ionic.

His decision was further strengthened after returning to Laurier House from a stormy interview with Governor General

Tweedsmuir. King had told Tweedsmuir, whom he preferred to call John Buchan, that he wanted to be released from the obligation to wear his Commander of the Order of St. Michael and St. George (CMG) and his King's Jubilee medal. He asked Buchan to obtain the King's permission, for he felt it was not dignified for the prime minister to be dressed in "baubles." He also told the Govenor General that the government would no longer approve the British crown bestowing honours or knighthoods on Canadians. Buchan said he was amazed that King thought he could run a successful civil service without the promise of honours. Obviously King had been storing up many grievances, he then angrily denounced Buchan's recent speech in praise of Byng without any reference to King ("...a slap and a way to bring up old controversies" 25 March 1936). Finally King told Buchan he was "deeply hurt" by his attitude towards King's eager friendship. He had wanted Buchan to spend happy days with him roaming Kingsmere — "...but now...I did not care if I ever saw it again — that the whole joy of what I had in mind was gone" (25 March 1936).

In this unsettled frame of mind King returned to Laurier House and sought the consolation of God's blessing for all that had happened at Rideau Hall. He did not have long to wait. He soon recorded he had been spiritually "touched," the justness of his cause confirmed: "I felt a release from an artificial thraldom ...certain that I am now experiencing what I did about this time a year ago, a marvellous evidence of a great Divine guidance and purpose." Then he remembered the B.N.A. Bank Note Company pillars and, in a flash, equated their significance and connection with the night's events: "I believe I will secure these columns and will be able to put them up at Kingsmere — a sign — a symbol as the ruin was...They will correspond to the St.

National Archives of Canada/PA 42629

British North American Bank Note Building.

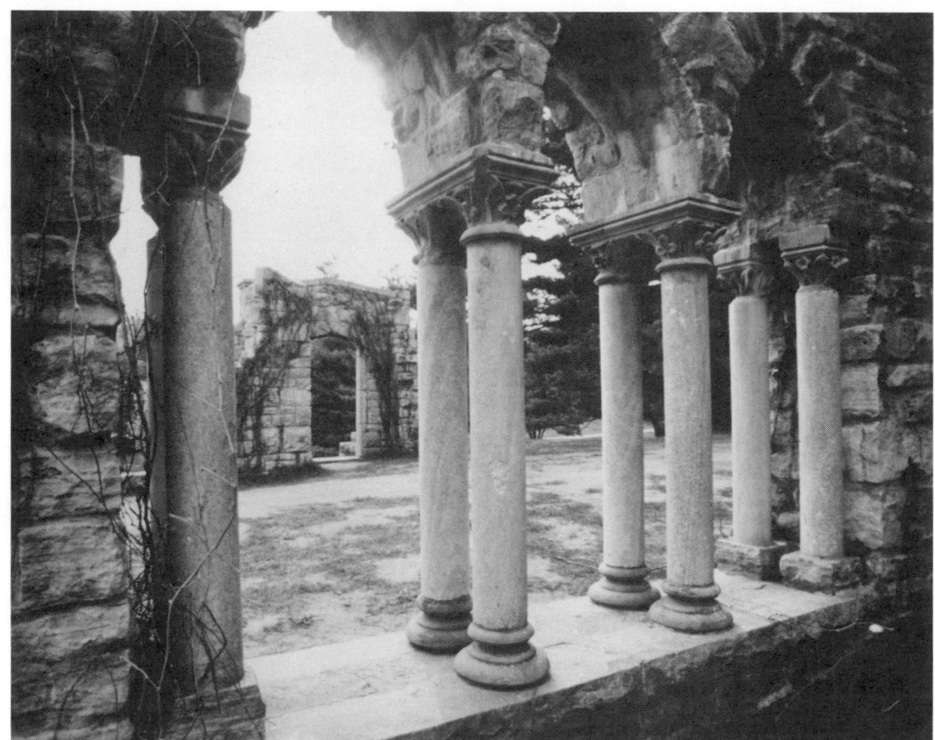
National Capital Commission

Looking through the colonnade at the Abbey ruin.

Michael Gate and the St. George Gate — will be the true St. Michael & St. George...certainly placed somewhere as a sign — that it was a divine leading which caused me to take the stand I did." (March 26, 1936).

King's pleasure, however, was soon marred by an article in the *Ottawa Citizen* noting his purchase and his plans for the columns. He said the item caused a shudder to go through his body: "I had dreaded publicity on this, fearing that people will misunderstand, and that it will raise a question in minds of sums of money, and lead them to think of graft" (11 April 1936). Although five years had passed, the Beauharnois scandal was still a painful memory, a "nightmare" he said. The Beauharnois issue had exploded in 1931, leading, as King expressed it, the Liberal Party and himself into the "valley of humiliation." A few Liberal senators had played unethical roles regarding power concessions on the St. Lawrence which King's government had granted to the private Beauharnois Power Company. Accusations of bribery, corruption, and tainted campaign donations tarnished King's reputation and ruined the careers of others. Although King was cleared, he never forgot the lessons, nor the adverse, damning publicity.[41] After 1931 King's nervousness over large, personal expenses was not wholly caused by his habitual frugality — the public "accountant," he felt, was now always peering over his shoulder.

His unhappiness over the publicity and the expense of the B.N.A. Bank Note Company columns was eventually dispelled by his enthusiasm to use them to build an arch. However, when King first saw the size and height of the columns up close, he was horrified. He soon recovered and found the perfect site at the bottom of the Moorside grounds, bordering on the forest in an area he called "Diana's Grove." After the construction was finished, he named the arch the Arc de Triomphe to commemorate "the place of victory and triumph of July 1, 1936, and all that has led up to that moment, and which marks it as a place of new beginning" (3 July 1936). He felt the Arc memorialized Canada's work for peace at the recent League of Nations meeting, his thoughts on the future of Kingsmere, his decision to build a new records building in Ottawa and to pursue other civic beautification measures. As well, he added another layer onto the already complex association he had devised: his overwhelming feeling of spiritual renewal.

A few nights after the Arc was completed, he held a dinner party at Moorside. He thrilled to see the ladies walk out on to the lawn: "When I saw them in front of the arch I was in raptures — the beauty of the figures in their light garments about the stone was like a Roman or a Grecian tableau" (4 July 1936). Even a year after its construction, the Arc prompted nostalgic memories as he gazed at his ruin under the light of a bright evening star: "In the one open space between them [the columns] shone the loveliest, the brightest Star of the heavens at this season, my "L'Etoile" — I thought of the Arc de Triomphe in Paris as I sat beneath it years ago after seeing Tannhauser at the Opera and singing The Evening Star — It was as if mother spoke to me from the skies, had placed God's seal there, the seal of certainty & truth on all I had seen and felt" (21 August 1937).

At the same time, King attempted to design a smaller ruin from other salvaged B.N.A. Bank Note Company building pieces. He liked a piece resembling a sarcophagus so much, he thought he would highlight it by placing a small window on it. After a trial placement he had it taken down, fearing that "there is just the danger of having too much done in the way of reproductions about the lawn" (27 June 1936). King fussed in his diary, acknowledging that all the attention spent on this mistake was anticlimatic and detracted from the joy of the arch. However a few days later, he found the perfect site for a small ruin between the ornamental flower borders and the Hidden Garden area. The resulting, successful construction incorporated the "sarcophagus" base, four small pillars and a lintel to form what King named his

National Capital Commission

Arc de Triomphe with the pagan gargoyles at their base.

"window on the forest." He was pleased with the final effect: it framed a forest view and served as a focal point for the formal gardens.

In 1937 King searched for more historic Canadian stones and relics. Someone told him that there was a salvage yard on Lyon Street where stone from demolished government buildings had been dumped. There he hoped to find enough stones to build another addition to the Abbey ruin — this time he wanted to build a wall of Gothic windows, a desire probably influenced by his June visit to the Melrose Abbey ruins in England. He noted in his diary that he "studied" the ruins "...particularly the long gothic aisles, the tracery of the windows, etc." (21 June 1937). This ruin, repaired and reconstructed by Sir Walter Scott in 1822, was a subject of many nineteenth century engravings and pictures. Scott exulted over his find: "There are such rich bits of old-time sculpture for the architect, and old-time story for the poet. There is as rare picking in it as in a Stilton cheese, and in the same taste — the mouldier the better."[42]

Well-primed, King happily discovered stone and carvings from the original Parliament buildings at the salvage yard. He found much more than he expected — he had been told that most of the burned debris had been thrown into the Ottawa River below Parliament Hill.[43] King was delighted to buy some fine bronze-coloured stone, small columns, as well as a fireplace and mantle from the old Parliament building. Ewart was again brought out to Kingsmere to plan the latest addition, as King attempted to build his chapel wall by wall.

King's creative energies surged as he planned the next phase. He sought to clarify why he was building ruins on this lonely Gatineau hill, and what they meant to him. After reading an article Joan had given him on English follies, King mused that perhaps his ruins were "to improve the mind," as well as "...to help the spirit find a habitat that is congenial to it, something of the past, as well as present as one looks out to the future" (8 August 1937). As construction time drew near, King felt an immediate connection with a past, this time predating his Jacobean ancestors. In a line of thought, which did not reflect his life-long membership in the Presbyterian church, King tried to articulate an Eastern-tinged theory of the transmigration of souls:

> There is too some relating back of my soul to ancient times — with its building of temples & dwelling therin — it may be what has been retained through centuries of descent by good living on part of ancestors — As we increase in spiritual power, we go back in our knowledge as well as forward towards the no beginning at the one extreme and no end at the other, all a part of the presence of God (22 August 1937).

He also felt that the ruin's religious significance, revealed to him two years ago, guided his preliminary design ideas. His recent reading of "Rugby Chapel," and the works of the Romantics were another great influence: "I felt we should make the new ruin into a chapel — a Saint Michael Chapel...a little sanctuary 'in Memoriam,' a place to read, & reflect, and pray....It must now become a sort of Rugby Chapel, a memorial to leadership — spiritual guidance" (30 August 1937). The idea was bolstered by King and Joan's enthusiastic discussions: "We talked of cloisters, gothic windows, etc., etc., & of our visits [to England]..." (23 August 1937). His secretaries were ordered to find works on ecclesiastical architecture in the Parliamentary Library and then deliver them to Kingsmere.

His mind made up, he now had to justify the expense. This effort created a new theme not only in his financial rationalizations, but also in his theorizing over the ruin's significance. For a childless man, a man steeped in family history, and an insecure politician, the idea of creating a lasting legacy in the form of his Abbey ruin was tremendously appealing. In an almost ecstatic diary entry, King explored this new thought:

> I feel in some way I should not incur the expense, yet it seems to me, there is something 'larger' which justifies it. I am a national figure, my example will have its effect on the Nation when I am gone — to foster the ideal — to teach the lesson of preservation and redemption in terms to which it can be referred so as to impress youth, etc., is part of my work. I am speaking to my own & other generations, expressing my soul — reconstructing the past, with the truly spiritual note, and making meanwhile a sanctuary for one's own soul and the soul of others (1 September 1937).

After the philosophical and design foundations had been established, the work progressed rapidly. Ewart created a design with just the right touch of a chapel, "a cloistered effect," that King wanted. Three small Gothic windows were to be fashioned into a wall opposite the doorway structure.

That year, sharing the crate with the stone angels King had received from the Westminster salvage yard was a stone with the crest of the Speaker of the House of Commons of Westminster carved on it, and a stone tablet ornamented with the arms of England Lord Stanhope had given him. Garvock, the contractor, suggested embedding these pieces at the north end of the ruin into a wall which would also contain the fireplace salvaged from the Canadian Parliament building: Joan thought it was a "heavenly" idea, and King immediately elaborated upon the symbolic aptness of the combination "amid these resurrected walls." The fireplace symbolized a sacred fire, the hearth, an altar. He fused the two associations into a symbol of the joining of the sacred and the profane, of Christian and pagan worship, and of the "days when Government was by the church & the growth of government into the State, the association of the two is well worked out in the combination of Houses of Prlt. with an old Abbey structure" (4 September 1937). Although he wanted to imbed both stones above the mantle, only the Speaker's coat of arms stone was so placed. When told later the next year that the coat of arms (belonging to Speaker Shaw Lefevre, speaker of the British House of Commons from 1838-1859), was being replaced by an exact replica, King was overjoyed. This, he felt, greatly increased the historic value and significance of the ruin's fireplace wall.

As usual during construction, King alternated between despair and joy. He fussed and fiddled to get the proportions and composition just right. He "pulled out" one of the pillars in the window wall, to make it appear more rugged, and was thrilled to think he had "captured something of the atmosphere of Rugby Chapel" (10 September 1937). When King inserted three stones, picked up from the "ruin" of his grandfather's printing office, into the fireplace wall, he said he was convinced of the appropriateness of the placement: "that was where the fires of freedom for Canada were lighted" (10 September 1937). A few days later his joy was transformed into misery when he realized the fireplace wall, massive and heavy looking, did not reflect his idealization of it. To relieve the overly massive feeling, King insisted that a circular window be inserted to the right of the mantelpiece. He also ordered the contractor to remove the white stones near the coat of arms and replace them with darker ones. Then he decided yet another small window was needed on the opposite side of the mantelpiece. King said his corrections were inspired by a divine guidance, an "answer to prayer." King was delighted with the final effect: "...the moonlight last night on the stone was like white magic, ethereal — celestial..." (17 October 1937). Six years later Emil Ludwig, the writer, perhaps primed by King, remarked when visiting the ruin that it would be inspirational for future Canadians:

> This would be the place to write books which would help younger people. Some day, people will come here, will see these Ruins. They will talk about a man who has been a statesman; fond of social service work, and will be immensely interested in knowing how he passed his time, and that he was interested in doing things like this. That will make them feel a great interest and your example will be very helpful to them (26 August 1943).

Never again would King experience such joy in building ruins. After 1937 King's ruin-building abruptly halted, the Abbey never completed. He did, however, continue collecting bits and pieces of carving and stone.

The Second World War curtailed his landscaping projects, but it did not dampen his acquisitive urge to collect meaningful architectural fragments for future ruin-work. Canada House clerks in London, surprised to receive a cable late one night marked "most immediate" from the Prime Minister, referred it speedily to Lester B. Pearson, a counsellor at the High Commission. He was not terribly amused to read the Prime Minister's request for a few stones from Westminster Hall, reportedly bombed the night before. Although Pearson thought that this was hardly urgent compared to other pressing war work, reconstruction, and repair to the city, the request did come from the Prime Minister, therefore Pearson dutifully carried it out. The relics, however, did not reach Kingsmere until 1947. King delightedly unpacked railings from Buckingham Palace, pieces of sandstone and marble (including an altar table section) from St. Paul's Cathedral, timber, lath and plaster from Westminster Abbey, a Tudor rose carving and a section of the noticeboard from the House of Commons, as well as a lead finial from Westminster Hall.[44] Despite his revived interest after the war in landscaping and repairing lookouts and bridges, for unexplained reasons King never used the London relics in his ruins or displayed them on the grounds.

Although his ruin-building flagged during the late 1930s and early 1940s, his ruins continued, in King's mind, to dominate all other landscape improvements. The Abbey ruin, in particular, exerted an influence on King's Kingsmere life up to his death, and was always the highlight of estate tours given to visitors. Guests' thank you notes were full of praise for King's undoubtedly enthusiastic explanations of the Abbey ruin: "I want to tell you again how much both Ruth and I enjoyed our visit, and your story about the Roman ruins. It was a grand inspiration..."[45] or, "I shall never forget the thought behind your Roman symbols, so cleverly introduced, as we were strolling about your spacious grounds."[46] Reading Gray's "Elegy" amid the ruins became a yearly ritual, a ritual reminiscent of kissing the marble lips of his mother's statue each time he returned to Laurier House from a lengthy trip.

The sacredness of the ruin was further heightened when "the little dogs" were buried there. In 1940 when Derry, the Patteson's beloved dog, died, King had him buried next to the ruin. The next year Pat died. Attended by his estate staff and the Pattesons, the devastated King held a funeral at the ruin, complete with hymns and prayers. As Pat was buried next to Derry, King possibly quoted from a favourite poem in his collection, by

Rudyard Kipling — "The Power of the Dog:"

When the body that lived at your single will,
When the whimper of welcome is stilled (how still!)
When the spirit that answered your every mood
Is gone— wherever it goes — for good,
You will discover how much you care,
And will give your heart to a dog to tear.[47]

Annually the gardener was instructed to plant flowers, usually portulacea, on the graves. As well, King would often place bouquets there. Later he had the gardener place flat stones on Pat's grave and plant thyme between them. He was always delighted to see birds perching in the trees near the graves, an event usually interpreted as a Heavenly message of the dogs' continual "guidance and fidelity."

At one time King seriously considered his own burial in the ruin. One fine summer day as Joan and King sat and contemplated the Abbey ruin, King said he might place his tomb inside and mark it with a simple inscription: "William Lyon Mackenzie King, M.P., Prime Minister of Canada 1921-1925; 1925-1930 ...Born Berlin, Ontario, Dec. 17, 1874 — Died — (no degrees or anything else)." Then he reconsidered, confiding to Joan that perhaps it should be modelled on the sarcophagus-shaped window-base on the lower lawn, with the addition of some carving on the side. True to form, he added, "...some day I may think out a verse for the other side — and a bit of symbolism for either end" (29 August 1936). This magnificent last resting place was not to be. In the end he chose to be buried next to his mother in the family plot in Toronto's Mt. Pleasant Cemetery.

The Abbey ruin began to attract uninvited visitors — some out for a Sunday stroll, others with less pastoral pursuits in mind. In 1939 the ruin became even more ruin-like when tool-bearing vandals tried to destroy it. Before they were surprised, extensive damage was done. They smashed the finger in the hand (the one pointing prophetically, according to King, to Heaven) in the Speaker's Coat of Arms, smashed the carvings on the window pillars, and the carving on the Parliament building stones. They also pried up part of the steps leading to the entrance of the ruins. King confided in his diary that he was lost for a motive for such senseless violence and told Joan it was "part of the evil spirit that is operating in the world today" (14 May 1939).

The Abbey ruin also witnessed earthier sights. Elizabeth Smart, the poet and novelist, at age twenty-two staged a "Bacchanalian Orgy" (as she termed it in her thank you note to King) at the hilltop ruin. Her parents owned a Kingsmere cottage, but evidently Elizabeth required the spirit-infested atmosphere of King's ruin for her party. A journalist euphemistically called it a "Greek playlet," and further noted that it was attended by a Government House aide who "...appeared in a tiger skin and laurel wreath, while the rest of the cast were in knee length Greek costumes. A pleasant time was had."[48] This aide was actually a Guard's officer who, upon arrival, took off his uniform, and then proceeded to cover his long woolen underwear with a tiger-skin rug borrowed from a Rideau Hall floor.[49] Fortified by wine and hampers of food, Elizabeth's guests (promising civil servants, diplomats, bankers, and an assortment of young Ottawa society) danced around a huge bonfire to gramophone records of "L'après-midi d'un faune" and Ravel's "Bolero." They were costumed by individual inclination: some as nymphs, druids, and satyrs — all quite in keeping with King's ruin, but perhaps not quite interpreting the spirit of his Abbey. Elizabeth wrote King that her party was a great success: "The moon rose, our spirits rose, and the Revel rose to heights unprecedented. Had it not been for your generosity...There could have been no clashing of cymbals, no sacred pie, no barbaric music, no ink red wine....You have made possible the coming of Bacchus to Canada..."[50] King never mentioned the revel in his diary.

Until his diaries were released to the public, the collected ruins and their significance for King were a mystery. Before his death, they were rarely mentioned in the press. In 1938 a Montreal newspaper article characterized the Abbey ruin as the "premier's hobby," and cast King in the role of a rescuer of "beautiful bits of architecture" from the "razers."[51] After his death in 1950 when pictures of the ruins and brief details of his dabblings in spiritualism reached the public, there was speculation, some not particularly flattering, on the meaning of the ruins. An Ottawa journalist decried the ruins as anachronistic in such a young country as Canada, and psychologized that perhaps they were a "...materialistic link with some repression in his mind, a desire to create synthetic roots, an expression of nostalgia or his sentimental attachment to the past, adherence to tradition and custom and his respect for ancestral effort and accomplishment."[52] Not all his friends were attracted to the ruins. Violet Markham, an ardent British reformer and one of King's oldest friends, admitted to John Buchan, Lord Tweedsmuir, that she found King's prized ruins "distressing." His former aide, Reginald Hardy, advanced a bizarre theory supposedly revealed by King. Hardy said King liked to read on the hill, but found it too windy, so he collected stones to build a small windbreak, which eventually he transformed into the ruin.[53] Closer to the truth was Hardy's observation that the ruins were part of King's preoccupation with the "life beyond." As he noted: "Perhaps, somehow, King had discovered the secret of some sort of extra dimension. Perhaps those empty doorways which opened upon space and led to nowhere were for him, and him alone, the gateway to a very real and satisfying world."[54] Bruce Hutchinson, newsman and King observer, reflected that the ruins symbolized "the ambivalence of the Canadian mind:" at home in the rugged land of Canada, but ever nostalgic for its European origins.[55]

For the thousands of tourists who visit Kingsmere each year, the ruins continue to be objects of amazement or occasional humourous conjecture, but always the main attraction. The collection of ruins, although mediocre by European standards, were the most outstanding features on his landscape. King never surpassed them in symbolism or ornamentation. After his death the ruins were threatened with real ruination by hordes of tourists who wanted souvenirs. The National Capital Commission tried to curtail this by dumping pieces of stone near the Abbey ruin for souvenir hunters to pick up. In 1935 King had already prophesied its attraction. The only disadvantage of the ruin he noted was "that it may attract tourists or visitors. On the other hand, it will add something of special interest and inspiration for all" (9 May 1935).

CHAPTER SIX

King as Gentleman Farmer

THE MOOING OF SHEEP AND THE BAAING OF CHICKENS

When Paddy Murphy told King that Mrs. McGillivary was thinking of selling off the remainder of her property, he was especially intrigued by the thought of owning the farm house, barns and outbuildings: "The more I think of it the more I believe it wd pay me to keep a man & his wife & have a sort of little farm out there. — Might go in for horse & cart to do rough work, a cow & pigs & chickens & vegetables & apples — enough to meet expenses at all events" (30 December 1926). King, the neophyte farmer, seemingly did not care that the land was agriculturally marginal — the soil was thin and stoney, some areas inadequately drained, while other sections had reverted to scrub and bush.[1] Nevertheless, he continued to dream of self-sufficiency.

The call of the pastoral was like a siren song to King. He, like many non-farmers, idealized a farm as the ultimate picturesque, romantic element on a landscape. Owning more land had less to do with his mounting enthusiasm for the project than his romanticized thoughts on the activities of farming. This attitude sustained him through the trying negotiations with Mrs. McGillivary, described in Chapter Three, until he had secured the farm at his price. While he was negotiating, King searched for an experienced farm manager who could move in as soon as the deal was closed. Through local contacts he found a sheep farmer who had to leave the farm he was renting. King was immediately taken with this "fine looking Scotchman," a "delightful man" to have as an overseer: "It wd make Kingsmere a different place to feel he was here & looking after everything" (1 April 1927). McBurnie, King never mentioned his first name, at first did not want to come out to Kingsmere, perhaps an omen King should have heeded. However, King brought him around by promising to pay sixty dollars a month, provide the farm house rent-free, and buy fifty of McBurnie's sheep at twenty dollars a head. After the deed had been signed and McBurnie hired, a euphoric King was ready to begin the adventure of farming: "How I delight in these rural & pastoral pursuits" (25 April 1927).

His delight was tempered by a newspaper report, four short sentences, on his latest venture. The item noted King's recent land purchases — erroneously writing that King's estate was four miles "in depth" — and that he was going into the sheep business. Distressed, King wrote in his diary that the publicity would "...do great harm in circles that have been helping me with Laurier House & in creating suspicion in minds of public of graft, etc." (26 April 1927). King was terribly afraid of what his benefactors, who had set up a fund for the renovations and furnishings of Laurier House and for King's personal use, would think of his new hobby. He took Peter Larkin, his financial benefactor and supervisor of the trust fund, on a tour of the new property — its barns, outbuildings and orchard. King worried that Larkin, whom he had appointed High Commissioner to Britain, would think his latest venture a foolish extravagance. The wealthy Larkin, however, shrugged off King's fears saying he never denied himself anything and that the farm was a good investment in land and health — King obviously had once again paraded his usual justifications of the healing qualities of the Gatineau Hills on his body and soul.

Later that summer the healing balm of his beloved hills probably eased the pain when he read the *Montreal Standard's* satire on King the politician in the guise of King the "verandah farmer." After poking fun at his ambition, his frequent Kingsmere holidays, and his ego, the writer then ridiculed King's agrarian policies through his naïvete in farming matters:

> 'Farming from the verandah is the best way to farm. I am a verandah farmer first, last and all the time. I make no bones of it.'
>
> 'No rough work like ploughing and planting?'
>
> 'No, Bozzy, we leave that to a lower order of intelligence....'
>
> 'But,' I protest merely for the sake of argument, 'all the other farmers work.'
>
> 'And that,' smiles the Premier, 'is just where they are wrong. If they'd stick to the verandah and let others do the work they'd be much happier. It's hard work — and hard times — that made the Progressive party. When we get rid of the work we shall get rid of the Progressive Party.'...'The verandah farmer,' the Premier goes on with his boyish smile, 'is the kind of farmer we want. He doesn't carry a grouch. He is at peace with himself and the world. I look forward to the day when all the agricultural members of the Liberal party in Canada will be verandah farmers....What little farming I've done has put me inside the farmer's skin. I know now what he wants. When he has everything and spends nothing he will be happy as a clam at high water.'[2]

When asked by his fictional companion why he chose sheep, the Premier explained sheep-raising was selected for its political "application." Because sheep were blind followers, he would use them as an object lesson for the Liberal party:

> 'Well, if ever I have any rebels in the Liberal party I'll bring 'em out here to Kingsmere, dine 'em and wine 'em well and then I'll show 'em the sheep.'
>
> 'And what would the sermon be?'
>
> 'I'll say, look at the sheep. Observe how faithful they are to the hand that feeds 'em and always remember that the Government in power can provide better pasture than the party in Opposition. Copy the sheep.'[3]

King did not comment on this attack, merely filed it in his papers.

Perhaps a congratulatory letter from the Ontario Minister of Agriculture, John S. Martin, helped to relieve King's unhappiness over the derogatory publicity. Martin wrote that he was interested to hear King was going to "take a dip into agriculture." Martin was a leading breeder of White Wyandotte chickens, as well as an enthusiastic Shropshire sheep farmer: "I am very fond of sheep...I would hate to think of farming without them because they are the best weed exterminators that I have ever found."[4]

The realities of farming, especially sheep raising, were yet to dispel the romantic haze surrounding his newest enthusiasm. King's farming experience to date was limited to his childhood chores in the Woodside kitchen garden and with the family cow. At Kingsmere his agricultural experience had been confined to holding the horses' heads while his workers fastened the horses' chains to tree roots. King was a total urbanite. How he found himself calculating costs of building barns, housing sheep, and growing hay, was more a matter of fashion, class, and the sentimental rhetoric of the time rather than a deep-seated calling or profound need. King was not alone in his pursuit of the pastoral pleasures of hobby farming. Many of his affluent contemporaries supported barns and sheep and chickens on their country estates, their farming a component of fashionable country life in the 1920s and 30s.

European Influences

Hobby farming was not a North American innovation; it drew on a number of European intellectual traditions. The primary pastoral lure was rooted in the complex notion of Arcadia — a golden age when all meadows were sunlit and grazing sheep were continually serenaded by piping shepherds. Practitioners and theorists of the Picturesque Landscape Style delighted in assigning symbolic connotations to their landscape components, such as rotting stumps, memorial tablets, hermits, and ruins. The farm and its inhabitants were also included in the Picturesque's symbolic system. Cows and sheep and the humble farm worker were said to animate the landscape, adding a romanticized "local colour" to the country estate. The farm, echoing Arcadian sentiment, assumed connotations of the good, simple life — morally uplifting, innocent, and Romantically sentimental.

The farm, as a valued Picturesque component of the country estate, was to be ornamented and landscaped according to current theory and design. A "prettified" farm was called *ferme ornée* and, for a short time in the 18th century, were common elements on large estates. Marie Antoinette had a model farm, le Hameau, built near the Petit Trianon at Versailles where she and members of her court would dress up as shepherds and dairymaids and play at the Arcadian ideal — completely cleansed, of course, of the reality of farm operations.

In France, the *ferme ornée* was viewed more as a theatrical stage on which one could play at rural life.[5] The British *ferme ornée* was defined as the prettified property of an amateur farmer.[6] The term could also apply to an 18th century innovation: the small country house designed as an up-scale gentleman's villa, which was especially popular with those who did not have the wealth to establish themselves as full-fledged country gentlemen.[7]

Whether it was part of a larger estate or an estate in itself, the farm, operating or not, was to be landscaped as a garden, a *ferme ornée*. Hedgerows were to be augmented with ornamental vines, shrubs and trees; paths were to border the land; flower beds, especially rose beds, were to be placed about the farmyard; outbuildings were to match the style of the house or perhaps resemble a ruined monastery or Moorish castle; and a small serpentine river or pond, once created, was to be filled with ducks and geese.[8] Either one could build a farm complex on the most aesthetic site or renovate and relandscape the working farm. The object was to compose a picture, something essentially English, idyllic and romantic.

As a landscape style the *ferme ornée* did not survive its initial popularity — working farms did not translate well into entertainment sites. The romanticized attitude towards rural life and work, however, did not decline as rapidly as the concept of the *ferme ornée*. The British and French landed gentry and aristocracy had begun, in the late 1700s, to take a greater interest in the economic benefits of farming — an enlightened self-interest for their wealth was in large part created and sustained by their land. Woodlands were planted not only for picturesqueness, but also for the promise of wealth. They became "nurseries of game," providing fresh meat in the winter when other supplies were scarce.[9] Farming became fashionable for many reasons, one of which was the connection with hunting. As a landlord hunted over his estate, he could not avoid noticing problems of repair and maintenance. As well, agricultural pursuits became more popular, and estate owners, influenced by the revolution in agricultural techniques

> ...began to plant, drain and enclose, to run farms themselves and to encourage their tenants to improve the farms that were on lease. This new interest, besides greatly advancing farming techniques, and boosting food output, enabled landlords to perhaps double their income. Once it became clear that this was the case, improvement became exceedingly popular.[10]

Hunting and farming pursuits, no longer idle pastimes, had evolved into "virtuous and prestigious occupations."[11] Not only was great wealth to be gained from an economically-run estate, but social status was also enhanced. Land ownership was characterized as the safest and most prestigious form of investment: "Anyone who owned land had a permanent stake in the country."[12]

Canadian Arcadia

Canada did not have a hereditary rural aristocracy, nor a tradition of thousand-acre country estates, overseen and improved by an involved landlord. Most early farms were family affairs, sole proprietorships of uncertain duration. Farming, even after the pioneering era, was a hard business in Canada for all classes.

At the turn of the century, the Canadian economy was beginning to "boom." Economic "good times" were a mixed blessing, and caused unsettling changes in society. People began to worry about "materialism, selfish individualism, love of luxury and ease, urban poverty and crime, and political and business corruption."[13] The inevitable softening of the nation's spiritual, moral and cultural values was threatening to many Canadians. Some social commentators, fearful of what they defined as the degeneration of the nation, spiritedly praised the comforting traditional values embodied, they thought, in the rural way of life. Canadian intellectuals and social commentators vigorously promoted the concept of the countryside as "the cradle of essential social values."[14]

However, there was a problem with this simplistic view —

namely hundreds of country families were deserting central Canadian farms. They migrated to cities and towns searching for better living conditions, less social isolation, better financial prospects, and, sometimes, just "city lights." The exodus, defined as "the rural problem," was loudly censured. Social critics feared the nation's primary industry was in danger of collapsing. They did not publicly acknowledge that industry was fast overtaking agriculture as the country's dominant economic force. They clung to the notion of agricultural primacy — strongly bolstered by the comforting values within the Victorian sentimental version of country life and of the religious underpinnings of nature. The rhetoric of romantic nostalgia and religious sentiment not only influenced urban attitudes to country living, but was also used in the campaign to keep the rural population on the farm. Fresh air, clean living, innocent country pastimes, and healthful natural surroundings were commonly praised as benefits of country living. The countryside was glorified as the healthiest — morally, physically and spiritually — place to live, the city was benighted and its entertainments immoral. Industrialists and other city dwellers, so the argument continued, lived unhappily in the city in order to conduct business, but their hearts were always in the country.

Colonel Deacon (right) of Glenburn Farms near Unionville, Ontario was a highly-praised hobby farmer whose specialty was shorthorn beef cattle.

To create a vibrant, forward-looking and settled rural society, agricultural leaders began a campaign of rural regeneration. This movement was initiated and fostered by the faculty and administrators of the Ontario Agricultural College [now the University of Guelph]. These agricultural educators and leaders wanted to develop a "new agriculture" led by a forward-looking generation of farmers. Farming would be conducted along the latest scientific and technological lines by a farmer who was a "gentleman." The new farmer would be well versed in literature, poetry, music and religion, as well as social etiquette, speaking skills and the latest agricultural information. Thus equipped, he (women were still to serve as helpmates) could assume a leadership role in his community, forge new links between city and country, and eradicate the pejorative definition of farmer — an uncouth, dull-witted rural rube. If the Canadian farmer seized the opportunities of new markets, education, and technological advances, a regenerated rural society, supported by traditional moral and spiritual values,

National Library of Canada/NL 16858

The idea of a *ferme ornée*, or landscaped farm, was an 18th century landscape fad which could still be found on some early 20th century estates — most often in an abbreviated form. Pictured here is Donalda Farm, near Toronto, a 20th century Canadian example.

would result. Prosperity, only one advantageous outcome, would help to create a rural utopia characterized by indoor plumbing, electricity, telephones, good roads, wider food range, and well-built, beautifully landscaped homes.[15]

The rhetoric of the agrarian reformers also influenced urban perceptions of country life. This rhetoric, coupled with the other inducements to visit the wilds of nature, was quite persuasive. Some wealthy urban families answered the siren call of the farm, seeking to rejuvenate their constitutions and to enjoy real living, amidst the pastoral beauty of surrounding hills, stream and meadow. It was, of course, yet another measure forward on the social yardstick. Owning a city residence as well was the best of both worlds, but this was downplayed in articles extolling the country estate. However, it was recognized that not all transplanted urbanites might want to farm their country properties. A country estate, it was proposed, could be quite enjoyable and picturesque "without the care and responsibilities of a farm:"[16]

> Things go wrong...farming may easily exceed the most fantastic nightmare for the unpredictable and absurd...It seems too simple to plow, to seed and let the sun and rain do the rest; so simple to bundle in the feed to comfortably housed stock. Yet each operation is highly complex, attended in all cases by the ravages of disease and sickness, subject to mismanagement, and, worst of all, a world competitive price structure which is so often no structure at all.[17]

The most fashionable model for those who succumbed to the lure of the farm was that of the British landed gentry. When the pastoral qualities of a country home were praised, it was often in the British context: "like our relatives across the water, we were bound to discover eventually that cities are for business and the country for living."[18] For example, the country house of Peter Sims, Mackenzie King's friend, was said to be set in a "characteristic English country house setting — a quiet expanse where sheep graze under the elms."[19] The term "gentleman farmer" came to have two definitions — one identifying the cultured working farmer and the other denoting the rich hobbyist who often left the daily working of the farm to a manager. In addition to the healthful benefits (sports, hobbies, and hospitality) of owning a country estate, farming was said to give the hobby farmer a golden chance to study "the country's basic economies at close range."[20]

Mackenzie King certainly thought farming would put him in touch with the "basic economies." In a rare interview at Kingsmere, King explained to a very sympathetic reporter why farming (he had just begun) held such interest: "There is an interesting angle in this for me....You know I have to buy implements, I have to reckon the cost. It gives me an insight into the problems of the farming people of the country. It gives me a closer realization of the difficulties with which agriculture has to contend."[21]

National Library of Canada/NL 16859

On the more affluent farm estates, the architecture could be grandiose, such as Sir Henry Pellatt's Lake Marie Farm, near King, Ontario. Its grey stone dairy building looked like a chapel.

Many of King's hobby farming friends and colleagues, the new breed of gentlemen farmer, supposedly found farming "zestful," a relaxing hobby and a means of regaining health. The gentleman farmer, the new "Cincinnatus," experienced the curative power of "the companionship of living things," and discovered in it the "antidote to a self-centred life."[22] He could also gain self-knowledge by acknowledging that "deep down in his heart every man is a son of the soil." The greatest compliment was to be called a good farmer.[23] Other recruits to rusticity were drawn to farming by a spirit of adventure — the same spirit that prompted some to go big game hunting or sail their yachts across the ocean: "the sport comes in trying to make the place pay."[24] Some never made the effort, writing it off under amusements, as yet another expensive hobby. Mackenzie King was not immune to the romanticism of farming nor the social cachet of being a gentleman farmer. His holdings were not as extensive as the more enthusiastic hobby farmers; nevertheless, his farming experiences were a consuming interest until the onset of the Depression.

King's Farming Experiences — The Sheep

Mackenzie King had probably admired the picturesqueness of country estate farms on trips to Britain as well as on visits to Ontario and Quebec estates. The sight of barns, hedgerows, grazing sheep and gently rolling hills — the perfect English pastoral scene — had a powerful, romantic attraction for King:

"...took much pleasure at the pastoral scene of cattle in the fields — the low lying meadows — the views from the [King] Mountain side..." (18 September 1931).

Early in his Kingsmere life, before King had begun interpreting his dreams, he had dreamed Arcadian scenes. In one dream he travelled by train through a beautiful stretch of countryside seeking his ideal woman — pure, good and lovely with golden hair, beautiful features and the figure of Venus di Milo. He had learned she lived on a farm, beyond a body of water, near a lily pond and a grove of trees (4 December 1904). Unfortunately he awoke before we could learn his response to the Arcadian ideal of nature and woman.

Professional farming, when Mackenzie King began, was not a dream world nor a frozen tableau of rustic scenes to please the viewer. It had become a complex undertaking, evolving from a way of life into a highly mechanized, highly organized way of making a living. Marketing agencies, breed associations, professional organizations, technological and scientific advances, government red tape and legislation, and specialization characterized the farm of the 1920s. The mixed farming King attempted was fast becoming outdated. His farming activities followed the model of his parent's feeble attempts at animal-keeping and garden-tending during their Woodstock years, rather than modern operations.

King, however, surpassed his parents' holdings on his first day of farming. Chickens, sheep, horses and cows not only had to be cared for but also needed proper housing. The original barns were dilapidated and sited in a place King did not like. All spring he mulled over the possibilities before deciding to renovate the old buildings. To the barn he added a two-storey picturesque addition, ornamented with a dormer window and colonnaded porch.[25] He noted exuberantly in his diary that this planning was "great fun & I got a real delight" designing the "H"-shaped complex with Paddy Murphy and McBurnie. Worried about the costs, King consoled himself with the thought that perhaps McBurnie would make the livestock pay. As well, he produced one of his usual rationalizations — the improvements would prove to be a good investment: "The expense is large but I can afford the outlay today, and it is laying up for tomorrow in a way I believe will tell in dividends as well as health of body mind & peace of heart & soul" (8 July 1927).

The slow pace of barn-building allowed King's anxieties to plague him once again: "Perhaps I am all wrong in getting into the farming business. I have been adding to instead of lessening my responsibilities" (24 June 1927). The mood passed and within a week King was rhapsodizing over the slowly rising barns: "The cluster of barns look well, the design is a pleasing one, and I believe the arrangement is good" (12 July 1927). With a satisfied air, he wrote that the barns "will do credit to a gentleman's farm" (8 July 1927). M.N. Cummings, an Ottawa contractor whom King appointed to the Senate, offered to give him a new chicken house. The whole lot of them, Cummings, King, Joan, Godfroy, McBurnie and Paddy Murphy conferred on the design and siting of the new house. All agreed on the details so quickly that the house was built in the next four days. A second chicken house was created from an old log house King moved in from elsewhere on the property. The removal and renovations were costly both in effort and money. King justified the expense by appealing to his romantic feelings toward old buildings: "Sentiment is expensive, but it is I think worth preserving" (13 July 1927).

By mid July King happily wrote that "...the barns are taking on the appearance of a first class summer cottage of rather good proportions" (18 July 1927). Typically he then began to dither about the siting of the barns, wondering if it would not have been better to leave them in their old position. He resisted temptation and left them alone. When the buildings were finished, he painted the clapboarding yellow with white trim to harmonize with the other estate buildings. The barn complex was divided into sheep pens, garage, feed storage, and stalls for horses and cows.

As soon as the barn complex was finished, it was integrated into his romantic appreciation of the estate: "...went over the moors coming suddenly upon the sight of the barns in the distance. They looked lovely in the morning sun..." (7 September 1927). This "distant view" of his estate in general (contented sheep on a far hillside, beautiful stalls sans animals, the forest backdrop) seemed to please King more than the reality — he loved the form but not always the content of some of his romanticized rural pursuits. But then in 1927 he had a lot of reality to contend with. The rose-coloured spectacles he wore during the initial stages of his farming career were soon to be abruptly torn off.

National Archives of Canada/PA 124432

King took great delight in designing the barns on his new farm, enjoying their aesthetic look "on the skyline."

Before the barns were ready, King had been acquiring livestock. After hiring McBurnie, King immediately organized moving him and his sheep to the Farm. His initial enthusiasm was slightly dampened when he saw McBurnie's sheep up close for the first time. King confided in his diary that the sheep were not only much larger than he imagined sheep to be, but were "less beautiful than I had thought sheep were" (3 April 1927). This glimpse of reality did not deter King from establishing an Arcadian retreat in the wilds of the Gatineau hills. In addition to the flock of sheep, King also bought two horses and two cows for $226. These animals never seemed to be a part of King's sentimental regard for his farm holdings. They ate and ate and seemingly produced little, although King determined to sell milk to Joan at ten cents a quart. King also had to buy all kinds of new equipment for these animals: whipple trees, harnesses, cow chains and fittings, horse shoes, etc.[26]

King rented two trucks, one of them an army truck, to transport the sheep. On the day of the sheep transfer, King, greatly excited, helped supervise the unloading, oblivious, as he would not be in the future, toward dire omens. Alerted by "a guiding & protecting Providence," he was terrified, as the truck pulled into the Farm, to see fiery sparks shooting out near its exhaust pipe. The fire was successfully contained and the only casualty was an over-excited sheep which nearly broke its leg disembarking. King's happiness, however, was soon deflated when McBurnie informed him later in the day that two ewes would have to be killed, in King's vague wording, "because of some sickness developed in the sudden change of weather" (28 April 1927). King, heartsick once again, feared he had taken on more than he should have. However, his mood lifted when, still enveloped in a protective pastoral dream, he saw McBurnie and the lambs the next night:

> It was a delight to see the sheep browsing about the grounds in the vicinity of the barns, the little lambs skipping and at play — jumping into the air all four feet at once...It was a lovely sight and a not unpleasing sound to hear the little lambs calling for their mothers & the mothers replying. McBurnie in the midst with his bag of feed over his shoulder made a lovely pastoral scene, the sort of thing Jules Breton and Millais delighted in. It was inspiring (29 April 1927).

The disquiet brought on by his over-excitement, the sick sheep and the gradual realization of what he was blindly venturing into, slowly began to blunt his euphoria. Worry began to gnaw at him, worry that his supporters would, rightly, think he was indulging in a rich man's hobby, and rather presciently, that further mishaps would occur.

First the sheep strayed into places where they should not. The pasture fencing was not yet completed, so a boy was hired to prevent the sheep from straying onto the road. Instead he allowed them to roam everywhere else. The sheep "...were out on the moors — all the moors — as far as the woods — had been under the fence into Williamson's property, eaten his flowers, sweet William, iris & other plants" (1 May 1927). King evidently thought sheep could be treated like his little Pat, for he noted that when McBurnie returned, the straying sheep seemed to "mind him at once." When they were herded into their rightful pasture, King's annoyance was replaced by an aesthetic appreciation of their distant beauty on the landscape. He fervently hoped the sheep would "...become contented & not stray too far" (1 May 1927). Soon after King had to steel himself to order a lamb killed for a Laurier House dinner: "I feel genuinely pained at the thought & doubt if I can eat it. I love to see the little creatures on the hill side. It is a reposeful picture in one's mind & they are as children" (9 May 1927). King seemed to be stressing the "gentleman" in gentleman farmer, rather than cultivating the realistic attitudes of one who wanted to make his farm pay.

As King began to reconcile his squeamishness over the less romantic aspects of sheep farming, the next calamity struck. One of his ewes was killed by a dog — a $20 loss said King — followed the next day by the killing of two lambs. King was abruptly introduced to the vulnerability of sheep to predators (wild animals and dogs) and was soon to learn of the ever-present menace of parasites.[27] Sheep-killing dogs, the bane of rural Canada, were the subject of great debate in the agricultural journals from the 1890s up to the time of King's farming. Fines, by-laws, lawsuits were all discussed as possible retribution against negligent owners. By 1930 legislation was passed in Ontario and Quebec protecting the sheep owner. The owner could receive compensation for killed sheep from the local government and the guilty dog owner.

After King's staff had traced the guilty dog, King instructed his Quebec lawyer to take action. The lawyer took the problem to the Hull Council which advised that a fine could be levied against the owner, a Mrs. R.J. Devlin, and the dog could be destroyed under the Revised Statutes of Quebec. King, not wanting to draw further attention to his farming endeavours, told the lawyer not to sue, but to have the dog destroyed and the owner sent to him. Mrs. Devlin duly appeared in the Prime Minister's office. King, who said he dealt with her "quietly and carefully," told Mrs. Devlin that the dog had to be destroyed. She then pleaded with the Prime Minister to allow her to move the dog to a county outside the province, for if the dog was destroyed, it would be the end of her crazy son, Bob. After hearing her rural Gothic tale, King let her leave early to spirit the dog away before the law came to kill it. There were no further incidents until early fall when Pat and Derry, King's and Joan's dogs, killed a lamb. Earlier King had found it "interesting" teaching Pat not to worry the sheep, but this interest was replaced by revulsion when he saw how the dogs had torn the lamb's throat. He said he gave Pat a severe thrashing.

National Archives of Canada/C 9051

Mackenzie King feeding his sheep — he loved the look of them on the landscape.

Two weeks later, the sheep lost their picturesque appeal when they were shorn with a shearing machine borrowed from the Central Experimental Farm. King was thrilled, however, to earn $91.40 from the sale of the wool to the Quebec branch of the Canadian Co-operative Wool Growers.[28]

McBurnie further raised King's hopes for farming success when he told him that he had a contract to sell the lambs at $10 each. King believed the sheep would pay for themselves by autumn. But the next day his optimism was deflated when he saw McBurnie's accounts. Adding the amount paid to McBurnie for his sheep to the setting-up expenses plus the land purchase price, King reached the "very considerable sum" of $10,000. Soon after McBurnie once again raised King out of the slough of despond and into the realm of hope and glory by cutting out raspberry bushes and other scrub on the farmland moor: "I could hardly believe my eyes. I am going to have a perfectly beautiful property...McBurnie is a wonderful man, worth his weight in gold" (23 June 1927). By July King had even relaxed enough to comment on his agricultural motivations: "It is amusing even to me how I seem to have drifted into this farming business, to have almost gone into it as if by unseen compulsion. It is I believe all going to work out for the best" (8 July 1927).

Within a month McBurnie's golden weight had plummeted, again taking King's optimism with it. McBurnie reported that the sheep were not doing well, some had worms, and one sheep which had eaten mica had to be killed. King was furious, faulting McBurnie for making him bring so many sheep to the Farm, and then restricting them to one pasture which King had learned increased the risk of infection. King metaphorically tore his hair: "I felt again tonight I had tackled too much in this farm" (9 August 1927). He quickly enlisted Dr. Marriott, an animal specialist from the Experimental Farm, to examine the sheep. Marriott reported that the lambs were faring better, but the flock was weakened by parasites and needed a change in pasture. King and McBurnie were said to be greatly relieved. King, however, began retrenching by selling one cow and one horse. It is not clear what happened to the other two.

By October the sheep were said to be in much better health. King even ventured out into the flock to feed some of them by hand. Godfroy Patteson took pictures of the great event, one of which appeared in a laudatory article by a *Toronto Star Weekly* reporter. King took the reporter, Frederick Griffin, over hill and across the moors looking for his sheep. When he found them, King, with a "proprietary glow in his voice," said, "Have you ever seen a picture more peaceful and beautiful?" To demonstrate his active interest in the sheep, King explained to Griffin the care of orphan lambs. Then attempting to call a lamb over to be petted, King was slightly dismayed: "Usually he will come right over when you call, but to-day he seems to be on his dignity."[29] King liked the lengthy article so much he framed copies of the artist's proofs and sent copies to friends and colleagues. King obviously enjoyed the flattering allusions to himself as a "son of the soil," and the accuracy, in King's mind, of the reporter's interpretation of what Kingsmere meant to King: "It was hard to imagine that the bare-headed man who strode along pointing with pride to this or that feature of the land was the first citizen of the land. Rather did he seem just a well-to-do farmer, whose greatest problems were fencing and the raising of sheep."[30]

Unfortunately the highly flattering article provoked ridicule in the House of Commons:

> Not long ago I saw in the *Star Weekly* a picture of the Prime Minister tending his sheep. I wonder if he is going to put the sheep industry entirely out of business, and then find himself without a vocation during his summer holiday tending his sheep.[31]

King sent a copy of this portion of *Hanzard* to the editor of the *Toronto Star Weekly* to demonstrate why he was so reluctant to publicize his Kingsmere estate: "Not that I mind in the least any of the satire or ridicule as far as my public work is concerned. What I dread is the invasion of one's privacy and personal life by a horde of intruders who have no kindly purpose at heart, and are actuated by motives only of curiosity or of mischief."[32]

The adverse publicity did not, however, diminish King's delight with the picture of himself feeding his sheep. He sent a framed copy as a Christmas gift to Governor General Willingdon, along with his new book, *The Message of the Carrillon*, a collection of speeches: "I sd in my letter to His Ex there was high authority for truth that shepherds were watching flocks when the Message of the Angels song was heard & I was sending him a symbol of both" (24 December 1927). God may have been in his heaven, and all's right with the world, but a dark cloud was slowly moving across King's sheep pastures, for McBurnie handed in his notice to quit the next spring. King, ruefully acknowledging that this part of farming was much more difficult than raising plants and flowers, now classed McBurnie as "a real disappointment."

Disappointment changed rapidly to horror and indignation when King inspected the sheep in April, a few days before McBurnie was to leave. King discovered that this "half knave & half fool" had been highly neglectful of the sheep. King believed McBurnie, now described as dishonest and quarrelsome, had from the first substituted his sick sheep for King's healthy ones, and had sold off King's sheep all the while swearing they had died. The worst jolt of all was seeing the weakened condition of the animals, herded on top of their own manure, dirty, coughing, and infested with ticks: "It is the most cruel & wicked piece of business I have ever seen" (30 April 1928). When J.H. Grisdale, Deputy Minister of Agriculture, and a veterinary surgeon from the Experimental Farm came out to look them over, they reported to King that the sheep had been starved: "Two of them were lying dead, one beautiful little lamb of last year dying & another older one so thin it could not move" (30 April 1928). Grisdale angrily told King McBurnie "should be in jail."

National Archives of Canada/PA 134815

Throughout his life, King loved picturesque rural scenes on his estate. He once wrote: "As the working men or the dogs or horses move about on the landscape, the scene is just too beautiful for words."

King could not understand why McBurnie had acted so spitefully. Perhaps, King reasoned, McBurnie only made it appear sheep could not live at Kingsmere, but then having gotten what he could out of King, abused the sheep from some obscure motivation to "get even" with King. Meanwhile the veterinarian condemned the sheep and their pasture. King philosophically accepted the reduction in the size of the herd, but, fantastically, he still wanted to keep a few on the landscape "for appearances."

King changed the sheep's pasture and attempted to redeem some of the damage. He sent an urgent request for sheep dip to the Canadian Co-operative Wool Growers' in Toronto and borrowed a sheep-dipping outfit loaned by the Quebec government to the farmers of Hull County. He sold the wool, ranging from low medium standard to medium, seedy, light, for $80.22. Although by the end of May he thought the sheep were looking better, his agricultural spirit was broken: "The whole livestock end has been a disappointment, failure & annoyance" (3 June

1928). A month later King sold all his sheep to a neighbouring farmer, Michael Mulvihill, at half the amount he had originally paid for them. After returning from a European visit that summer, King was further disheartened to see the neglected, dirty condition of the farm. He immediately, almost petulantly, exclaimed that the farm had been "...a mistake, a costly experiment with more worry than pleasure, & undue publicity" (4 November 1928).

Chickens

In 1927 King also began poultry raising, an activity he found alternately thrilling and distressful, but compared with his sheep raising, rather more successful. He bought thirty-five chickens, 160 eggs and an incubator, as well as a new chicken house and run. The chickens were not at first a part of King's idealization of a farm landscape. However, a flock of chickens was a common farm feature, often the responsibility of the farm wife, providing her with "pin money" from the profits of selling eggs and chickens.

Unfortunately King's chicken raising initially provoked unpleasant press attention, rather than remunerative rewards. King had remarked to F.C. Elford, Dominion Poultry Husbandman at the Central Experimental Farm, that he had taken a "fancy" to White Wyandottes. Elford had then passed this on to the Conservative Ontario Minister of Agriculture, John S. Martin, a leading authority and breeder of White Wyandottes. Martin offered to send the eggs, which he would sell for $25, to the Experimental Farm, so that the C.E.F. could supervise the hatching. He also offered to give King, free of charge, a trio of mature chickens. Motherwell wrote to King explaining the offer, saying $25 dollars for pedigreed eggs was not out of the way at all, and was even more of a bargain with the rooster and hens thrown in.[33] King, never one to refuse a bargain, immediately wrote, enclosing a cheque and elaborate thanks, and then hedged a bit, saying that neither McBurnie nor he were expert breeders or raisers of Wyandottes, but that he hoped at some time to make a "...worthy exhibit and reflect some further credit upon the donor...if you still feel that you would be willing to risk your reputation along with mine...I shall be happy indeed to accept your gift...."[34] When a rival (Liberal) White Wyandotte breeder heard that King had bought eggs from Martin, he offered King some of his Wyandottes ("which do not associate with Mr. Martin's birds ...they are strong Liberals..."). Under a picture of a Wyandotte on his letterhead, John M. Bell had typed: "A Liberal, with plenty of GRIT."[35]

Delighted as King was with his expanding poultry flock, he was furious when an over-zealous Experimental Farm employee released the story of the hatching of his Wyandottes to the press. The press release was included in the C.E.F.'s publicity campaign for the upcoming International Poultry Congress. The short article noted that the eighteen chicks which had hatched (two did not survive) would probably make a good showing at the Congress Live Bird Exhibit. An editorial writer for the *Ottawa Journal* reacted in a rather jaundiced tone:

> We can see where this business of having a shepherd Premier is going to be an infernal nuisance. Every time a hawk threatens one of the Prime Minister's chickens a communique will come from Kingsmere....We have no objection to our Prime Minister going back to nature, whether it be by playing the role of the lone shepherd on the mountains or communing with the stars from a Gatineau porch. But too much of that sort of thing is

more than enough. If our morning papers are going to be filled up with the gamboling of Mr. King's lambs... then we object. A little less news from Kingsmere and a little more from the West Block would be better for everybody.[36]

The comment in the *Toronto Star* was more satirical. In an article entitled "American Eagle is Hon. W.L.M. King's Prize Poultry," it was noted: "Exhibits entered in the name of Hon. W.L.M. King will be few in number if the hawks are permitted to steal the chickens out of Hon. W.L.M. King's hen-run as Mr. King's favourite poultry, the American Eagle, is permitted to steal opportunities for employment out of the lives of Canada's boys and girls and the fathers of these boys and girls."[37] The author further observed that King should be represented at the Congress by an exhibit of "Buff (or is it Bluff?) Orpingtons."

With barely concealed fury King wrote Motherwell demanding that he personally find the person responsible for giving the story to the press ("very annoying publicity"), and forcefully make "...him clearly to understand that there is to be no further reference to this subject."[38] He further noted that he had thought to exhibit the birds given him by Mr. Martin at the Congress, but now King felt that "...to call further attention to my Kingsmere interests, directly or indirectly, will not only serve to rob me of whatever enjoyment I obtain there through privacy, but will also prove directly prejudicial to the Government."[39]

King enjoyed the frequent re-siting, according to standard poultry practice, of the chicken houses, devoting his time to the aesthetic and practical considerations of each move. King was not troubled when ordering chickens killed or eating them. In fact, he found it quite thrilling to eat his chickens, especially when accompanied by other produce of his farm: vegetables, fruit and milk.

Certainly his poultry-raising did not involve the same bitter trials as the sheep. This venture, however, was not without its distressful moments. By the end of 1927, McBurnie had informed King that the Wyandotte rooster John S. Martin had given him was immature, or as King euphemistically explained to Elford: The rooster "...had not measured up to expectations entertained of him."[40] Elford, without informing King, told Martin who immediately sent along another, more vigorous, rooster. King, overjoyed, thanked him effusively, not only because Martin sent along another rooster, but also because he generously allowed King to keep the original one. The increased egg output was sabotaged when McBurnie let the chicken eggs freeze — a sign of his growing dissatisfaction at Kingsmere. After the next caretaker King hired in 1928 also neglected the chickens, they were then taken to the C.E.F. to be "looked after." These chickens and their offspring (84) were not returned until the summer of 1929.

When he hired Edward Schnizel (whose name he constantly misspelled in the diary) as caretaker, the chickens were admirably tended. King once again enjoyed roasting fowls and scrambled eggs. He also began selling chickens to Joan. The flock remained healthy until the fall of 1935, when active tuberculosis was diagnosed by the Chief Pathologist of the Central Experimental Farm. King stoically received the disheartening news that the entire flock had to be destroyed.

He also tried ducks, and even built a duck pond near the barns, however they were not mentioned in diary or letter after 1927. King also experimented with pheasant raising, probably as a result of seeing them at the Poultry Congress. In September

1927 Charles McCrea, Ontario Minister of Mines, sent King pairs of Golden pheasants, Lady Amherst pheasants and English Ring-necked pheasants. King had his estate workers build wire netting enclosed runs (16' x 12' x 6'/5m x 4m x 2m), and large open coops for each bird pair. The pheasants were met in Ottawa and brought out to Kingsmere by a Department of Interior employee in charge of the Migratory Birds Act. Soon after, King wrote him, noting that the pheasants were "...decidedly happy" and "seem to be thoroughly at home in the Laurentian hills."[41] King also remarked that he was keenly interested in making a success of pheasant-raising.

Traditionally pheasant-raising was connected to field sport and shooting. Victorian gentlemen took pride in their pheasant flocks and the possibilities of a good day's shoot on their land. In Canada raising pheasants for hunting persisted up into the 20th century. Colonel A.O.T. Beardmore built a pheasantry of seven runs on his country estate eighty kilometers from Toronto. From seventy-five ring-necked pheasants, he expected to produce between three and four thousand eggs annually. Some were to be sold to the provincial government for restocking purposes and the rest were to be released into Beardmore's woodlands. He said it was not only a fascinating hobby, but benefitted the local economy through the sale of hunting licenses.[42]

King never considered raising pheasants as hunting stock — again he acquired the form of a country pursuit, but not the substance. However, he enthusiastically entered into this newest farming adventure. King reflected that the pheasants were just as keen to succeed: "It is interesting to have in mind the wild birds — the pheasants — doing their part — sitting on eggs..." (14 May 1928). These particular eggs (one dozen silver pheasant eggs) were given to King by a donor who "requested that there be no publicity."[43] In 1928 one of his hens died. In 1929 when King over-wintered his pheasants under the expert care at the Central Experimental Farm, he still lost a cockerel. He was so disheartened, for he only had two hens left, that he had his private secretary phone the Farm to tell them to keep the hens indefinitely.[44] From then until 1940, King had intermittent supplies of pheasants which regularly died off due to the depredations of winter, predators, hunters and other hazards. The C.E.F. continued to be heavily involved in his pheasant-raising for many years, but even its expert care could not keep all the pheasants alive.

In 1937 H. Lloyd, an ornithologist connected with the Museum of Man, sent King a pamphlet, "Instructions for the Handling of Pheasants and Their Eggs," hoping it would be of help. However when Joan told him the latest batch of pheasants, a gift from H.C. Nixon, Ontario Minister of Game and Fisheries, seemed to be unhappy in their cages, King immediately had them set free: "I had been writing of liberty & decided to go over & let them have their freedom. They should never have been deprived of it." He was a bit dismayed to see the birds fly off in all directions: "...hope they yet find each other & be a happy family together" (8 August 1937). Happily a few weeks later one of the neighbouring farmers told King the pheasants were still alive and well. King immediately instructed Schnizel to lure them back to his estate — he enjoyed seeing them wandering across his landscape. He thought they could be trained to parade (perhaps substituting for peacocks) around the Farm grounds.

In 1939 an Ontario government official presented King with yet another dozen pheasants which had been exhibited at a provincial government exhibition. At first King thought he would have a run built close to the farm house so that he could watch them from his window, but then changed his mind and again set the pheasants free. The next year King was rewarded when the remaining pheasants paraded across his farm grounds: "Later I heard the cock pheasant just near the house; he walked towards the barn and I later saw him coming up the path; still later the two hen pheasants came and walked up to the back door and I looked at them out of the window....The first real happiness has been to see these birds free and enjoying their freedom..." (9 June 1940).

National Archives of Canada/PA 178406

King had an old log house moved from one part of the estate to the farm to be used as a second chicken house. Aesthetics and sentiment played a large role in this expensive decision.

Although the Experimental Farm played a major role in his pheasant-raising, King did not request as much help with another small farming venture — bee-keeping. In 1931 King hired his caretaker's brother, Henry Schnizel, a private gardener who did bee-keeping on the side, to look after the hives. He made at least eight trips to Kingsmere each year, replacing damaged hives, feeding the bees, restocking queens or drones if needed, and then preparing them for winter. In 1944 King received a startling communication from Schinzel that all his bees had died from starvation during a sudden warm spell in spring which had brought them out of hibernation too soon. The Dominion Apiarist at the Experimental Farm was quickly contacted and agreed to supply two new hives within the week.[45] During the war Schnizel had great difficulty in making the required number of trips to the estate due to gas and tire rationing. He appealed to King to have his gas rationing upgraded to the farming category, so that he could continue servicing King's bees. King replied, through his private secretary, that he could not endorse anything of the kind. However, when the bee season was about to open, Schnizel was to telephone King to see what arrangements could be made. These unwritten arrangements were translated into chauffeured trips to Kingsmere in King's own car. Finally in 1945 Henry Schnizel quit, saying he was not as young as he used to be and found he was not "able to run around as in previous years."[46]

The Kitchen Garden and Orchards

By 1929 King had abandoned any hope of being a successful livestock farmer. Despite the flurries of pheasant-raising and bee-keeping, he now concentrated on the plant, rather than the animal, kingdom. He occasionally rented animals from neighbours; he also frequently rented out his own pastures. Although King had ceased raising livestock, they still gave him trouble. He wrote Michael Mulvihill, a neighbouring farmer, complaining that Mulvihill's cattle were enjoying the illicit pleasure of grazing on King's land and in his gardens:

> "...I should be glad...if you could arrange to have those [cattle] that are at present on my property taken home. I might say that yesterday they broke down part of one of the fences around the garden, and got into the grounds, and did not a little damage to some of the plants and flowers. The servants and I were up most of the night trying to keep them out."[47]

The cow he rented from Mulvihill proved to be a poor milker. It needed to be coddled and kept in the barn, resulting in a red entry in the farm ledger. He rented a pair of work horses from his fellow Kingsmere cottager, Jackson Booth, the same summer. These horses proved to be quite useful and in King's eyes ornamental as well. They unfortunately became very popular with the staff who continually fed them across one of the stone walls. King had to stop this because the horses, in their enthusiasm to get the treats, began dislodging the stones, pulling the walls down.[48]

In his "Memorandum Re Country Residence" (ca. 1928), King stated that "The purpose of the farm is to keep my house in the city and my cottage in the country supplied, as nearly as possible the year round, with vegetables and eggs, and during the summer, with milk and cream, and to some extent as opportunity offers, with butter."[49] He no longer harboured any illusions of running the farm for "profit and gain," but mainly now for "recreation and health."[50] Although he had given up the business side, he was thrilled that year to receive a certificate making him an honourary member of the British Society of Agriculture.

King did attempt to cultivate field crops, under the guidance and advice of the deputy minister of Agriculture, J.H. Grisdale, who made a thorough survey of the 200 acre (494 ha) farm in April 1927. His findings were not enthusiastic. Grisdale noted that a "...very small proportion indeed of the whole of the cleared area [is] of such character as would permit of its being brought under the plow for either grain, hay or root crop production."[51] Grisdale would only recommend the two or three small fields at the far end of the south-east corner of the property for cash crop planting. He divided these 4 1/2 acres (2 ha) into three sections and devised a four year crop rotation plan: roots — grain — hay — roots. King had his staff follow these suggestions and by late August King could comment: "The oats are cut on the nearby field. They are not too thick, indeed rather thin, but the clover etc. beneath has caught well" (11 August 1927). Within two years King was writing like a seasoned grain grower about the ploughing in of his buckwheat crop to fertilize the soil. His office staff also received a farm education. His private secretary often had to phone the C.E.F. for details on various operations at Kingsmere. For example, in 1928 he had to find out for King the correct implement to use when sowing oats and fine seed, and then type up the information in detail. King's Parliament Hill staff also learned the proper way to disk-harrow, sow, and roll a field to oats, peas, vetch, and clover.

Although King found this phase of agriculture interesting, he was most enthusiastic about the extensive kitchen garden and orchard planted during his first year of farming. The kitchen garden, a huge plot, was sited between the farm house and bordering fence. He once again asked J.H. Grisdale for advice, this time for vegetables and fruit. He stated his three objectives for the following year, requesting information on how to proceed and where to procure the right varieties:

1. I wish to lay out an orchard of fruit trees, some apple, plum cherry and pear trees. About fifty, or one hundred in all.
2. I wish to make an asparagus bed.
3. I wish to plant strawberries, raspberries and currants.[52]

Farm officials cautioned him not to begin any of these projects in the fall, but to wait for spring. Five C.E.F. booklets on fruit cultivation were sent along, together with the addresses of dependable fruit tree and asparagus suppliers, with whom King had several delightful exchanges.

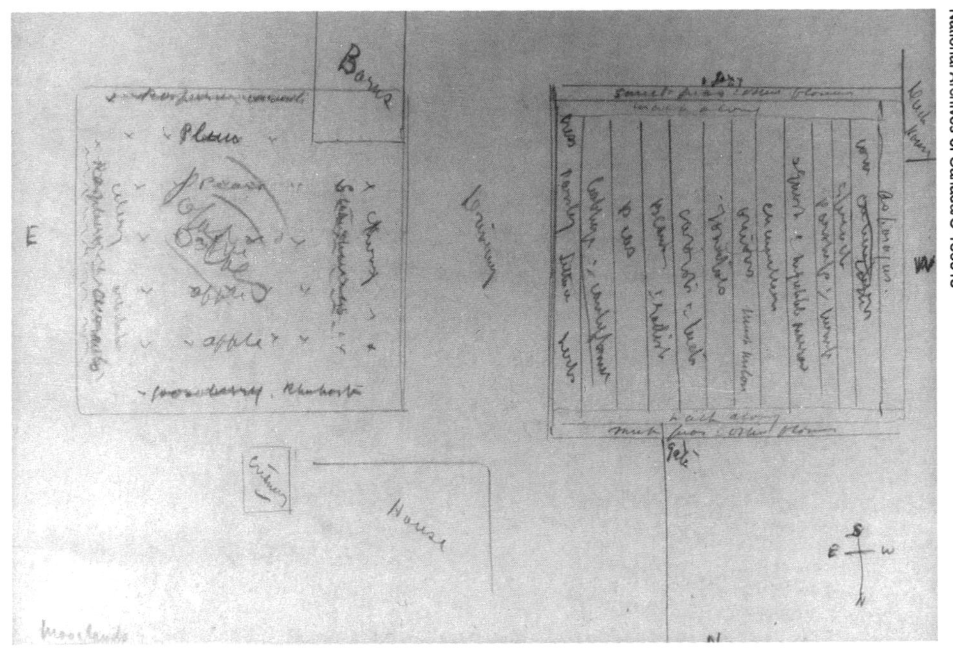

National Archives of Canada/C 136613

King's plan of an early vegetable garden at the farm.

He happily recorded his first harvest in September 1927: "We have now all we need of apples, tomatoes, potatoes, cabbage, carrots, beets, turnips etc." (24 September 1927). However, the ever-vigilant King had to reprove his Kingsmere staff for wasting food: "There is a tendency to waste much that has been grown which annoys me very much. Also a failure to even send to the house the vegetables as grown" (19 September 1927). To this end, King went out and picked apples himself with the maid, Ada, and then proudly sold the surplus to F.A. McGregor, one of his secretaries. Within four years, King was selling apples and raspberries to a distributor. His gross sales of $67 inspired him to speculate: "...believe one could develop a fine fruit growing industry here were one so inclined" (29 September 1931).

He was delighted with an exchange with a southern Ontario strawberry grower, Harry Tinney of Havelock, Ontario, who, when sending an order to King, remarked that his wife said that the plants were true "Grits" and would grow well for him. King replied that the plants were excellent, thriving in spite of the late planting, and offered the use of his name "as a testimonial." He also used the letter for a bit of electioneering:

> Please tell Mrs. Tinney I was delighted to receive her message. I thought the plants were "Grits" when I looked at them, and I had no doubt that you yourself must have the best of wives, recognizing how well cared for all the plants appeared to be...I have now to begin on the work

Paul Horsdal/National Archives of Canada/PA 134778

The farmhouse and nearby garden.

Canadian agriculture: "Should it fit in with the plans of the Department of Agriculture to have a few varieties in the orchard, I, of course, would greatly welcome the practical benefits which would come to myself or others later on from a step of the kind."[55]

The kitchen garden and orchard expanded under the expert care of Schnizel, then Nicol and later the Kellys. Mrs. Kelly remembered the kitchen garden as being as "big as a field...that whole lawn."[56] Picking fifty boxes of raspberries before breakfast was not unusual she said. The Pattesons, especially Godfroy, were very involved with King's fruit and vegetable growing. Godfroy advised on the timing of selling potatoes in a lengthy memo to King in 1928. In 1931 when King's dentist asked for particulars on the types of muskmelons grown at Kingsmere ('Golden Champlain,' 'Benders Surprise,' and 'Montreal Green Nutmeg'), King did not have a clue. He turned to Godfroy for details on the varieties and their cultivation — a complicated procedure involving hilling up earth, protecting seedlings in small wooden cold frames, and pinching runners to provoke greater production. In later years some of Godfroy's happiest moments, when he was not feeding wild birds, were when he supervised the kitchen garden. It certainly was one of the most successful ventures King attempted at the Farm. King's records one year show an amazing amount of vegetables, fruits and herbs distributed between the Farm, Shady Hill and Laurier House. When he occasionally rented out the cottages, King would send surplus berries over to the tenants. King delighted in offering guests his own produce. In 1935 he

> of the campaign. Tell Mrs. Tinney that I am glad to know we are in the fight together.[53]

After his defeat in 1930, Mackenzie King asked Grisdale if the C.E.F.'s aid would continue: "I wonder if, not withstanding I am now in opposition, I might continue on personal grounds to have the benefit of your good offices and judgment with respect to some of my farm adventures."[54] Evidently this was no problem for Experimental Farm officials continued to help him at Kingsmere throughout his years in Opposition and up into the 1940s. In late 1939, M.B. Davis, the Dominion Horticulturist, offered to send out a number of fruit trees (apple, pear and plum) for an experimentation plot. King was delighted, needless to say, to see himself as an altruistic benefactor in the larger scheme of had Vincent and Alice Massey to lunch and gave them a "Kingsmere double treat" — a Kingsmere Lake trout and fresh garden asparagus.

Farm House Renovations

As he aged, King yearned for year-round access to the estate — closing up each fall was a sad occasion for him. The farmhouse seemed the logical dwelling to renovate. During the first eight years he owned the farm house, he rented it out to his caretakers and their families.

Then, while he was in the midst of planning his Abbey ruin in May 1935, King began to seriously consider winterizing the typical one and a half storey frame home. When he decided, for a mixture of political and financial reasons, not to proceed with the ruin, King turned to the farmhouse. Joan and he spent cosy evenings planning additions to the structure:

National Capital Commission

The outbuildings.

> She was for making the living portion at the back, facing south & getting views of the mountain & the Ottawa distance. I had been for fitting up the front portion, but it faces the road and is not nearly so good. Only servants will be crossing front quarters etc. — Still I think Joan is right for what we want & to keep the front as it is. We plan for upstairs with bathroom etc & a good bedroom, facing south, which would get the all day sun in October & November & in March & April & May & a conservatory beneath (26 May 1935).

With grand plans once again dancing in his head, King approached Ewart and Cummings for estimates. He wanted to complete the alterations while he was still leader of the opposition; less attention, he thought, would be focussed on this construction than when he became prime minister again. However, King was not pleased with Ewart's plans: "...I experienced some disappointment in the failure to connect the whole part with the new and what is likely to prove of more considerable cost than I had anticipated. Also, certain features of the plan did not seem to me as artistic as I had expected..." (5 June 1935). King spent a few more nights with drawing paper, pen, and reference books, trying to illustrate just what he wanted. When Cummings and Ewart submitted their estimates — just under $5,000 — King was horrified and immediately canceled their participation: "I have felt all along it was unwise to get an architect into the project, and that the work on the farmhouse, if carried out,

The renovated farmhouse.

should be done, as other work at Kingsmere has been done, pretty much with local men and in accordance with one's own plan" (20 June 1935). Accordingly King contacted a Chelsea contractor and carpenter, R.J. O'Neil: "He is just the man for the job, much better than fussing with an architect. We did more in an hour together in the matter of reaching right decisions than would have been possible with an architect in a week. There is no mystery about everything. It is possible to talk frankly, no professional secrets to guard or etiquette to observe" (8 July 1935).

When O'Neil discovered rot in the foundations and other structural damage, King's nervousness over the expense increased. He finally justified it by telling himself that a weekend in the country was necessary year round — "insurance against fatigue and impaired health." The only way to provide this was to do the house over properly and install an oil furnace and modern bathroom fixtures. Beyond this rationalization was a more class-oriented justification: "Besides the old farm house was no longer habitable even for farm hands, and unworthy the home of servants of one in my position" (19 July 1935). The ink was barely dry after writing these thoughts when King abruptly changed his mind and rehired Ewart to supervise O'Neil and to plan the renovations.

Interestingly during his farm activities, from livestock-raising to choosing bathroom fixtures, King did not seek or experience "signs" or otherworldly confirmations of his decisions and plans. In the late twenties, King was not as active in recording or experiencing "psychical" phenomena as he would be in the early thirties. Also, his farming was overshadowed in the mid-1930s by his intense preoccupation with ruin-building. Perhaps the intensity of the signs and visions related to the ruins siphoned off or suppressed any spillover into his farming activities. However in August 1935 after certain decisions had been made for the farmhouse, King happened to visit a Kingston estate, Cataraqui Grange, the former home of his maternal grandmother. Here he experienced a "psychic" sign. King was absolutely amazed by the similarities between this house and what he was planning to build at the Farm:

> It is incredible that in practically all particulars the two places are identical in what has been already planned on paper, or what has been in my mind, as the work of construction has gone on, as, for example, the wisdom

> of having fireplaces upstairs as well as down, and in both rooms downstairs, also, the additional room to serve the purpose of a kitchen....What was equally interesting was the way in which we finally decided to have the servants bath room and bedroom placed upstairs, instead of at the end of the kitchen, the staircase to run exactly as in the house at Kingston....I firmly believe I have unconsciously, and in a symbolical way, been repeating what my ancestors did a hundred years ago, and that I have been "impressed" to this and by their spiritual presence, just as I am repeating the work of my grandfather....in once more subjecting the Executive to the will of Parliament... (9 August 1935).

No matter how much care King took or how often he intervened in the renovations, things did not always proceed the way he wanted. He did admit on this project that some of his disappointments might be due to his frequent inclination to "idealize everything." He constantly fussed over Ewart's slowness in making decisions and then not implementing them fast enough to satisfy King's impatience. Also he could not resist changing his mind over the placement of various components. After deliberating a few nights over the unaesthetic look of the back addition, he made O'Neil extend it. One of his private rooms he thought could be made into a little chapel: "...a prophet's chamber Joan calls it, & that it may become. I believe it is what my soul calls for & needs, — a place I can keep sacred records, & think sacred thoughts" (3 November 1935). Later on another room, "the green room," was to be set aside for psychical research. When he won the 1935 election, his impatience increased, for he was terribly worried the press would publicize this latest round of improvements. And well he might worry, for the total amount spent was nearly five times Ewart's initial $5,000 estimate.

National Archives of Canada/PA 129854

King on the farmhouse porch in one of the last photographs taken before he died.

Originally King thought he would add a small wing which could be heated in the cold weather months, however, his plans expanded considerably. King added a basement blasted out of the Shield, two L-shaped additions, staff bedrooms, guest suites, library, a grander entrance foyer, new verandahs, elaborate ornamental plastering and mouldings, plus all new wiring, heating and plumbing fixtures.

Although Moorside continued to be the horticultural showplace of the estate, King did not neglect the landscaping around the farmhouse. He had a circular drive cut and sodded at the entrance to the house. Its grassed centre was ornamented by a circular flower bed and sundial. Aided by Sandy Stewart of the Federal District Commission, King planted shrubs and trees around the house. White board fences were erected to frame the orchard area to the rear of the house, trees were planted to soften the property boundaries, wide front and side lawns were cleared, stone walls and pillars were built at the entrance to the drive, and even a small balustrade was erected at the back of the house. The kitchen garden supplied the sweet peas, cannas, dahlias, and gladioli for the many flower vases used on the estate. Isabelle Kelly, wife of the last caretaker, was evidently very adept at arranging flowers and was often complimented by King on her ability: "He always said I did everything nice. He said, 'You know Mrs. Kelly, you've got a green thumb.' I would say 'I didn't know if I had a green thumb but I know it works a lot.'"[57] Every second day she would fill and arrange twenty-five vases of flowers for the farmhouse alone with King's preferred arrangements of mixed flowers. Mrs. Kelly would make four trips over to the Moorside gardens with her clippers and basket and collect annuals and perennials, as well as forest wildflowers and branches of flowering shrubs. In the spring she would fill the vases with daffodils and tulips, in the summer with roses.

The Second World War predictably changed the course of his life at Kingsmere. As much as he loved his new country home, the demands on his time in Ottawa understandably overruled his need to go to Kingsmere. Summer labourers were also in short supply, so King had to let the gardens go. In 1943 he dismissed Nicol, the caretaker, who had complained that he was becoming just an ordinary labourer not a gardener with the amount of grass he had to cut unaided. The Kellys were then hired to look after Kingsmere until the end of King's life.

During the war, King's infrequent trips to the Farm became even more special to him. When Pat, his first dog, died in his arms in 1941 in the farmhouse, the sacredness of the house was established. He never relinquished his belief in the health-giving atmosphere of the estate — whether he was recovering from sciatica, an election campaign, or the worries of the war. Not surprisingly in July 1950, King, suffering from a terminal heart condition, refused to go into hospital: "I said if now my condition was such that the summer at Kingsmere would not improve matters, I would rather end my days in the country in the Summer-time" (7 July 1950).

CHAPTER SEVEN

The Immortal Garden

MACKENZIE KING'S LEGACY

As the dying Mackenzie King gazed out the Farmhouse window and noticed the trees gently swaying in the wind and heard the songs of his beloved birds, he reassured himself that he had found the best solution for the future of the estate. Its disposition had pleasantly preoccupied him from 1924 onwards, as the estate grew over the years into a property of nearly 600 acres. King's land holdings had slowly crept up from the lake, spreading and expanding to include four cottages, a country home, numerous outbuildings, a hobby farm, the ruins and acres of garden, forest, stream and meadow.

In 1924 King had smugly admitted to himself that, with the purchase of Moorside, Kingsmere would someday be one of the finest estates in Canada. Smugness soon gave way to self-sacrificing justification — the estate would be his legacy to the Canadian people: "The foundations have been laid of a real estate, which thro' the years will be associated with the family name and the position I have held in the country. God grant that it may be the means of great usefulness on my part to the people of the country" (24 September 1924).

What form this legacy would assume changed over the next thirty years, as King considered one idea after another. Yet every plan always incorporated the idea of a King memorial as the basis of his gift to the nation. At one time King thought the estate should be used as a summer "rest home" for ill or needy civil servants: "for men & women who need an outing or a convalescing home & who have not the means to secure this help elsewhere" (1 July 1936). A year later he mused in his diary that perhaps the estate could be a "centre for a clinic some day," memorializing his dead brother and sister, with the Abbey ruin serving as a "...sign of healing — Medicine and Religion" (29

Eardley Escarpment in Gatineau Park.

August 1937). When John W. Dafoe, Liberal supporter and journalist, mentioned to King in the late 1930s that the estate would be the perfect spot for King's retirement, King archly replied it would be a "...good spot for Conferences for the Liberal party & that I hope to make it more so" (16 June 1937). As the threat of a second world war mounted, King returned to the clinic idea, expanding the concept into a convalescent home for Canadian soldiers, and, after the war, for injured war veterans. King also thought at another time that the estate would be a worthy summer home for future prime ministers.

Although commemorating his family's "associations and traditions" was uppermost in his plans, the emphasis slowly shifted. As the estate expanded and King lavished effort, money and emotion upon it, he began favouring a personal memorialization, a concrete expression of the "*bona fides* of my political faith & teaching" (8 April 1934). As noted in Chapter Five, after building the Abbey ruin, King thought he might erect the ultimate memorial—his tomb in the centre of the ruin. The tomb was never built, but the idea of a commemoration of his life gained strength. He had before him the resonant examples of the "shrines," as King called them, of prominent men: George Washington's home, Mount Vernon; Thomas Jefferson's Monticello; and William Gladstone's Hawarden. However, when King mentioned his Kingsmere plans to his friend, John D. Rockefeller, Jr., he was gently chided for wanting a few too many "shrines" — at the same time Woodside was under consideration for historic designation and restoration.

King enjoyed these gentle musings, but his pleasure, as with other estate projects, was always blunted by worry or guilt. In this case, it was not an anxiety over money, but a worry that his gesture would be misunderstood. He feared his altruism might be interpreted as an indication of communist sympathies. The estate, he insisted in his diary, would be given to the people of Canada not along "...socialist lines, but out of a sense of personal obligation & christian motive" (18 July 1935). He wanted to "...give back to the State in these Kingsmere properties the equivalent of all that I have had paid to me in salary as deputy Minister or P.M. etc., so that my life might be given to Canada, in its services, entirely without compensation other than that of the large opportunities of public service & the positions I had enjoyed" (17 July 1939).

A year before he died, King read an article about the American author, Washington Irving. King fervently hoped that what was written about Irving and his home, "Sunnyside," would hold true for himself and Kingsmere: "'His Spirit still pervades his beloved Sunnyside and as long as the house stands it will breathe the story of its world renowned Master who during his occupancy was ever striving to improve it as he strove to improve the lot of his fellow man'" (11 September 1949).

National Archives of Canada/PA 32110

Toronto's Mount Pleasant Cemetery, where King is buried, opened in 1876. It was directly influenced by the rural cemetery movement which had originated in France.

The Park Movement

In the end, the estate did not house war veterans nor sick civil servants, it was given to the people of Canada as a national park. At times during the thirty years of deliberation, his intentions did not seem entirely altruistic. King often invoked the idea of a gift to the nation to quiet his financial anxieties or to suppress his guilt feelings of owning too much land, too many possessions. He finally came to terms with these conflicts. In his will, he tried to communicate his feelings of "joy and inspiration" and why these feelings had prompted him to will it to the people of Canada as a park:

> I had not been long in office before I conceived the idea of acquiring sufficient land to make the Kingsmere properties into a park which would be worthy of its location in the immediate vicinity of Ottawa and which some day I might present to my country as a thank-offering for the opportunities of public service....If I have been able to carry on in the service of the State for the length of time I have, I shall always feel it was due in no uncertain measure to the enjoyment I have derived from developing these properties over the years, and having simultaneously in mind their ultimate presentation to the people of Canada as a public park....I express the wish that the lands at Kingsmere may be maintained as nearly as possible in their present state; that they will be developed as parkland, and that they will form a wild life sanctuary and will continue to have the character of a natural forest reserve.[1]

King had persistently supported the idea of a national park established in his beloved hills — an enthusiasm he separated from his deliberations over the fate of his estate. He worked to secure the preservation of the Gatineau's forests and wildlife in

National Archives of Canada/PA 10003

Rockcliffe Park is one of Ottawa's oldest public parks.

order to safeguard this enriching and beautiful environment for Canadians.

King certainly was aware of the central role of park creation within the preservation, conservation and beautification movements of his day. By the 1920s creating public parks would not have been found unusual. Parks were an innovation of the nineteenth century. While open areas for public use were not novel — the town square probably is as old as settlement itself — the concept of government setting aside land for public recreation was new. Prior to this, the term "park" meant the private grounds of a gentleman's estate which were definitely not open to the public — a connotation which persisted in garden writing up into the 20th century. Country homes enclosed by extensive landscaping and wooded areas were often described as set in "park-like" surroundings.

Landscaped parks entered North America in the 1830s as part of the "rural cemetery" movement. In many cities and towns the cemetery was the only bit of landscaped land open to the public with paths or roads to stroll upon. Family picnics and Sunday promenades were common in cemeteries such as the Old Burying Ground in Saint John, New Brunswick. Unfortunately many early burying grounds became unsafe when urban congestion and increased use overtaxed their land area.[2] In some cases the cemeteries were worrisome health hazards in an age of yellow fever, cholera and typhoid epidemics.

In Europe available urban land had become so scarce that social commentators advised buying land adjacent to cities for non-denominational burials. The French, influenced by the English landscape garden, became innovators of a new style of cemetery landscaping on these lands.

Père Lachaise Cemetery was opened in 1804 on the northeastern boundary of Paris. By the 1820s it had become a magnificent garden cemetery, a popular tourist attraction for North Americans and Europeans alike. The naturalistic ideas of the 18th century English Landscape Style were applied to the hilltop site, resulting in winding, picturesque roadways, tree-lined paths, irregular ground, grassy meadows, thickly planted "bosquets," artfully arranged shrubs and flowers, as well as beautiful monuments, funeral architecture and gravestones.[3] The idea of a designed landscape ornamented with memorial objects was neither novel nor distressing. The influence of the Romantics, the exaltation of mourning and the heightened contrast between city and countryside all converged to promote the building of landscaped cemeteries.

Early public park creation in Canada occurred sporadically. One of our earliest urban parks, the Halifax Public Gardens, dates from the 1840s when the Nova Scotia Horticultural Society created a botanic garden. Admission to the garden, featuring fountains, archery courts and buildings, was by annual subscription. After returning from a European holiday, an energetic alderman promoted the idea of public parks, noting how impressed he was by Parisian public open spaces.[4] In 1867 the Halifax Public Gardens, under municipal supervision, was opened to the people of Halifax. On land adjacent to the private botanic garden, trees, flowers, winding gravelled walks, two seals in the pond, and a fountain were combined into a pleasing space. A magnificent bandstand hosted popular Sunday afternoon band concerts. In 1875 the two park sections were united when the Horticultural Society sold their garden to the city.

National Archives of Canada/PA 10130

Central Park in Ottawa was elaborately landscaped in the Victorian style.

Canadian park building was also influenced by the highly publicized creation of Central Park in New York City in the 1860s. This was the first American park to be landscaped for recreational and aesthetic enjoyment, developed with public funds, sited on public land and open to all.[5] Its creator, the founder of American landscape architecture, Frederick Law Olmsted, fervently upheld the Victorian belief in the beneficial contact with nature. In 1874 he designed Montreal's Mount Royal Park utilizing many of the design criteria he had developed for Central Park. By this time he had more than a decade of experience in designing parks, college campuses, private estates and residential subdivisions.

By 1900 park creation was a major activity within the City Beautiful movement. For example, eight small parks were created between 1893 and 1897 in Winnipeg. Occasionally professionally designed, early parks were frequently laid out by dedicated amateurs, who, determined to beautify their towns and villages, devoted cheerful weekends to planning and planting. These new parks were not often built on the scale of Mount Royal, but were usually small, some merely ornamental squares.

The most intense period of park creation occurred before

National Archives of Canada/PA 25059

Early tourists bathing in the hot springs at Banff National Park.

World War I. Justifications for park building during this time continued to include Olmsted's spiritual bond-with-nature philosophy and breathing-spaces-for-the-worker rationales. In addition, the booster mentality of the era also influenced park creation. Parks were touted as visible proof of a prosperous community, a community concerned about the welfare of its residents.

National Parks

Belief in healing nature, vested interests and idealistic philosophies also came together in the promotion of national parks. The national park movement in the United States was initiated by the opening of Yellowstone National Park in 1872. Those advocating the creation of Yellowstone National Park, as well as the forest reserve in New York's Adirondack Mountains in 1885, did so to prevent private ownership and exploitation. In Yellowstone, it was the geysers, hot springs and waterfalls, and in the Adirondacks it was an adequate water supply for New York canals and rivers that had to be protected — the wilderness aesthetic and values were not mentioned.[6]

Like its American counterparts, the first Canadian national park, Banff Hot Springs Reserve, was not primarily established as a wilderness park. After three Canadian Pacific Railway workers discovered the hot springs in 1883, word spread among the construction workers, eventually coming to the notice of federal Department of the Interior officials. There was considerable to-ing and fro-ing of letters, some visits to the site, and many recommendations for its use. Interested M.P.s and a high-ranking CPR official strongly advised the government to reserve the ten square miles around the spring as a park. This support solidified the government's wish to prevent private ownership and exploitation, and to use the land as a financial asset. Sir John A. Macdonald sold Parliament on the idea of Banff as a resort, saying it would attract tourists away from American and European resorts:

> "It has all the qualifications necessary to make it a great place of resort....There is beautiful scenery, there is prairie sport and there is mountain sport; and I have no doubt that that will become a great watering-place.... Then there will be a rental of the waters; that is a

perennial source of revenue, and if carefully managed it will more than many times recuperate or recoup the Government for any present expenditure...."[7]

To shape it into a resort park, massive landscape changes were proposed: roads, townsite, baths, and hotels. Macdonald wanted wealthy clientele to build aesthetically-correct, government-approved villas on the township site. Macdonald did not want Banff to become "just another spa" frequented by a "doubtful class of people."[8] Banff became a Canadian prototype of the national park as a repository of scenic health-giving beauty, as well as a playground for the wealthy. The affluent were the only ones who could afford the extensive and expensive trips so far from home.

Early national and provincial parks were revenue generating sites for government and private enterprise. Controlled hunting, logging and mining were permitted in certain areas. Tourists brought in revenue as well. The western parks especially were used to popularize and promote the Canadian Pacific Railway, which carried tourists to the parks. The federal government also received a share of the tourist dollar. Raw, untouched nature was found to directly benefit the visitor and indirectly the economy.[9] The national park was characterized as a resource, like a coal deposit, to be utilized for the maximum benefit of interested parties.

The rise of the urban landscaped park movement had influenced how people defined "park" — an idea not always synonymous with wilderness. The influential Frederick Law Olmsted had defined a park as "...being a space of ground differing from a garden in spaciousness and the broad, simple and natural character of its scenery, and from the wood in the more scattered arrangement of its trees and greater expanses of its glades."[10] City people, taught to view park scenery as tamed nature, were often taken aback when visiting national wilderness parks: "'They call it a 'park,'...you are surprised to find it a wilderness.'"[11] Others quite happily accepted the "wilderness" as a novelty, a respite from their city life.

At first our natural resources seemed limitless. Many did not see the conflict between the needs of commercial interests and the demands for wilderness protection. By the 1890s, however, concern mounted over the increasingly obvious depletion of many natural resources, especially forest reserves and wildlife. The RCMP by the early 1880s had remarked on the diminishing wildlife in the Northwest Territories. In 1889 the Police Commissioner advised the Minister of the Interior that wildlife was decreasing at an alarming rate due to sport and native hunters.[12] A few years later reports of stump-filled eyesores, garish billboards obstructing scenic views, and less game to be hunted infuriated concerned wilderness supporters. They used these reports to support wildlife protection measures. These measures had an economic impact because wildlife was a major tourist attraction.[13] Additional emotional weight was given to conservation writings when the last passenger pigeon died in 1911 in a Cincinnati zoo, and the last remnants of the great buffalo herds were rounded up on the prairies and placed on protected lands.[14] Nature, "a storehouse of animate and inanimate wealth,"[15] needed to be protected, harvested sparingly, allowing its "stores" to be replenished so that future generations could utilize these riches. This orientation, a "wise-use" policy, characterized early conservation thought.

In 1911 the Parks Branch was set up in the Department of the Interior. It was the first government organization in the world established to deal solely with the management and development

King at the opening of Prince Albert National Park in 1928.

National Archives of Canada/PA 178403

of national parks.[16] Although before this date there had been some provincial and federal regulatory legislation to protect wildlife and forests, it was now hoped that a new age of protective governmental policies had begun. Greater protection of parks and wildlife throughout the Dominion seemingly was assured.[17]

James B. Harkin, the first commissioner of the Parks Branch, eloquently promoted the ideals of wilderness preservation and appreciation. He firmly believed in the rejuvenating properties of nature and in the primary role wilderness parks could play in offering close contact with "primordial" nature. National parks were "priceless works of art," Harkin believed. They were preserves of original Canadian landscapes, which, when seen, would instill in all Canadians "a love of the country and pride in its natural beauty."[18] Heritage, health, beauty, spirituality, and conservation were the selling points for national and provincial parks — values which did not exclude controlled hunting and logging in some parks.

The nature-worshiping Mackenzie King would have had little difficulty accepting Harkin's ideals of park creation and nature preservation. Harkin once noted, in words close to King's own feelings, that "the day will come when the population of Canada will be ten times as great as it is now but the national parks ensure that every Canadian...will still have free access to vast areas possessing some of the finest scenery in Canada, in which the beauty of the landscape is protected from profanation, the natural wild animals, plants, and forests preserved, and the peace and solitude of primeval nature retained."[20]

Up into the 1920s many pieces of legislation were passed to establish additional national parks and to promote conservation and preservation. As well, a Commission of Conservation was established in 1909. King would have been aware of its programs. The Commission was an independent, non-partisan advisory committee which explored the major issues of natural resource conservation. It was empowered to disseminate information and to make recommendations to Parliament. Before disbanding in 1921, the Commission powerfully influenced measures for and public awareness of wildlife protection, reforestation, and establishment of national parks and wildlife sanctuaries.[19]

During King's lifetime nearly sixteen national parks, seven Ontario provincial parks, and five Quebec provincial parks were created. In 1928, when he was prime minister, Prince Albert National Park was established in his riding a few hours north of Prince Albert, Saskatchewan. The park, a "playground for the people of Saskatchewan," encompassed 1,400 square miles including myriad rivers and fifty interconnected lakes. The *Calgary Albertan* spiritedly praised the formation of the park which "...protects a large area of our best forest and lake country in Saskatchewan...reserved areas in which the Canada known to explorer, hunter and pioneer may still be found, will be treasured by children, not only for their recreational, health and scientific value, but as perpetuations of the Canada of an earlier day."[21] King was thrilled when a lake and connecting river were named after Kingsmere: "What a privilege to be able as P.M. to make a gift of this kind to one's constituency, to a Province & to one's country" (5 August 1928). At the park's dedication King spoke of his profound belief in the "significance of the beautiful the retention of Nature as from the hand of God." After linking the park to Canada's early history of voyageurs and explorers, he dedicated it "to the Glory of the Creator whose bounty was mirrored in its lakes & rivers & forests and to the highest good of the people of Canada for all time to come" (10 August 1928).

National Archives of Canada/PA 178404

The lakeside cabin, presented to King at the opening of the Prince Albert National Park, was furnished for Lord and Lady Cromer's trip there the following year.

King was presented with a small lakeside cabin. He said he was delighted, but confided in his diary that he hardly knew if he should keep it or not. A year later, however, he obviously had not made up his mind. He still had the cabin for he alerted the superintendent of the park, J.A. Wood, to prepare it and an itinerary for Lord and Lady Cromer who would be visiting in August. The superintendent soon wrote that the cabin was nearly furnished, pieces had been supplied by various towns and cities of Saskatchewan: the dining room by Moose Jaw, the living room by Regina. Wood, promoting wilderness ideals, also suggested that King himself visit the park: "...I am quite sure you would be rested both physically and mentally, if you would spend two weeks with us."[22]

Evidently the Cromer's trip through Prince Albert National Park was a great success. The weather was perfect, the fish were biting, and the camping and scenery were all that British tourists hoped it would be. Wood, knowing that a romanticized glimpse into the life of native people and voyageurs would be enjoyed, arranged for native guides "...to carry their canoes in real Indian fashion, and I had two of my wardens build up back packs and head packs, in order that our distinguished visitors might obtain an idea of just how packing was done in the North country."[23] King hereafter sent other friends to his little cabin until he gave it up a few years later.

In 1931 during the Depression Mackenzie King vigorously defended the park when the Commons debated to reduce funds for national parks and historic sites. After assuring members of Parliament that he had the interests of the entire province in mind and not only the residents of his riding, King, as Leader of the Opposition, asked the Minister of the Interior to make his "last cut" before reaching the Prince Albert park. He argued that the preliminary developments of basic sanitary improvements and subdivision of lots should be carried out before cutting funds. The park was very popular: "The thousands of people who visited the park last year and the year before were very much embarrassed by the fact that the arrangements generally were not at all adequate to the needs of such numbers of people visiting the park and not at all such as to permit of persons resident there for any length of time."[24] His "special plea" for the Prince Albert park received a non-committal answer from the minister, saying he deeply regretted any cutbacks on the funds for such places of beauty and relaxation.

Gatineau Park

The rhetoric surrounding the creation of national parks and his direct participation in the Prince Albert park, further strengthened King's belief in the idea of parks as part of Canada's national heritage. From the late 1920s onward, he envisioned his Kingsmere gift as a part of the national park movement, encompassing wildlife conservation as well as the ideal love of nature. Willing his Kingsmere estate to the nation as a park was mentioned more frequently in his diaries. At the same time King championed the wider concept of reserving land in the Gatineau Hills as a national park.

The notion of creating a national park in the Gatineaus dates from the 1903 city plan report of the landscape architect, Frederick Todd, hired by the Ottawa Improvement Commission. The O.I.C. was established in 1899 as a result of Laurier's interest in creating a grand capital for the nation — a "Washington of the North." It was empowered to "purchase, acquire and hold real estate in the city of Ottawa and vicinity thereof for the purpose of public parks or squares, streets, avenues, drives or thoroughfares, and for their maintenance."[25] The O.I.C.'s program of beautification began by brush clearing and garbage removal. However, it did clean up the banks of the Rideau Canal, turn King Edward Avenue into a broad, tree-lined boulevard, and build a scenic drive alongside the Canal.[26]

Todd recommended far-reaching changes including urban parks connected by parkways, beautification of boulevards, establishment of playgrounds, and the creation of "large natural parks or reserves" near the capital. He noted that Canada was famous world-wide for her forests, thus it would be appropriate to reserve forest land near the capital for future enjoyment: "Not only will those reserves be of inestimable value to future generations as an example of the original forest, but they will also provide a place where nature may still be enjoyed, unmarred by contact with humanity."[27] He further recommended that this reserve should be within easy driving distance of Ottawa. The reserve land should be typical Canadian forest growth, containing "as picturesque and as diversified scenery as possible...there should also be included the rugged mountain and the pastoral valley."[28] He especially recommended reserving the Gatineau River valley, land between Wright's Bridge and Chelsea, and land around Meech Lake, as well as building a parkway to connect the reserve to the cities. Fifty years onward, Todd warned, when the Ottawa-Hull population would be five times as large as in 1903, it would then be too late to reclaim the untamed forest lands where "...the wildest birds are at home, and where nature's mossy carpet is still luxuriant and unworn."[29] Todd counselled the O.I.C. that the cost should not weigh heavily on the city's ratepayers for "...it will be impossible in fifty or one hundred years to place a value on such reserves, or to calculate the good which they have accomplished, or the people who have been benefited mentally, physically and morally by having access to such a complete change from the exacting cares of business and the impure air of crowded streets."[30]

Such stirring sentiments for the public good and the preservation of Canada's natural heritage evidently did not strike a responsive chord. One member of the Improvement Commission noted that the report seemed to frighten the association, its concepts were considered too big to grasp. Some members singled out the recommendations for a Gatineau reserve as "ridiculous."[31] Direct action was not taken for another thirty-three years despite minority reports to the government and city plans in 1912 and 1916 reaffirming the need for a national park.

Sir Herbert S. Holt, prominent in the Montreal business community, chaired the planning committee of the 1916 city plan commission. The report, issued under his name, in particular promoted the acquisition of land in the nearby Gatineau Hills for a park:

> One of the attractions of Ottawa is to be found in the slopes on the north side of the river which stretch away to a sky line of distant forest-clad mountains. Nature, which has not made this tract of land fertile, has made it beautiful. Much of it is still covered with forest. Since it has little commercial value it could be acquired at slight cost and a great tract of it, consisting of 75,000 or 100,000 acres, should be secured as a national park. Here, at the very door of the Capital, should be preserved for all time a great area in the state of nature.[32]

The park would provide employment for local farmers and hunters as wardens, and in "wise-use" terminology, also be a "haven of pleasure to foresters and men of the rod and gun."[33] However, World War I and the rebuilding of the Centre Block of the Canadian Parliament, which burned in 1916, prevented forward movement on the park issue.

In 1926 Mackenzie King involved himself in Gatineau beautification and preservation, after learning that the C.P.R. wanted to lay track alongside the Gatineau River. He wrote the Quebec government and other concerned organizations urging them not to pursue the project. Using his prime ministerial leverage, King obtained a promise that the highway rather than the railroad would follow the water "to secure scenic properties of route etc." (15 May 1926).

King slightly, but more publicly, advanced the national park idea in 1927 by introducing a bill creating the Federal District Commission [replacing the Ottawa Improvement Commission.] The F.D.C. was given the power to pursue beautification and city planning on both sides of the Ottawa River — in effect to establish a federal district. When outlining the need for extending the boundaries of the Commission's jurisdiction, King said that a national park near Ottawa-Hull was "very much in the public interest" and that action should be taken on the proposal, however, appropriation could not be included in this particular bill.[34] The bill received much bipartisan support during second and third readings, but Dr. J.W. Edwards, Conservative M.P. for Frontenac, opposed the measure, noting that "...certain persons are interested in the other side of the river through having a summer home there. Is it the idea to make beautiful driveways up to the homes of those persons some of whom sit in this house."[35] King countered by noting that he was the only one he knew in the House who had a summer residence "on the other side of the river" and that he would "strongly oppose" any money spent in improving a driveway approaching his property. This seemed to pacify his opponents and the bill passed.

The next year King pushed his campaign to promote a national park a little further by proposing, in a lengthy Parliamentary speech on May 24, 1928, to amend the Federal District Commission Act of 1927. Holding a copy of the Holt Report "aloft," he vigorously defended an appropriation of $3,000,000 for the Commission. With this funding it could plan and implement regional beautification: "Ottawa is the focal centre of the Dominion...which is acknowledged as the first of the dominions of the British Empire. It is the heart of a nation that has grown great not only in its own affairs but in the affairs of the world at large...."[36] He referred to the planned capitals of the world, such as Paris and Washington, D.C., as worthy of emulation, and pleaded for an architecture and landscaping which would symbolize the greatness of Canada as seen in her capital. As part of his vision of a grand capital, King mentioned once again the need to create a national park which would be "...a fitting adjunct to the capital of our country."[37]

King did not lose "the vision" of protecting the natural landscape of the Gatineau hills despite the F.D.C.'s slow action during the early 1930s. Nearly ten years before King had bemoaned tree cutting in the Gatineau Hills, noting in his diary that it broke his heart to see how the forests were being thinned out and cut down: "Were I a wealthy man I would purchase them outright. Had I a majority in prlt. I wd expropriate them for the State" (23 May 1926).

Just before he returned to power in 1935, King again lamented over the forest cutting which had proceeded without restriction. This time King made headlines, rather than diary entries, when he denounced the wanton destruction of the Gatineau forests. He had previously joined (as honourary president) a recently organized association, the Federal Woodlands Preservation League, along with other prominent Ottawans and Premier R.B. Bennett (another honourary president). Governor General Bessborough was its patron. The League worked against indiscriminate cutting of privately-owned tracts of the Gatineau forests. King was appalled when he viewed slides of this "frightful devastation." After touring these areas, King used what he had seen as powerful ammunition during a debate on national park expenses in May 1935. He felt the ravages rivalled pictures of the devastation of the First World War:

> I think hon. members would be horrified if they could see what has happened within the last two years within a radius of ten or fifteen miles of the city of Ottawa. Whole hillsides which face the approaches to Ottawa from other parts of the country have been completely denuded of their trees. There have been left devastated areas which

> are nothing else but barren rocks and eroded soil...Streams and springs are drying up, and the wild life of woods and waters disappearing.[38]

King spoke from firm conviction on the preservation of the Gatineau forests, as well as from actual practice for he had just planted nearly 1,000 trees on his estate as part of a Quebec government reforestation plan.

King was delighted with the newspaper reports of his energetic championing of forest preservation. He felt his strong showing was "significant and prophetic," because the newspaper reports appeared on Victoria Day. King then decided he wanted to do something even further to beautify the nation's capital on Victoria Day, so he wrote Premier Taschereau and the Quebec Minister of Lands and Forests urging the Quebec government to take action on the preservation of the "woodland beauty" of the Gatineau hills.

National Archives of Canada/PA 110893

Lumbering in the Gatineau region.

Reforestation was one of the watchwords in early 20th century Canada. By the 1880s reports had been submitted to the Ontario government outlining the need for replanting and preserving the province's forests. Forest fire, misguided settlement practices and indiscriminate cutting, had created scrubby waste lands, in some cases "sand plains." However, little action was taken until 1908 when a few forest reserves were established, some reclamation programs were initiated, and education programs on woodlots and forest conservation were run for farmers.

By the 1930s there was some forward progress.[39] Then the Depression hit and further destruction of privately-owned forest stands was caused by farmers needing the money from selling cut timber. Mackenzie King noted in his spirited House of Commons speech in 1935 that local farmers were so hard up that they eagerly accepted meager returns from businessmen bent on making a profit from the cutting:

> Times being hard, they have found a number of people who were prepared to accept their proposals and sell and cut the wood at that figure, and as I have said owners have been selling wood in many cases at as low a figure as from forty cents to one dollar per cord depending on the quality of wood cut....It has been only within the last two years that what has been happening along the roadsides, the river banks and the lake shores has taken place....[40]

King noted that the aim of the Federal Woodlands Preservation League was not to prevent private owners from making money on their woodlots. The League wanted three assurances: that the owners would not strip entire hillsides, they would cut trees only of a certain size, and would not cut within prescribed distances from public roads. The impassioned King reminded the House that the government had spent "a considerable sum of money" to beautify Ottawa and if something was not done to protect the Gatineau hillsides "much of the effort thus far spent will prove to have been in vain; for, as I have said, it is impossible to separate the city itself from its immediate environments."[41] King urged compensation for the woodlot owners, a forest survey and relief programs connected with reforestation. He was delighted to push Prime Minister Bennett (who King thought was jealous of his leadership on the issue) into promising, on record, that the chairman of the Federal District Commission would work on the problem along with representatives from Ontario and Quebec, since the federal government had no jurisdiction over provincial timber cutting (27 May 1935).

The issue lingered in his mind over the summer, prompting a "vision" in mid-July which he interpreted as an indication that he was on the right track:

> The part of the vision I recall most vividly was being on a roadway which led into a forest, along the sides of the most beautifully wooded hills I have seen. I was trying to explain what it meant to the country to preserve these wonderful resources, the trees were like massive oaks, gnarled, thick bark, beautiful leaves, then came a flower upon them more lovely than I could describe (16 July 1935).

King's conviction never wavered. Whenever appropriate he pleaded for forest conservation. He even included forest protection as a war-time patriotic measure: "The safeguarding of forest resources, adequate to the country's needs, is a service towards which all can contribute. In times of peace, it is a service which ministers to popular enjoyment of God's-out-of-Doors. In time of war, it becomes a form of patriotism which no nation or people can afford to neglect."[42] Understandably when he saw a demonstration of "Mr. Adair's new invention" — a hand-held, electrically-run tree-cutting saw, King was horrified: "It made me sad, however, to think of what may become of our forests — forests everywhere, with a device like that, doing in an hour the work of ten if not 20 or more men" (13 October 1949).

He was happy, on the other hand, to see an immediate effect of the League's intense lobbying — a survey of the lower Gatineau woodlands carried out by the Department of the Interior at the request of the Chairman of the Federal District Commission. The survey report supported the League's findings: the cutting was economically provoked and needed to be controlled; clearing had been so massive that tree cutting on that scale would not be possible for another twenty to sixty years. As well, recreational use had been curtailed by clear-cutting. The report's strongest recommendation was "for the outright purchase of lands for forest protection, for inclusion in a federal district."[43] By the time the report was distributed, King was prime minister. He had included a strong environmental platform in his election campaign: "afforestation, the preservation of our present forest wealth, scenic development, the establishment of more national parks, etc. etc."[44] King was once again in a position to further his vision of the enhancement of the nation's capital, as well as preserve the scenic beauty of his beloved Gatineaus.

Meanwhile the members of the Federal Woodlands Preservation League had been actively campaigning for the formation of a national park. In December 1935 the editor of the *Ottawa Citizen*, Charles A. Bowman, spoke to the Ottawa Local Council of Women on the need for preservation of the Gatineau woodlands. Bowman cited the beauty of the hills, and their appropriateness for skiing, hiking, and camping, to justify the seemingly contentious issue of buying land for a national park. He ended by praising Mackenzie King's efforts to save the woodlands and his efforts to secure action from Taschereau's government on preservation and recreation in this area. Bowman hinted he would not be surprised if King's summer home would some day become the property of the people of Canada: "It would be a rare national heritage to treasure, by lake, mountain and woodlands, where the spirit of Canada is truly reflected."[45]

National Capital Commission

Brown Lake in Gatineau Park.

At the same time the Clerk of the House of Commons, Dr. Arthur Beauchesne, had entered the controversy, joining the side of woodlands protection and the creation of a national park. When testifying before a parliamentary committee on constitutional reform, he made headlines by suggesting that a federal district be established on both sides of the Ottawa river. Not only should the government form this district, he counselled, but it should also establish a great national university, as well as acquire 100,000 acres for a national park in the Gatineaus. Bennett had already noted in 1935, that setting up a federal district and establishing a national or federal district park in the Gatineau Hills would necessitate "...some modification of the existing provisions of the British North America Act..."[46] Beauchesne, however, had a solution for this: Parliament should summon a constituent assembly "for the special purpose for drafting a new constitution for Canada."[47] He was commended for bringing the issue before the committee in "such a bold way," but it had little effect.[48]

In 1936 the issue of a connecting parkway between Ottawa and the Gatineau Hills was once again publicly debated. Charles Bowman appealed to the public to build the parkway to memorialize the 100th anniversary of the "birth of national unity between Upper and Lower Canada" and the 100th anniversary of the accession of Queen Victoria to the throne." The parkway would allow families to picnic where "children can spend a happy day in the sweet security of Canadian lakelands."[49] Bowman promoted a circular route which a motorist could drive in a day's outing: the sightseer would travel through Ottawa, cross over to Quebec and drive through Hull, then circle back via Kingsmere, Meech Lake, Philippe Lake and Wakefield. He also encouraged the building of woodland paths connecting to one another and the parkway — noting the example of such arrangements in the national parks of the Canadian West.[50] The *Ottawa Citizen* also surveyed six "prominent members" of Parliament from the three main parties who, not surprisingly, thought the idea a fine one. They all stressed, however, that the parkway should also, despite the obvious enhancement of the Ottawa-Hull environment, ensure jobs as part of an unemployment relief program.[51] Bowman concurred, writing that the construction of a parkway "would be a national investment in well-being to set men to work" on it.[52]

King probably worked behind the scenes promoting the park and parkway. He always took personal responsibility for the Federal District Commission in Cabinet.[53] His numerous diary entries on beautification schemes in connection with the F.D.C. confirmed King's continuing interest in its programs. King had dropped the parkway idea after being attacked in 1927 for a personal interest in the scheme. Once back in power, however, King evidently felt much more confident of success. In August 1937 King gave a luncheon speech before Ottawa's prominent citizens to honour the Central Canadian Exhibition's fiftieth anniversary. The theme of his talk was the need for a federal district including a parkway and park. He emphasized that the federal district should also include land on the Quebec side of the river: "This would give the Capital a chance to expand into Quebec, which is very necessary....Then we would have one of the finest cities in the world." He even bravely mentioned Kingsmere in the speech, noting in his diary it was the first time he had done that: "...from now on I shall refer to it more & more — much as Hawarden might have been referred to by Gladstone — making it a part of the public 'life' of Canada — giving to it its proper setting in our national life." He felt the speech was very successful and capitalized on the "enthusiasm that has been aroused in getting the civic improvements under way." He wrote further that guiding the Federal District Plan through to completion would be a great achievement within his life's work and political career. He also noted that he would not mind being chairman of the F.D.C. when he retired, in the same way Laurier had hoped to be chairman of the Ottawa Improvement Commission: "This would be carrying on his work, and would be a great achievement for all time. Its seed at all events has been sown, we shall see how it develops." [19 August 1937].

King had concurrently been overseeing beautification measures in the city of Ottawa. His major contribution was the siting of the War Memorial on Confederation Square adjacent to Parliament Hill. Charles Bowman publicly lobbied in the April 1937 *Ottawa Citizen* to have it placed on a ridge near Kings-mere, commanding an impressive site like the war memorial on Vimy Ridge. Under the cover of this campaign, Bowman valiantly continued pressing for a parkway and park: "Visitors to the memorial could travel along a via sacra beautifully adorned, particularly with the poppies of Flanders....A national memorial park near Ottawa could also serve a national purpose for Canada such as Arlington Cemetery does for the United States at Washington. It is the place for monuments to statesmen and other national figures."[54]

In June 1938 King and public pressure had its way. The House of Commons debated, then passed a resolution to acquire land for a national parkway into the Gatineau hills as a first step in creating a national park. The motion was led by M. Leduc,

M.P. for Wright County, Quebec, the area where the parkway would be built. It was hardly a debate — the question whether this meant the establishment of a national park was asked but not directly answered. The $100,000 appropriation was passed quickly and quietly. Construction did not begin immediately because threatened woodland had to be bought and in some cases expropriated. Surveying the parkway route was the major action taken that first year as the F.D.C. determined to discover the feasibility and cost of a parkway.[55] The federal Department of Mines and Resources, probably with King's blessing and prompting, loaned personnel and equipment to aid the F.D.C.'s survey: a surveyor and engineer, transportation vehicles, equipment, a drafting office and aerial survey.[56]

By 1939 16,000 acres (6,480 ha) had been purchased and placed under the Federal District Commission's administration. As well, a Gatineau District Relief Project was initiated to create jobs for the area's unemployed: secondary roads were constructed on the new park land, trails were cut, the forest was underbrushed and several scenic lookouts were built. However, land purchases and other forward movement on the parkway and park ceased during World War II.

King did not let the vision die. In 1945 he submitted broad guidelines to parliament for a new national capital plan. The Federal Woodlands Preservation League had also been active at the same time lobbying the government to buy more land in the Gatineaus. Firmly embedded in King's suggestions as well was the expansion and development of a park in the Gatineaus. King invited Jacques Gréber, a French city planner he had met during his visit to the Paris exhibition of 1936 to oversee the planning. Gréber had formerly been retained by King in 1937 to advise on the National War Memorial and Confederation Square. He wanted to place the memorial outside the downtown core, but was overruled by King.[57] Gréber's work halted when he returned to Europe at the onset of the Second World War. King invited him back in 1945 and gave him an institutional connection to the F.D.C. and a mandate to provide a plan for the capital region.[58] Gréber highlighted Gatineau Park as "the essential feature of the whole plan for the National Capital of Canada," and "an invaluable natural asset."[59] He proposed the conservation of panoramic scenes of Ottawa and Hull as seen from the Gatineau Hills, and the completion of the parkway. He also proposed that the total area of the Gatineau Park should reach 83,000 acres. He directed the F.D.C. to follow the "same overall policies of maintenance and restrictions...in this added territory, through direct ownership, or otherwise; that is, to parkway systems, to the installation of lookouts, picnic grounds and controlled recreation centres, to the more efficient closer protection of the forest, fish and game, and to direct control of the use of the land in general; in a broad sense, more facilities and accommodation for the public in general, and less for the individual."[60]

This dream was realized very slowly. However, by the time King retired from office in 1948, Gatineau Park had become a definable entity. The Park was touted as a "democratic" park, in contrast to some of the western and maritime national parks, characterized as "the almost exclusive preserve of the well-to-do."[61] Gatineau Park was "within easy reach of a quarter of a million people by car, bus, bicycle or on foot, it is truly a recreation ground for all. No toll-gates mar its entrances. No schemes to part the traveller from his funds are even permitted within its boundaries."[62]

Evidently there were conflicting opinions within the F.D.C. regarding land acquisition which was not resolved by the time of

King's death. Accusations spread that a written policy had not been developed to aid land acquisition, rather it was done piecemeal. Parkland continued to surround private property and land prices skyrocketed because the Commission refused to act decisively. R.P. Sparks in 1955 submitted a "memo" on these problems. Sparks, who had property at Kingsmere, had been enthusiastically involved in the creation of the park for over twenty years. He was appalled by the inaction and sloppy stewardship of the Commission. He felt that the trouble was due to "...certain influential people, owning property in the area covered by Gatineau Park, have objected to its development in a manner which will make it what it should be — 'the show place of Canada.'[63] The Commission had, by then, acquired 50,000 acres (2,020 ha). The parkway, however, had not been built, nor had the facilities for diversified recreation been sufficiently developed. Today 1,600 hectares of Gatineau Park's 35,600 hectares remain in private hands.[64]

Wildlife Sanctuary

King was pleased to preside over the formation of Gatineau Park, but he also found intense joy in the legalizing of wildlife protection within the reserve area. King dearly wanted to provide an asylum for all varieties of wildlife. He even declared in his diary that if large numbers of deer could be encouraged to live in his woods, he would allow them "to tear up part of the garden to see this wild life at liberty here" (5 August 1938). Not the usual sentiments of a gardener.

In his later years King recorded each thrilling sight of wildlife on his property. His bee and pheasant-raising activities often led to glimpses of Gatineau wildlife. In 1941 King had chanced ("to my amazement, and keen delight") upon a black bear ambling near the ruins: "For sheer delight, I have not, for a long time, experienced anything equal to the sensation of seeing that bear in his wild state on my own grounds" (14 September 1941). His apiarist, Henry Clegg of Chelsea, in 1946 killed a bear which had torn King's hives apart. The carcass was brought to the Farm house for King to examine. He supposedly remarked as he examined the dead bear "with interest:" "I hope the bees will be safe from now on."[65] There was also an apocryphal story about King chasing a bear away from his hives, beating it with his cane to the delight of onlooking servants. One doubts that the Prime Minister, cane or not, would have lived to tell that tale.

One day King was told that his just-released pheasants were spotted and deer were also sighted on the property. He marvelled that in 1937 such a sight could still be seen in the Gatineaus — only 24 kilometers from the Parliament Buildings: "Ere long this will read like a fairy tale" (23 August 1937). But the magic held, and more deer over the last years were spotted. On one such sighting King rather hysterically noted that he could have "screamed for delight" when he saw the deer leap into the air, flicking their white tails: "To have seen this bit of primeval life on one's own property, at this day, is something that causes me to rejoice" (5 August 1938). Joan, Godfroy and the servants always reported any sightings of wildlife, often breaking into King's study to tell him to come out and look. At one point King mused on the possibility of "taming" the deer by feeding them in the winter, so that they would venture closer to the house.

King was always more comfortable viewing nature from a distance. The crueler side of nature was often beyond his sentimental understanding: "I was sorry to find yesterday that some animal had stolen two of the eggs from the little birds' nest by the side of the Abbey ruin. How cruel Nature seems to be in the way in which one life preys upon another. I could not help feeling the sorrow that will be in the breast of the little bird who has been seeking to bring his [sic] little ones to life" (16 July 1938).

Godfroy Patteson seems to have had a direct influence on King's concern for wild birds. Under Godfroy's influence, King erected on the Moorside grounds bird houses to attract purple martins. Godfroy, according to King, had a remarkable "knowledge of birds, their habits & ways" (16 April 1938). King said he was touched to watch Godfroy's "concern" for the birds. Godfroy often arranged suet, peanuts, hard peas and chopped apples on trays which he then put into the trees surrounding Shady Hill. As well one spring Godfroy spent a morning hanging strands of horsehair in nearby shrubs for the birds to use as nesting material. It seems King enjoyed watching Godfroy as much as the birds.

King could not have been unaware of the issues surrounding wildlife preservation. There was much activity in Ottawa, locally as well as federally, on wildlife conservation. Much of it centred on birds. Bird house competitions were sponsored by the Federal District Commission in 1929 to "inculcate in boys and girls a direct interest in the Capital and its beautification and the conservation of bird life."[66] Even earlier in 1915 the Dominion entomologist, Gordon Hewitt, wrote that he and his department were instrumental, along with the Ottawa Improvement Commission, in establishing bird sanctuaries in the heart of Ottawa: the entire Central Experimental Farm and a wooded section in Rockcliffe, a suburb of Ottawa.[67]

Hewitt, a major Canadian wildlife conservation activist, during his short life was able to affect change in federal conservation legislation. Born in England, he was asked, while teaching at Manchester University, to become the Dominion entomologist for Canada's Department of Agriculture. He married Prime Minister Robert Borden's niece in 1911. By 1917 he had fought for and won the passage of the Migratory Birds Convention Act.[68]

The public debate over the economic and sentimental aspects of bird conservation stimulated a heightened interest in wildlife and protective legislature. As well, local natural history clubs and wildlife organizations expanded their memberships and displayed a broader interest in animal life and wildlife protection.[69] The idea of establishing wildlife sanctuaries became more popular — a public enthusiasm probably fostered by the early efforts of Department of the Interior officials, specifically James Harkin, to establish wildlife sanctuaries within expanding national park areas.

One of the popularizing elements in the conservation movement was the work of the ardent wildlife conservationist John "Jack" Miner of Kingsville, Ontario. Miner established Canada's first bird sanctuary in 1908 on his property, which in 1917 became a provincial Crown reserve. Miner earned an O.B.E. for his conservation work. He practiced reforestation, bird tagging to determine migration patterns (an earnest Christian, he printed Bible verses on the bird tags), and wildlife conservation before it was a fashionable, popular movement.[70] King collected articles on Jack Miner's work and once proclaimed in a public speech in favour of a wildlife sanctuary in Ottawa: "the people of Ottawa should take to heart the words of Jack Miner."[71] In 1948 King declared an annual national wildlife week in early April as a memorial to Jack Miner.

King, who was later to write in his will, "I express the wish that the lands at Kingsmere...will form a wild life sanctuary and will continue to have the character of a natural forest reserve,"[72] was delighted when the F.D.C. instituted some wildlife protection measures on their land in the Gatineaus. Not all Kingsmere area residents, however, were happy when Gatineau Park was designated as a wildlife sanctuary. In 1946 an angry beekeeper wrote to the *Ottawa Journal* complaining about the damage bears were inflicting on Gatineau valley sheep and apiaries. He especially blamed the Federal District Commission's appropriated lands, characterizing the area as a "first-class breeding ground for them. Certain it is that our troubles coincide with the establishment of this restricted area."[73] The writer concluded by noting that King probably would have signed a petition for removing the bears. The beekeeper, however, did not know his man and his thrill of sighting wildlife at Kingsmere. In 1951, after King's death, the F.D.C. took further action to develop his entire estate as a bird sanctuary.

Mackenzie King's conviction that his activities over fifty years at Kingsmere would earn him praise — "future generations will bless me" — has been amply proved. The estate continues to be a wildlife sanctuary, a protected forest area, and a monument to the man, who in his at times quirky fashion, has left us a legacy of accessible wilderness, mysterious ruins and a personally-designed landscape. "Some day the whole city will come out to see the autumn forests in all their beauty," King once prophetically told Joan. However, they would also drive out to see what one dedicated man fashioned out of the harsh Canadian Shield.

William Lyon Mackenzie King was a complex man. Weighted down by burdens, many self-imposed, he had many demons nipping at his heels. He was lonely, guilt-ridden over the death of his mother, burdened by having to live up to his grandfather's legacy, and also by the achievements expected of him as the eldest son. His political career was punctuated by set-backs, as well as by glory. He was a seemingly dull man, charming at times, egotistic and tyrannical at others. But if his contemporaries could have looked inside him, seen beyond the facade and the neuroses of the man, and gazed into his imaginative being, they probably would have seen King striding around a technicolour garden, enacting the roles of gardener, farmer and environmentalist.

Mackenzie King participated in many of the same horticultural and cultural activities as his contemporaries, and created a landscape reflecting the common designs of early twentieth-century Canadian gardens. However, his gardens were individualized not only by the romantic ruins, but also by the diaries themselves which record the intentions underlying his gardening efforts. The diaries give both his inner life and its outward expression — his Kingsmere landscape — greater depth and resonance. For King, the diaries allowed him to present himself and his varied Kingsmere activities in the best possible light: the gardener as hero.

Later, recognizing that gardens and their makers are transitory, King guaranteed himself and his Kingsmere estate immortality by willing his property to the nation. The landscape he created was, as he described his boathouse in 1917, his "spiritual creation," a "little child of his thought and spirit." He lives on not only in yellowing pages of *Hansard*, but also in a vibrant, renewing landscape — a place of repose and beauty.

ENDNOTES

Introduction

1. Esberey, Joy E., *Knight of the Holy Spirit: A Study of William Lyon Mackenzie King*, University of Toronto Press, Toronto, 1980, p. 8.
2. Nicolson, Murray W., *Woodside and the Victorian Family of John King*, Parks Canada, Ottawa, 1984, p. 84.
3. Jennie married, had children, and seemingly lived a long and happy life in Barrie, Ontario.
4. Nicolson, p. 8.
5. Ibid., p. 9.
6. William Lyon Mackenzie King Papers, National Archives of Canada, MG 26, J 6, Vol. 31, File 241.
7. Nicolson, p. 52.
8. Ibid., p. 53.
9. von Baeyer, Edwinna, *Rhetoric and Roses: A History of Canadian Gardening, 1900 -1930*, Fitzhenry and Whiteside, Toronto, 1984, p. 9.
10. Snelgrove, H.J., "President's Address," *Annual Report of the Horticultural Societies of Ontario*, Toronto, 1909, p. 12.
11. Newton, Norman T., *Design on the Land: The Development of Landscape Architecture*, Harvard University Press, Cambridge, 1971, p. 268.
12. Wright, John R., *Urban Parks in Ontario: Part II: The Public Park Movement 1860–1914*, Ottawa, 1984, p. 1.
13. Woods, Jr., Shirley E., *Ottawa, The Capital of Canada*, Doubleday Canada Ltd., Toronto, 1980, p. 282.
14. Wright, Janet, "Architectural and Landscape Report," in Marc de Caraffe and Janet Wright, *Le domaine Mackenzie-King, Kingsmere, Québec*, Commission des lieux et monuments historiques du Canada, Agenda Paper, Parks Canada, Ottawa, n.d., p. 210.
15. See von Baeyer, Chapter Four on the City Beautiful movement, Chapter Six on the development of the Canadian nursery industry and Chapter Seven on the horticultural media.

Chapter One

1. King Papers, MG 26, J 17, Vol. 7, File 10.
2. Thomas, Keith, *Man and the Natural World, Changing Attitudes in England 1500-1800,* Penguin Books, London, 1983, pp. 260-1.
3. Ibid., p. 265.
4. Ibid., p. 259.
5. See, Atwood, Margaret, *Survival: A Thematic Guide to Canadian Literature*, Anansi, Toronto, 1972, pp. 49-66.
6. Berger, Carl, *Science, God, and Nature in Victorian Canada*, University of Toronto Press, Toronto, 1983, p. 31.
7. Ibid., p. 9.
8. Lampman quoted in Altmeyer, George, "Three Ideas of Nature in Canada, 1893-1914," *Journal of Canadian Studies*, Vol. II, 1976, pp. 24-25
9. As quoted in, Cole, Douglas, "Wilderness Values and Canadian Taste, 1895-1930," a paper for the Society for the Study of Architecture in Canada, May 1976.
10. Capt. Mac, *The Muskoka Lakes and the Georgian Bay*, 1884, p. 13.
11. Ibid., p. 14.
12. Henry Albert Harper Papers, National Archives of Canada, MG 30, A 28, Vol. 1, King to Harper, 19 July 1892.
13. Dubé, Philippe, avec la collaboration de Jacques Blouin, photographe, *Deux cents ans de villégiature dans Charlevoix: l'histoire du pays visité*, Les Presses de l'Université Laval, Québec, 1986, p. 91.
14. *Toronto Daily Star*, July 17, 1890, as quoted in Wolfe, Roy I., "The Summer Resorts of Ontario in the Nineteenth Century," *Ontario History*, Vol. LIV, No. 3, 1962, p. 158.
15. Thomas, pp. 247-48.
16. Pimlott, J.A.R., *The Englishman's Holiday: A Social History*, Faber and Faber, London, 1947, p. 27.
17. Ibid., p. 150.

18. Dewar, Keith, *Resort Development in the Rideau Lakes Region of Eastern Ontario, 1826-1955*, M.A. Thesis, Carleton University, 1983, p. 43.
19. Sangster, Charles, from "The St. Lawrence and the Saguenay," in Klinck, Carl F. and Reginald E. Watters, eds., *Canadian Anthology*, 3rd edition, Gage Educational Publishing Ltd., Toronto, 1974, p. 71.
20. Dubé, p. 76.
21. Ibid., p. 69.
22. Ibid., p. 77.
23. Ibid., p. 72.
24. Ibid., p. 104.
25. Frechette, Annie, "Summer Resorts on the St. Lawrence," *Harpers*, July 1884 [?], p. 199
26. Hinshelwood, N.M., *Montreal and Vicinity*, Desbarats & Co., Montreal, 1903, p. 101.
27. Ibid., p. 93.
28. Lanken, Dane, "Summers Down the St. Lawrence," *Canadian Geographic*, April/May 1987, pp. 61-62.
29. Knott, Leonard L., "An Ancient Seigneury at Murry Bay, Quebec," *Canadian Homes and Gardens*, April 1932, pp. 40, 42.
30. Frechette, p. 207
31. Ibid. p. 209
32. Bradley, A.G., "The Humours of a Canadian Watering Place," *MacMillan's Magazine*, May/October 1904, p. 429.
33. Leacock, Stephen, "The Love Story of Mr. Peter Spillikins," in *The Arcadian Adventures with the Idle Rich*, New Canadian Library No. 10, McClelland and Stewart, Toronto, 1959, p. 84.
34. See, Smith, M. Aileen and Phoebe Anne Magee, eds., *St. Andrews Heritage Handbook: A Homeowner's Guide to Exterior Renovation and Maintenance of Local Buildings*, St. Andrews Civic Trust Inc., St. Andrews, N.B., n.d.
35. *Lour Lodge and Cottages*, Digby, N.S., n.p., ca. 1913, p. 3.
36. Ibid., p. 11.
37. Wolfe, Ron I., "The Summer Resorts of Ontario in the Nineteenth Century," *Ontario History*, Vol. LIV, No. 5, Toronto, 1962, p. 152
38. Ibid., p. 152
39. Haddock, John A., *A Souvenir of the Thousand Islands of the St. Lawrence River...*, 2nd ed., Weed-Parson, Alexandria Bay, New York, 1896, p. 63.
40. Ibid., p. 63.
41. See, Moon, Barbara, *The Illustrated Natural History of Canada: The Canadian Shield*, N.S.L. Natural Science of Canada Ltd., Toronto, 1970.
42. Wolfe, "Summer Resorts...," p. 152
43. Ibid. p. 156.
44. Anderson, Allan and Ralph Beaumont, *Postcard Memories of Muskoka*, The Boston Mills Press, Cheltenham, Ont., ca. 1978, unpaged.
45. Boyer, Barbaranne, *Muskoka's Grand Hotels*, The Boston Mills Press, Erin, Ont., 1987, p. 27.
46. Ibid., p. 108.
47. Haddock, p. 15.
48. Boyer, p. 108.
49. Berry, James P., *Georgian Bay: The Sixth Great Lake*, Clarke Irwin & Co., Toronto, 1968, p. 108.
50. Wall, Geoffrey, and John S. Marsh, "Recreational Land Use in Muskoka," in *Recreational Land Use: Perspectives on its Evolution in Canada*, Carleton University Press, Ottawa, 1982, p. 145; and see Boyer.
51. Berry, p. 148.
52. Wolfe, "Summer Resorts...," p. 159.
53. Benidickson, J. "Paddling for Pleasure: Recreational Canoeing as a Canadian Way of Life," in *Recreational Land Use...*, p. 325.
54. Ibid., p. 326.
55. Dawson, R. MacGregor, *William Lyon Mackenzie King: A Political Biography 1874-1923*, University of Toronto Press, Toronto, 1958, p. 40.
56. King Papers, MG 26, J 6, Vol. 15, File 118/119. The Gerrys were a prestigious American family. The boys' grandfather, Elbridge Gerry, was a Governor of Massachusetts, a signer of the Declaration of Independence, the fifth Vice-President of the United States, and the originator of the concept of "gerrymandering" — where political boundaries of an area could be rearranged to suit a particular political party. The boys' father, Elbridge T. Gerry, was a lawyer, who held a variety of chairmanships on charitable boards in New York City.
57. Gill, Brendan and Dudley Witney, *Summer Places*, McClelland & Stewart, Toronto, 1978, p. 33.
58. Wharton, Edith, *A Backward Glance*, Reprint, Charles Scribner's Sons, New York, 1985, p. 82.
59. Ibid., p. 80.
60. Mallet, Gina, "The Cottages of Newport," *City & Country Home*, October 1986, p. 80.
61. Ibid., p. 65.
62. "Notes by the Marchioness," *Ottawa Free Press*, September 10, 1902, p. 6.
63. "Something About Ottawa's Summer Resorts," *Ottawa Free Press*, June 16, 1900, p. 9.
64. Gard, Anson, *The Hub and the Spokes, or, The Capital and its Environs*, The Emerson Press, Ottawa, 1904, p. 36.
65. Taylor, Eva and James Kennedy, *Ottawa's Britannia*, Britannia Historical Association, Ottawa, 1983, p. 46.

66. Gard, , p. 13.
67. Ibid., p. 13.
68. Taylor, p. 46, 87.
69. Ibid., p. 58.
70. "Something About Ottawa's Summer Resorts," p. 9.
71. Taylor, p. 360.
72. "Something About Ottawa's Summer Resorts," p. 9.
73. Ibid., p. 9.
74. "City of Ottawa — Capital of the Dominion of Canada," *Ottawa Free Press*, Ottawa, 1899, p. 24.
75. Ibid., p. 9.
76. Connolly, John J., "Chelsea-Quebec," *Up the Gatineau!*, No. 2, June 1976, p. 2.
77. City of Ottawa..., p. 59.
78. Lambton, Gunda, "Irish Surnames of the Gatineau," *Up the Gatineau!*, No. 13, 1987, p. 13.
79. Gard, p. 370.
80. Connolly, p. 7.
81. King Papers, MG 26, J 6, Vol. 150, File 14, "'Yarrow' Goes to the Country," Yarrow (Mary McKay Scott), *From the Gatineau Hills*, n.p., n.d., p. 26.
82. Ibid., "Lilac Time on the Gatineau," p. 30.
83. Ibid., "An Appreciation," p. 8.
84. King Papers, MG 26, J 10, Vol. 25, File 6, Lanctot, Gustave, "Kingsmere in Chronology," 1936, pp. 1-2.
85. Ibid., p. 3.
86. "The Summer Exodus," p. 1.
87. Berger, Carl, p. 18.
88. King Papers, MG 26, J 6, Vol. 150, File 15, "Edwin Chamberlain's Memories," *Ottawa Evening Citizen*, March 25, 1939.
89. Bourinot, Arthur S., *Some Personal Recollections and Historic Facts about Kingsmere*, A paper read at Moorside, Kingsmere, October 8, 1963, pp. 5-6.
90. Bourinot, Arthur S., "Kingsmere and the Poets," *The Quick and the Dead: Views and Reviews on Poetry*, Rockcliffe Park, Ont., 1955, p. 17.
91. Lanctot, p. 3. It is not clear when King Mountain was named or after whom. Some evidence states it was named "King" by an English officer in the early 1800s because of its towering presence over the other hills. Bourinot, *Some Personal Recollections*, p. 4.
92. King Papers, MG 26, J 6, Vol. 150, File 14, *From the Gatineau Hills*, "'Yarrow' Goes to the Country," p. 26.
93. King Papers, MG 26, J 17, Vol. 7, File 10.

Chapter Two

1. King Papers, MG 26, J 17, Vol. 7, File 10.
2. Ibid., Sept. 6, 1901.
3. Smythe, Robert, *Kingswood: A History of the Little Cottages, Mackenzie King Estate*, Vol. 2, National Capital Commission, Ottawa, 1982, p. 247.
4. Jennie King to Isabel King, August 8, 1904, quoted in Dawson, pp. 117-18.
5. Although we generally think of siting homes or cottages to take advantage of a view as particularly British, the practice is known to date back at least to the Romans. Pliny in the 1st century A.D. advised that villas should be sited to have a view of "...cities, land and sea, a spreading plain and the known peaks of the hills and mountains." Berrall, Julia S., *The Garden, An Illustrated History*, Penguin Books, London, 1978, p. 111.
6. Neatby, H. Blair, *William Lyon Mackenzie King: 1932-1939, The Prism of Unity*, University of Toronto Press, Toronto, 1976, p. 100.
7. Wright, Janet, "Architectural and Landscape Report," *Le domaine Mackenzie-King, Kingsmere, Québec*, with Marc de Caraffe, Agenda Paper, Commission des lieux et monuments historiques du Canada, Parks Canada, Ottawa, n.d., p. 212.
8. Dawson, R. MacGregor, *William Lyon Mackenzie King: A Political Biography, 1874-1923*, University of Toronto Press, Toronto, 1958, p. 117.
9. Ibid., p. 173.
10. Ibid., p. 192.
11. McGregor, F.A., *The Fall and Rise of Mackenzie King: 1911–1919*, Macmillan of Canada, Toronto, 1962, p. 4.
12. Smythe, *Kingswood...*, Vol. 1, p. 10.
13. King Papers, MG 26, J 10, Vol. 23, File 6, King to John Murphy, 10 May 1916, p. 3.
14. Esberey, Joy E., *Knight of the Holy Spirit: A Study of William Lyon Mackenzie King*, University of Toronto Press, Toronto, 1980, p. 91.
15. King Papers, MG 26, J 10, Vol. 27, File 7, King to Elizabeth Moore, 1 November 1917 and King to Willie Murphy, Oct. 1918.
16. King Papers, MG 26, J 10, Vol. 27, File 7, King to W.P. Murphy, 17 April 1916.
17. King Papers, MG 26, J 8, Vol 21, File 1, Marjorie Herridge to King, 13 February 1912.
18. King Papers, MG 26, J 10, Vol. 27, File 7, King to Willie Murphy, 30 June 1916.
19. King Papers, MG 26, J 10, Vol. 28, File 13.
20. Klinck, Carl F., *Wilfred Campbell, A Study in Late Provincial Victorianism*, The Tecumseh Press, Ottawa, 1977, p. 75.
21. Ibid., p. 75.

22. Quoted in Hunter, Robert, "The Wilson Estate, Meech Lake, Gatineau Park, Quebec," Building Report, Federal Heritage Buildings Review Office, Parks Canada, Ottawa, 1984, p. 13.
23. Quoted in Bourinot, Arthur S., "Kingsmere and the Poets," *The Quick and the Dead...*, p. 16.
24. King Papers, MG 26, J 3, Vol. 12, File 1, King to Arthur S. Bourinot, 24 December 1929.
25. King Papers, MG 26, J 10, Vol. 23, File 4, King to R.M. Coulter, 29 June 1918.
26. Smythe, *Kingswood...*, Vol. 2, p. 242.
27. King Papers, MG 26, J 6, Vol. 135, File 8, "She Was Sure the King Didn't Come to Canada," *Saskatoon Star-Phoenix*, June 29, 1929.
28. King Papers, MG 26, J 10, Vol. 28, King to Lady Bourinot, 21 June 1916.
29. King Papers, MG 26, J 10, Vol. 28, File 3, George P. Harris to community, 22 Oct. 1924.
30. King Papers, MG 26, J 10, Vol. 27, File 18, George P. Harris to Mrs. T.A. McGillivary, 1 May 1925.
31. Ibid.
32. King Papers, MG 26, J 10, Vol. 28, File 3, George P. Harris to community, 22 October 1924.
33. King Papers, MG 26, J 10, Vol. 28, File 3, Harris to King, 25 June 1925.
34. Ibid.
35. See, Abella, Irving and Harold Troper, *None is Too Many: Canada and the Jews of Europe, 1933-1948*, Lester & Orpen Dennys, Toronto, 1986.
36. Woods, Jr., Shirley E., *Ottawa the Capital of Canada*, pp. 182-83.
37. All information on this estate comes from: Hunter, Robert, "The Wilson Estate, Meech Lake, Gatineau Park, Quebec," Building Report, Federal Heritage Buildings Review Office, Parks Canada, Ottawa, 1984.
38. Bond, Courtney C.J., *City on the Ottawa*, National Capital Commission, Ottawa, 1967, p. 33.
39. King Papers, MG 26, J 10, Vol. 28, File 3, Harris to King, 5 May 1927.
40. King Papers, MG 26, J 10, Vol. 28, File 3, Harris to King, 9 June 1927.
41. King Papers, MG 26, J 10, Vol. 28, Lady Bourinot to King, 26 June 1916.
42. King Papers, MG 26, J 6, Vol. 135, File 3, "Premier King Wields an Axe for Recreation," *Toronto Star*, July 23, 1924.
43. Ibid.
44. "William Terrill Macoun B.Sc.," typewritten draft, Department of Agriculture, Ottawa, 1933.
45. King Papers, MG 26, J 10, Vol. 26, File 3, Isabella Preston to King, 30 August 1922.
46. Ibid.
47. King Papers, MG 26, J 10, Vol. 26, File 3, King to Isabella Preston, 30 September 1922.
48. Ibid.
49. King Papers, MG 26, J 10, Vol. 26, File 3, King to W.T. Macoun, 30 September 1922.
50. Although Macoun died unexpectedly in 1933, the plant supply continued into the 1940s.
51. King Papers, MG 26, J 10, Vol. 25, File 7, Memo to King from WHM, n.d.
52. King Papers, MG 26, J 10, Vol. 26, File 3, King to W.T. Macoun, 9 July 1923.
53. King Papers, MG 26, J 10, Vol. 26, File 3, W.T. Macoun to King, 22 May 1924.
54. Griffin, Frederick, "Kingsmere," *The Toronto Star Weekly*, "General Section," February 4, 1928, p. 1.
55. Jekyll, Gertrude and Lawrence Weaver, *Gardens for Small Country Homes*, Reprint, Antique Collector's Club, Ltd., Baron Publishing, Woodbridge, Suffolk, 1981, p. 179.
56. Main, A.V., "Pergolas in the Garden," *The Canadian Florist*, March 14, 1913, p. 67.
57. Thonger, Charles, *The Book of Garden Furniture*, John Lowe, The Bodley Head, New York, 1903, p. 48.
58. Main, A.V., "Have a Pergola in Your Garden," *The Canadian Florist*, July 14, 1916, p. 122.
59. Jekyll, p. 181.
60. Ibid., p. 47.
61. Ibid., p. 42.
62. King Papers, MG 26, J 10, Vol. 26, File 3, W.T. Macoun to King, 31 May 1926.
63. Main, A.V., "Pergolas in the Garden," p. 67–68.
64. "Fences in Variety," *Canadian Homes and Gardens*, July 1932, p. 31.
65. Smythe, *Kingswood...*, Vol. 1, p. 117.
66. Ibid., pp. 17-18.
67. Berrall, p. 265.
68. Ibid., p. 106.
69. Smythe, *Kingswood...*, Vol. 1, p. 127.
70. King, W. L. Mackenzie, *Industry and Humanity: A Study in the Principles Underlying Industrial Reconstruction*, Reprint, University of Toronto Press, Toronto, 1973, pp. 107-108.
71. Thonger, p. 63.
72. Jekyll, p. 227.
73. Jones, James Edmund, "Sundials and Their Mottoes," *Canadian Homes and Gardens*, Oct.-Nov. 1934, pp. 29, 52, 54, 56.

74. Henslow, T. Geoffrey W., *Ye Sundial Book*, W. & G. Foyle, Ltd., London, 1935.
75. For example: "Construction of a Cheap Sun-Dial," *The Canadian Florist*, May 17, 1918, pp. 87-88.
76. Altree-Coley, G.E., "The Sundial in the Garden," *Canadian Homes and Gardens*, August 1930, p. 48.
77. Dawson, p. 239.
78. Thonger, p. 3.
79. Northend, Mary H., *Garden Ornaments*, Duffied & Co., New York, 1914, p. 110.
80. See, Stephenson, Sue Honaker, *Rustic Furniture*, Van Nostrand Reinhold Co., New York, 1979.
81. *Catalogue*, The Rustique Work Manufacturing Co., Belle Ewart, Ont., ca. 1877.
82. King Papers, MG 26, J 10, Vol. 24, File 9, King to N. Platt, 20 January 1932.
83. King Papers, MG 26, J 10, Vol. 24, File 9, Memo. from WHM to King, 8 August 1929(?)
84. King Papers, MG 26, J 10, Vol 24, File 9, Memo. from WHM to King, August 11.
85. Bourinot, Arthur S., "Kingsmere: Where Two Premiers Tramped the Woods," *Saturday Night*, Oct. 24, 1927, p. 5.
86. Smythe, Robert, *Kingswood...*, Vol. 1, p. 19.
87. King Papers, MG 26, J 10, Vol. 26, File 4, King to Stanley Thompson, 22 May 1925.
88. King Papers, MG 26, J 10, Vol. 26, File 4.
89. Ibid., King to Rogers, 9 July 1925.
90. Smythe, *Kingswood...*, Vol. 1, p. 112.
91. Smythe, *Kingswood...*, Vol. 2, p. 205.
92. Humphreys, Phebe Westcott, *The Practical Book of Garden Architecture,* J.B. Lippincott Co. Philadelphia, 1914, p. 100.
93. Ibid., pp. 109-10.
94. Haddock, John A., *A Souvenir of the Thousand Islands of the St. Lawrence River from Kingston and Cape Vincent to Morristown and Brockville...*, 2nd Edition, Weed-Parsons, Alexandria Bay, New York, 1896, p. 398.
95. King Papers, MG 26, J 10, Vol. 129, LeMoine to King, 2 August 1924.
96. Smythe, *Kingswood...*, Vol. 2, p. 263.
97. Smythe, *Kingswood...*, Vol. 2, p. 259.

Chapter Three

1. King Papers, MG 26, J 10, Vol. 27, File 16, W. Herridge to King, 10 April 1924.
2. Molson's Bank later merged into the Bank of Montreal. See, Stacey, C.P., *A Very Double Life*, Macmillan of Canada, Toronto, 1976, p. 119.
3. As described in, Stacey, pp. 121-22.
4. King Papers, MG 26, J 10, Vol. 27, File 18, King to Mrs. T. McGillivray, 31 December 1926.
5. King Papers, MG 26, J 10, Vol. 27, File 18, Mrs. T. McGillivary to King, 10 January 1927.
6. Gagnon Pratte, France, *Country Houses for Montrealers, 1892-1924, The Architecture of E. and W.S. Maxwell*, Meridian Press, Montreal, 1987, p. 19.
7. Wright, Janet, *Architecture of the Picturesque in Canada*, Parks Canada, Ottawa, 1984, p. 57.
8. Jameson, Anna Brownell, *Winter Studies and Summer Rambles*, McClelland & Steward, Inc., Toronto, 1990, p. 202.
9. *Canadian Homes and Gardens*, May 1929, p. 56.
10. Le Moine, J.M., *Maple Leaves: Canadian History — Literature — Ornithology*, Quebec, 1894, p. 21.
11. Ibid., p. 22.
12. Buggey, Susan and John J. Stewart, "Lakehurst and Beechcroft: Roches Point, Ontario, Canada," *Journal of Garden History*, Vol. 1, No. 2, 1981, p. 150.
13. Culham, Gordon, "We Make a Plan for the Estate," *Canadian Homes and Gardens*, May 1930, p. 56.
14. Gianelli, Adèle M., "Oak Hall — A Mansion in the Clouds of Niagara's Glory," *Canadian Homes and Gardens*, September 1930, p. 19.
15. Gagnon Pratte, p. 60.
16. Ibid., p. 60.
17. Ibid., p. 130.
18. Lawson, Harold, "Pioneer Architecture for Country Houses," *Canadian Homes and Gardens*, August 1931, p. 22.
19. See, Bain, David, "William Mundie, landscape gardener," *Journal of Garden History,* Vol. 5, No. 3, 1985, pp. 298-308.
20. Grimwood, Paul, Owen R. Scott, Marilyn Watson, "George Laing — Landscape Gardener, Hamilton, Canada West," *APT Bulletin*, Vol. IX, No. 3, 1977, see pp. 53-64.
21. Crawford, Pleasance, "Taylor, Edwin," manuscript, October 1988.
22. As quoted in, Crawford, Pleasance, "Charles Ernest Woolverton (1879-1934) Ontario Landscape Artist," *Landscape Architectural Review*, June 1982, pp. 17-20.
23. Ibid., p. 19.

24. Jacobs, Peter, "Frederick G. Todd and the Creation of Canada's Urban Landscape," *APT Bulletin*, No. 4, 1983, pp. 27-34.
25. Some of his extant works are the "garden suburbs" of Shaughnessy Heights and Point Grey in Vancouver; Battlefields National Park on the Plains of Abraham, and the Garden of the Way of the Cross at the St. Joseph Oratory in Montreal.
26. Dubé, pp. 237-250.
27. Bradley, A.G., "The Humours of a Canadian Watering-Place," *MacMillan's Magazine*, May/October 1904, p. 426.
28. Dubé, p. 174
29. Knott, Leonard L., "English Summers in French Canada," *Canadian Homes and Gardens*, June-July 1935, p. 29.
30. Ibid., p. 46.
31. King Papers, MG 26, J 8, Vol. 38, File 2, H.J. Sims and Family, H.J. Sims to King, 21 December 1931.
32. Girouard, Mark, *Sweetness and Light: The Queen Anne Movement 1860-1900*, Clarendon Press, Oxford, 1977, p. 153.
33. See, Elliot, Brent, *Victorian Gardens*, B.T. Batsford, Ltd., London, 1986, pp. 199-201.
34. Ibid., pp. 200-201.
35. Ibid., p. 201.
36. Hodgins, J. Herbert, "Shadowbrook — Estate of Vibrant Colour," *Canadian Homes and Gardens*, January 1929, p. 17, 50.
37. The firm was started by Laurie and Howard Dunington-Grubb whose commissions were pan-Canadian, spanning city planning to cemeteries to residential gardens. They also established Sheridan Nurseries, Toronto, which operates to this day.
38. Grey, Mary, "Rosemary and Lavender," *The Canadian Magazine*, July 1925, p.176.
39. Hodgins, p. 50.
40. Gianelli, Adèle M., "Edgemere, Country Estate of James Ryrie, Esq.," *Canadian Homes and Gardens*, January 1927, p. 62.
41. *Canadian Homes and Gardens*, December 1936, p. 27.
42. Ibid., p. 28.
43. Perkins, Dorothy, "The Rockery and Japanese Garden at Villa Fiora," *Canadian Homes and Gardens*, May 1927, p. 37.
44. Ibid., p. 37.
45. Ibid., p. 60.
46. *Canadian Homes and Gardens*, June-July 1936, p. 26.
47. Elliott, pp. 74-78.
48. Knowles, Valerie, *First Person: A Biography of Cairine Wilson, Canada's First Woman Senator*, Dundum Press, Toronto, 1988, p. 35.
49. Ludwig, Emil, *Mackenzie King: A Portrait Sketch*, Macmillan Co. of Canada Ltd., Toronto, 1944, p. 57.
50. Gladstone was involved in "rescuing" prostitutes, as King also attempted during his University of Toronto days.
51. King Papers, MG 26, J 10, Vol. 25, File 6, "Kingsmere in Chronology."
52. Smythe, Robert, *King of Kingsmere, A selection of diary entries, correspondence and photographs from the W.L.M. King papers and collections*, National Capital Commission, Ottawa, 1981, unpaged.
53. "The Prime Minister's Health," *Ottawa Journal*, September 30, 1927. quoted in Smythe, Robert, *King of Kingsmere...*
54. Elliot, *Victorian Gardens*, p. 176.
55. Ibid., p. 190.
56. Hadfield, Miles, *A History of British Gardening*, John Murray, London, 1969, p. 418.
57. *Canadian Homes and Gardens*, February 1929, p. 45.
58. Morgan, F. Cleveland, "Rock-Gardening in the Province of Quebec," *Rock Gardens and Rock Plants, Report of the Conference...*, Chittenden, F.J., ed., Royal Horticultural Society, London, 1936, p. 21.
59. Negus, Raymond E., "Rock Gardens," in Jekyll, Gertrude and Lawrence Weaver, *Gardens for Small Country Houses*, p. 240.
60. Morgan, "Rock-Gardening in the Province of Quebec," p. 29, and "The Lore of Rock Gardens," *Canadian Homes and Gardens*, July 1927, p. 32.
61. von Baeyer, *Rhetoric and Roses,* pp. 124–125.
62. Byng, Viscountess, of Vimy, *Up the Stream of Time*, The Macmillan Co. of Canada Ltd., Toronto, 1946, p. 81.
63. Ibid., p. 81.
64. Macbeth, Madge, "Building a Garden on Creation's Rocks," *Canadian Homes and Gardens*, September 1927, p. 40.
65. Ibid., p. 41.
66. King Papers, MG 26, J 8, Vol. 33, File 4, King to J.D. Rockefeller, Jr., 23 April 1948.
67. King Papers, MG 26, J 10, Vol. 27, File 1, plant lists, typed and handwritten.
68. Brickell, C.D, and B. Mathew, *Daphne, The Genus in the Wild and in Cultivation*, The Alpine Garden Society, Woking, Surrey, 1976, p. 82.
69. King Papers, MG 26, J 10, Vol. 26, File 3, L.W. Brockington to King, 3 October 1933.
70. The rock garden has recently been restored by the National Capital Commission which oversees the King estate.
71. de Caraffe, Marc and Janet Wright, "Le domaine Mackenzie-King, Kingsmere, Québec," Commission des lieux et monuments historiques du Canada, *Agenda Paper*, 1984, p. 214.
72. King Papers, MG 26, J 10, Vol. 23, King to J.D. Hunter, 24 April 1928.

73. de Caraffe, p. 210.
74. Perkins, Dorothy, "Uplands, A Country Estate of Great Interest," *Canadian Homes and Gardens*, December 1927, p. 60.

Chapter Four

1. King Papers, MG 26, J 6, Vol. 42, File 309, "Misc. Pamphlets," Sheridan Nurseries, "The Art of Garden Design," Toronto, n.d., p. 7.
2. Jack, Annie, *The Canadian Garden: A Pocket Help for the Amateur*, Musson, Toronto, 1910, p. 40.
3. King Papers, MG 26, J 10, Vol. 26, File 4, W.T. Macoun to Grisdale, 21 October 1929.
4. Elliott, *Victorian Gardens*, p. 240.
5. Macpherson, Mary-Etta, "Batterwood House," *Canadian Homes and Gardens*, May 1931, pp. 17-18.
6. King Papers, MG 26, J 8, Vol. 16, File 1921-50, "Mrs. Fulford and Her Staff."
7. King Papers, MG 26, J 3, Vol. 132, File 1, King to Flora Scrim, 27 March 1936.
8. King Papers, MG 26, J 10, Vol. 26, File 3, King to Mrs. John Moss, 9 May 1929.
9. King Papers, MG 26, J 10, Vol. 27, File 1, undated handwritten list.
10. King Papers, MG 26, J 10, Vol. 26, File 3, Memo, WHM to King, 1 May 1928.
11. "Obituary," *Canadian Florist*, April 21, 1947, pp. 26-27.
12. King Papers, MG 26, J 10, Vol. 27.
13. King Papers, MG 26, J 10, Vol. 26, File 3, Arthur Miles to King, 11 April 1928.
14. King Papers, MG 26, J 3, Vol. 135, File 3, Frank Skinner to King, 25 October 1940.
15. King's mother was actually named Isabel. Why he suddenly wanted her remembered by her middle name is unexplained, unless King wanted to distinguish her from his sister, also named Isabel.
16. Kingsmere Interviews, typescript, Mrs. Isabelle Kelly, August 13, 1983, National Capital Commission, Ottawa, n.d.
17. Paterson, Allen, *The History of the Rose*, Collins, London, 1983, p. 234.
18. King Papers, MG 26, J 10, Vol. 26, File 3.
19. King Papers, MG 26, J 10, Vol. 26, File 6, King to G.H. Ferguson, 17 December 1931.
20. King Papers, MG 26, J 10, Vol. 26, File 6, Paul Angle to King, 25 August 1936.
21. King Papers, MG 26, J 10, Vol. 26, File 6, Norman Scrim to King, 25 April 1936.
22. King Papers, MG 26, J 10, Vol. 26, File 6, M.B. Davis to King, 23 March 1936.
23. King Papers, MG 26, J 10, Vol. 27, File 1, "Garden — Plants," "Garden — Seeds."
24. King Papers, MG 26, J 10, Vol. 25, File 5, King to W.S. Meredith, 11 September 1933.
25. Ibid.
26. King Papers, MG 26, J 10, Vol. 25, File 5, King to Meredith, 19 September 1933.
27. King Papers, MG 26, J 10, Vol. 25, File 5, King to Meredith, 11 October 1933.
28. Northend, *Garden Ornaments*, p. 33.
29. King Papers, MG 26, J 8, Vol. 29, File 2, King to Joan Patteson, 12 October 1938.
30. King Papers, MG 26, J 6, Vol. 170, File 3, Press Release, "Sir William Mulock, KCMG, a Brief Appreciation by the Prime Minister of Canada," October 1944.
31. See for fuller discussion, Jackson, J.B., "The Sacred Grove in America," in, *The Necessity for Ruins and Other Topics*, University of Massachusetts Press, Amherst, 1980, and Stilgoe, John R., *Common Landscape of America, 1580 to 1845*, Yale University Press, New Haven, 1982, Chapter One.
32. Thomas, Keith, *Man and the Natural World...*, pp. 217-18.
33. Ibid., p. 213.
34. Kay, Edwin, "Garden Making in Eastern Canada," *Landscape and Garden*, Vol. 2, No. 3, Autumn 1935, p. 109.
35. Blackwood, Algernon, "The Man Whom the Trees Loved," *Pan's Garden: A Volume of Nature Stories*, Reprint, Books for Libraries Press, Freeport, New York, 1971, pp. 31-32.
36. King Papers, MG 26, J 10, Vol. 28, File 9, King to H. Mercier, 16 August 1934.
37. King Papers, MG 26, J 10, Vol. 28, File 9, J.O. Hélie to King, 2 May 1935.
38. See, Thonger, Charles, "Bridges," *The Book of Garden Furniture*, 1903.
39. See, Smythe, Robert, "Mackenzie King's Path to the Waterfall," typescript, for the National Capital Commission, 1983 and Hubers, M., "Trail Report," typescript, for the National Capital Commission, 1985.
40. Smythe, Robert, *King of Kingsmere...*, "Landscape/Publicity," Edward I. Wood to King, 22 August 1942.
41. Cunningham, Walter W., "Her Majesty, the Peony," *The Christian Science Monitor*, April 5, 1947.

42. King Papers, MG 26, J 3, Vol. 127, File 3, Orminston Roy to King, 3 January 1948.
43. King Papers, MG 26, J 3, Vol. 127, File 3, King to Ormiston Roy, 29 May 1948.
44. Smythe, "Mackenzie King's Path..." In 1953 the dam at Mulvihill Lake burst, the rushing waters swept away all of King's bridges, and eventually led to the straightening out of his intricate, picturesque stream and pools system.

Chapter Five

1. Neatby, H. Blair, *William Lyon Mackenzie King: The Prism of Unity, 1932-1939*, Vol. 3, University of Toronto Press, Toronto, 1976, pp. 70-72.
2. Esberey, *Knight of the Holy Spirit...*, p. 132. A full study of the extent of King's psychical interests will not be known until his spiritualism papers are released at the National Archives of Canada in 2001.
3. Mrs. Wreidt was noted in particular for her psychic contact with Queen Victoria which earned her not only the commendation of British psychics and spiritualists, but also titled patronage.
4. Neatby, *The Prism of Unity*, p. 73.
5. Ibid., p. 73.
6. Ibid., pp. 74–75.
7. King Papers, MG 26, J 10, Vol. 25, File 2, King to G.H. Ferguson, 27 April 1929.
8. Ibid.
9. King Papers, MG 26, J 10, Vol. 25, File 2, King to Ferguson, 18 May 1929.
10. King Papers, MG 26, J 10, Vol. 25, File 2, King to Ferguson, 4 July 1929.
11. Nevins, Deborah, "Flower Gardening in the American Way," *Fauns and Fountains: American Garden Statuary, 1890-1930*, The Parrish Art Museum, Southampton, New York, 1985, u.p.
12. Hale, Katherine, "Nymphs and Fauns as Magic Fountains in Canadian Gardens," *Toronto Star Weekly*, August 11, 1923, p. 18.
13. Tice, Patricia, *Gardening in America, 1830-1910*, The Strong Museum, Rochester, New York, 1984, p. 36.
14. Jekyll, Gertrude, *Gardens for Small Country Houses*, Baron Publishing, Woodbridge, Suffolk, 1981, p. 222.
15. Ibid., p. 219.
16. Tice, pp. 66-68.
17. Hale, p. 18.
18. Ibid., p. 18.
19. Dunington-Grubb, Laurie, "Sculpture as a Garden Decoration," *Canadian Homes and Gardens*, March 1927, p. 52.
20. Hale, p. 18.
21. Loring, Florence, "Sculpture in the Garden," *Canadian Art*, Vol. 1, No. 2, December/January 1943-44, pp. 64, 65.
22. King Papers, MG 26, J 10, Vol. 10, File 8, King to Robert Laurier, 7 May 1935.
23. King Papers, MG 26, J 10, Vol 10, File 8, Robert Laurier to King, 8 May 1935.
24. King Papers, MG 26, J 8, Vol. 29, File 6, J.C. Patteson to King, 30 December 1936.
25. King Papers, MG 26, J 8, Vol. 29, File 6, J.C. Patteson to King, 15 February 1937.
26. King Papers, MG 26, J 10, Vol. 25, File 2, J.A. Ewart to King, 8 May 1936.
27. King Papers, MG 26, J 10, Vol. 25, File 3, King to C.M. Bezeau, 11 June 1932.
28. Ibid.
29. Ibid.
30. King Papers, MG 26, J 10, Vol. 25, File 3, King to C.M. Bezeau, 26 July 1932.
31. *Kingsmere Interviews*, Dunlop, Mrs. Jean, typescript, National Capital Commission, Ottawa, June 27, 1983.
32. *Kingsmere Interviews*, King, Mrs. Marjorie, typescript, National Capital Commision, Ottawa, July 12, 1983.
33. Hardy, H. Reginald, *Mackenzie King of Canada: A Biography*, Oxford University Press, Toronto, 1949, p. 344.
34. King Papers, MG 26, J 10, Vol. 25, File 6, J.B. Harkin to Harry Baldwin, 27 January 1930.
35. King Papers, MG 26, J 10, Vol. 25, File 6, King to J.B. Harkin, 30 January 1930.
36. Robinson, John Martin, *Georgian Model Farms, A Study of Decorative and Model Farm Buildings in the Age of Improvement, 1700-1846*, Clarendon Press, Oxford, 1983, p. 105.
37. Jones, Barbara, *Follies and Grottoes*, Constable, London, 1974, p. 1.
38. Ibid., p. 1.
39. King Papers, MG 26, J 10, Vol. 25, File 2, King to Andrew McDonald, 5 April 1935.
40. King Papers, MG 27, J 8, Vol. 38, File 3, King to Peter Sims, 14 May 1935.
41. See, Neatby, H. Blair, *William Lyon Mackenzie King: The Lonely Heights, 1924-1932*, University of Toronto Press, Toronto, 1963, pp. 368-85.

42. Quoted in, Lowenthal, David, *The Past is a Foreign Country*, Cambridge University Press, Cambridge, 1985, p. 43.
43. King Papers, MG 26, J 6, Vol. 135, File 15, "Buys Carving from Buildings at Westminster," *Ottawa Journal*, November13, 1936.
44. Smythe, Robert, *King of Kingsmere...*, "War Relics."
45. King Papers, MG 26, J 10, Vol. 27, File 2, Ruth V. McDougald to King, 13 October 1947.
46. King Papers, MG 26, J 10, Vol. 27, File 2, Joan Gilmour to King, 14 October 1947.
47. King Papers, MG 26, J 6, Vol. 242, File 4.
48. King Papers, MG 26, J 6, Vol. 135, File 4, Jane, "Commóns Responds to Challenge of Beauty Contest by Preening," *Winnipeg Free Press*, May 30, 1936.
49. Ritchie, Charles, *My Grandfather's House: Scenes of Childhood and Youth*, Macmillan of Canada, Toronto, 1987, pp. 156-158.
50. King Papers, MG 26, J 10, Vol. 27, File 2, Elizabeth Smart to King, 20 May 1935.
51. King Papers, MG 26, J 6, Vol. 150, File 15, Cross, Austin F., "Kingsmere — And Its Ruins," *The Montreal Standard*, September 17, 1938.
52. King Papers, MG 26, J 17, Vol. 22, File 22, Stepler, Jack, "See King's Ruins as Link in his Spiritualistic Ventures," *Ottawa Citizen*, October 4, 1952.
53. Hardy, Reginald, "Our Fantastic Legacy from Mackenzie King," *Maclean's Magazine*, July 15, 1951, p. 39.
54. Ibid., p. 39.
55. Hutchinson, Bruce, *The Incredible Canadian, A Candid Portrait of Mackenzie King*, Longmans Canada Ltd., Don Mills, Ontario, 1952, p. 80.

Chapter Six

1. Smythe, Robert, *King of Kingsmere...*
2. William Lyon Mackenzie King Papers, National Archives of Canada, MG 26, J 6, Vol. 135, File 6, Gadsby, H.F., "Back to the Land Once More," *The Montreal Standard*, August 20, 1927, p. 37.
3. Ibid., p. 37.
4. King Papers, MG 26, J 10, Vol. 27, File 12, J.S. Martin to King, 19 May 1927.
5. Wiebenson, Dora, *The Picturesque Garden in France*, Princeton University Press, Princeton, New Jersey, 1978, p. 99.
6. Robinson, John Martin, *Georgian Model Farms...*, p. 1.
7. Ibid., p. 77.
8. Clifford, Derek, *A History of Garden Design*, Faber and Faber, London, 1962, pp. 138-39.
9. Williams, Robert, "Rural Economy and the Antique in the English Landscape Garden," *Journal of Garden History*, Vol. 7, No. 1, 1987, p. 88.
10. Girouard, Mark, *Life in the English Country House, A Social and Architectural History*, Penguin Books, London, 1978, p. 217.
11. Ibid., p. 215.
12. Ibid., p. 300.
13. Nesmith, Tom, "The Philosophy of Agriculture: The Promise of the Intellect in Ontario Farming, 1835-1914," Ph.D. thesis, Carleton University, Ottawa, 1988, p. 164.
14. Ibid., p. 164.
15. Ibid., p. 175.
16. "Lakewood on the Shores of Lake Ontario," *Canadian Homes and Gardens*, May 1934, p. 30.
17. Culham, Gordon, "That Little Place in the Country," *Canadian Homes and Gardens*, May 1940, p. 20.
18. Ibid., p. 58.
19. "Chicopee: An Estate in Western Ontario," *Canadian Homes and Gardens*, August 1933, p. 28.
20. "The Hermitage: A Pickering Estate," *Canadian Homes and Gardens*, May 1932, p. 16.
21. Griffin, Frederick, "Kingsmere," *The Toronto Star Weekly*, February 4, 1928, General Section, p. 1.
22. Meredith, R. Brian, "Lakeside Farm," *Canadian Homes and Gardens*, May 1930, p. 24.
23. Macpherson, Mary-Etta, "Glenburn Farms," *Canadian Homes and Gardens*, November 1931, p. 17.
24. Macpherson, Mary-Etta, "The Business Man Turns to Farming," *Canadian Homes and Gardens*, May 1930, p. 30.
25. Smythe, *King of Kingsmere...*
26. King Papers, MG 26, J 10, Vol. 26, File 2.
27. Reaman, G. Elmore, *A History of Agriculture in Ontario*, Vol. II, Ontario Department of Agriculture and Food, Toronto, 1970, pp. 131-32.
28. King Papers, MG 26, J 10, Vol. 26, File 2.
29. Griffin, p. 1.
30. Ibid.
31. Smythe, *King of Kingsmere...*, from the Debates of the House of Commons, February 20, 1928.
32. Smyth, *King of Kingsmere*, King to J.H. Cranston, 21 February 1928.
33. King Papers, MG 26, J 3, Vol. 106, File 2, W.R. Motherwell to King, 20 April 1927.

34. King Papers, MG 26, J 3, Vol. 106, File 2, King to J.S. Martin, 23 April 1927.
35. King Papers, MG 26, J 10, Vol. 27, File 13, John M. Bell to King, 5 May 1927.
36. "The News from Kingsmere," *Ottawa Journal*, June 3, 1927, p. 10.
37. King Papers, MG 26, J 6, Vol. 179, File 5, "American Eagle is Hon. W.L.M. King's Prize Poultry," *Toronto Evening Telegram*, June 4, 1927.
38. King Papers, MG 26, J 10, Vol. 27, File 13, King to W.R. Motherwell, 4 June 1927.
39. Ibid.
40. King Papers, MG 26, J 10, Vol. 27, File 13, King to J.S. Martin, 27 February 1928.
41. King Papers, MG 26, J 10, Vol. 27, File 12, King to Charles McCrea, 20 September 1927.
42. "Yellow Briar," *Canadian Homes and Gardens*, June 1939, p. 17.
43. King Papers, MG 26, J 10, Vol. 27, File 12, Memo.
44. King Papers, MG 26, J 10, Vol. 27, File 12, Memo.
45. Smythe, *King of Kingsmere...*, "Bees," King to Henry Schinzel, 8 March 1944.
46. King Papers, MG 26, J 10, Vol. 23, File 3, Henry Schinzel to King, 26 January 1945.
47. King Papers, MG 26, J 10, Vol. 26, File 2, King to Michael Mulvihill, 31 July 1929.
48. King Papers, MG 26, J 10, Vol. 25, File 3, King to Jackson Booth, 25 October 1929.
49. King Papers, MG 26, J 10, Vol. 28, File 13, "Memorandum Re Country Residence," p. 1.
50. Ibid., p. 2.
51. King Papers, MG 26, J 10, Vol. 26, File 2, "Memorandum re Kingsmere Property," April 29, 1927.
52. King Papers, MG 26, J 10, Vol. 26, File 3, King to J.H. Grisdale, 26 September 1927.
53. King Papers, MG 26, J 10, Vol. 26, File 2, King to Harry Tinney, 9 July 1936.
54. King Papers, MG 26, J 10, Vol. 26, File 4, King to J.H. Grisdale, 29 January 1931.
55. King Papers, MG 26, J 10, Vol. 28, File 9, King to M.B. Davis, 6 December 1939.
56. "Kingsmere Interviews," Mrs. Isabelle Kelly, typescript, National Capital Commission, Ottawa, August 13, 1983.
57. "Kingsmere Interviews," Mrs. Isabelle Kelly, August 13, 1983.

Chapter Seven

1. King Papers, MG 26, J 17, Vol. 2, File 1, W.L. Mackenzie King's will.
2. See, Coutts, Sally, "Easeful Death in Toronto: A History of Mount Pleasant Cemetery," *Society for the Study of Architecture in Canada Bulletin*, Vol. 11, No. 3, September 1986, pp. 8–10.
3. See, Etlen, Richard A., "Père Lachaise and the Garden Cemetery," *Journal of Garden History*, Vol. 4, No. 3, 1984, pp. 211–222.
4. Collins, Louis, "A Dream of Beauty, The Halifax Public Gardens," *Canadian Antiques and Art Review*, Vol. 1, No. 9, June 1980, pp. 23-24.
5. von Baeyer, *Rhetoric and Roses...*, p. 82.
6. Nash, Roderick, "Wilderness and Man in North American," in *The Canadian National Parks: Today and Tomorrow*, Proceedings of a Conference Organized by the National and Provincial Parks Association of Canada and the University of Calgary, Calgary, October 9-15, 1968, ed. J.G. Nelson and R.C. Scace, p. 73.
7. Brown, Robert Craig, "The Doctrine of Usefulness: Natural Resource and National Park Policy in Canada, 1887-1914," in *The Canadian National Parks: Today and Tomorrow*, p. 98.
8. Ibid., p. 99.
9. Foster, Janet, *Working for Wildlife: The Beginning of Preservation in Canada*, University of Toronto Press, Toronto, 1978, p. 16.
10. Ibid., p. 11.
11. Ibid., p. 11.
12. Ibid., p. 58.
13. Ibid., p. 27.
14. Altmeyer, George, "Three Ideas of Nature in Canada, 1893–1914," *Journal of Canadian Studies*, Vol. 2, 1976, p. 30.
15. Ibid., p. 29.
16. Foster, p. 77.
17. Ibid., p. 78.
18. Ibid., p. 79, 81.
19. Ibid., pp. 215-16.
20. Ibid., p. 81.
21. King Papers, MG 26, J 6, Vol. 174, File 5, "National Park Praised at Prince Albert, Sask. as Park Policy Advance," *The Calgary Albertan*, July 28, 1928.
22. King Papers, MG 26, J 3, Vol. 159, File 5, J.A. Wood to King, 18 July 1929.
23. King Papers, MG 26, J 3, Vol. 159, File 5, J.A. Wood to King, 27 August 1929.
24. Official Report of Debates, House of Commons, Second Session of Parliament, Vol. III, 1931, F.A. Acland, Ottawa, 1931, p. 3368.
25. Woods, Jr., Shirley E., *Ottawa, The Capital of Canada*, p. 191.

26. Ibid., p. 192.
27. *Report and Correspondence of the Ottawa Improvement Commission Relating to the Improvement and Beautifying of Ottawa*, Sessional Paper No. 51a, King's Printer, Ottawa, 1912, p. 23.
28. Ibid., p. 23.
29. Ibid., p. 24.
30. Ibid., p. 24.
31. Ibid., p. 40.
32. King Papers, MG 26, J 6, Vol. 150, File 15, "The Plans for Ottawa," *Ottawa Journal*, April 17, 1935.
33. Ketchum, Carleton J., *Federal District Capital*, n.p., Ottawa, ca. 1939, p. 41.
34. Smythe, *King of Kingsmere...*
35. Ibid.
36. Ketchum, p. 30.
37. Ibid., p. 34.
38. Smythe, *King of Kingsmere*, "House of Commons Debates, May 23, 1935."
39. See, Zavitz, E.J., *Fifty Years of Reforestation in Ontario*, Ontario Department of Lands and Forests, Toronto, ca.1959.
40. Smythe, *King of Kingsmere*, "House of Commons Debates, May 27, 1935."
41. Ibid., May 23, 1935.
42. King Papers, MG 26, J 6, Vol. 111, File 33, "Mackenzie King Urges Forest Conservation," *Montreal Gazette*, October 27, 1939.
43. Ibid., "Gatineau Park."
44. King Papers, MG 26, J 8, Vol. 38, File 3, Peter Sims to King, 25 October 1935.
45. King Papers, MG 26, J 6, Vol. 111, File 33, "Ottawa May Become Winter Sports Center of America Predicts Charles A. Bowman," *Ottawa Citizen*, December 17, 1935.
46. King Papers, MG 26, J 6, Vol. 110, File 17, "Prime Minister Asks Action By F.D. Commission," *The Ottawa Citizen*, May 28, 1935, p. 7.
47. King Papers, MG 26, J 6, Vol. 150, File 15, "Begin with Federal District," *Ottawa Citizen*, April 17, 1935.
48. King Papers, MG 26, J 6, Vol. 150, File 15, "The Plans for Ottawa," *Ottawa Journal*, April 17, 1935.
49. King Papers, MG 26, J 6, Vol. 110, File 17, Bowman, Charles A., "Gatineau National Parkway Would Open Scenic District," *Ottawa Citizen*, June 20, 1936, p. 27.
50. Ibid., p. 27.
51. King Papers, MG 26, J 6, Vol. 110, File 17, Hume, J.A., "Prominent Members of House Endorse Scheme for Park in Gatineau," *Ottawa Citizen*, June 20, 1936, p. 27.
52. King Papers, Bowman, p. 27.
53. Smythe, Robert, "Mackenzie King's Path to the Waterfall," unpublished paper for the National Capital Commission, Ottawa, 1983, p. 6.
54. Smythe, *King of Kingsmere*, "National Memorial Perspective," *Ottawa Evening Citizen*, April 15, 1937.
55. *Official Report of Debates of House of Commons*, Fourth Session, Eighteenth Parliament, Vol. I, King's Printer, Ottawa, 1939, p. 633.
56. National Capital Commission files, "Gatineau Park Report 1939–40."
57. Woods, p. 265.
58. Taylor, John H., *Ottawa, An Illustrated History*, pp. 187-88.
59. Gréber, Jacques, *Plan for the National Capital, General Report*, National Capital Planning Service, Ottawa, 1950, p. 244.
60. Ibid., p. 248.
61. King Papers, MG 26, J 6, Vol. 174, File 5, "Gatineau Park: A Great Achievement," *Ottawa Journal*, April 12, 1949.
62. Ibid.
63. King Papers, MG 26, J 17, Vol. 3, File 8, Sparks, R.P., "Memorandum Prepared for Submission to a Joint Committee of the Senate and House of Commons Set Up to Consider 'the financial and other relationships of the Government and the Federal District Commission with the City of Ottawa and neighbouring municipalities' (Speech from the Throne January 7, 1955)," Ottawa, 1955, p. 1.
64. Darragh, Ian, "Gatineau Park," *Canadian Geographic*, Vol. 107, No. 6, December/January 1988, p. 24.
65. King Papers, MG 26, J 6, Vol. 150, File 15, *Ottawa Evening Journal*, October 22, 1946.
66. King Papers, MG 26, J 6, Vol. 110, File 17, "To Start Judging 200 Bird Houses," *Ottawa Journal*, May 1, 1929.
67. Foster, p. 138.
68. Ibid., p. 144.
69. Ibid., p. 158.
70. King Papers, MG 26, J 6, Vol. 168, File 2, "Jack Miner's Life Was Colourful and Varied," *The Essex County Reporter*, November 9, 1944, p. 8.
71. King Papers, MG 26, J 6, Vol. 222, File 20, *Ottawa Citizen*, March 1, 1928.
72. King Papers, MG 26, J 17, Vol. 2, File 1.
73. King Papers, MG 26, J 6, Vol. 174, File 5, "Bears Have Become Pest Short Distance From Ottawa," *Ottawa Journal*, November 20, 1946.

INDEX

Page numbers in **boldface** indicate pictures.